Editor
Emily R. Smith, M.A. Ed.

Editorial Project Manager
Elizabeth Morris, Ph.D.

Editor-in-Chief
Sharon Coan, M.S. Ed.

Cover Artist
Denise Bauer

Art Coordinator
Kevin Barnes

Imaging
Alfred Lau

Product Manager
Phil Garcia

Publishers
Rachelle Cracchiolo, M.S. Ed.
Mary Dupuy Smith, M.S. Ed.

Managing Technology in the Classroom

Contributing Authors

Deborah Shepherd Hayes

Jan Ray, Ed.D.

Teacher Created Materials, Inc.
6421 Industry Way
Westminster, CA 92683
www.teachercreated.com
ISBN-0-7439-3500-4
©2002 Teacher Created Materials, Inc.
Made in U.S.A.

Table of Contents

How to Use This Book 4

    About the CD-ROM 6

    Your Circle of Support 8

Introduction to Computers 10

    What is a Computer? 10

    Types of Computers 11

    Hardware vs. Software 12

Your Computer System 13

    Input Devices 14

    Processing Devices 17

    Output Devices 18

    Storage Devices 21

Purchasing Educational Software 23

    Know Your Computer System 23

    My Computer System 34

    Know What You Want 35

    Software Evaluation Instrument 36

Getting Started with Software 39

    Paint, Draw, and Graphics Software 39

        Sample Lesson: A Cartoon Story—Storytelling 41

    Word Processing Software 46

        Sample Lesson: It's Negotiable: A Conflict Resolution Activity 48

    Spreadsheet Software 52

        Sample Lesson: Righty or Lefty?: An Introduction to Charting 55

    Database Software 64

        Sample Lesson: Animal Classification 67

    Presentation Software 72

        Sample *PowerPoint* Lesson: Nutrition 74

        Sample *HyperStudio* Lesson: The Apple Doesn't Fall Far from the Tree 80

Table of Contents *(cont.)*

Getting Started with Software *(cont.)*

Visual Learning Software 92

    Sample *Inspiration* Lesson: Getting Set for Storytelling 102

    Sample *Kidspiration* Lesson: Sorting Solid Shapes 108

The Internet and E-mail 113

    Sample Internet Lesson: The 5 W's of Website Evaluation 120

    Sample E-mail Lesson: My School, Your School 129

Search Engines 132

Typing Software—Teaching Little Fingers to Keyboard 139

Installing Software onto Your Computer System 143

Managing Your Classroom Software Library 148

Managing Your Computer Placement 157

One Computer—Thirty Students? 158

Classroom Computer Pod 168

Team Teaching with Technology 169

The Computer Lab 174

Teaching with Technology 176

Checklist Technology vs. Integrated Technology 176

Technology Standards 179

Simple Student Projects 185

Simple Student Activity Sheets 194

Basic Sheets for Any Assignment 218

Grading Rubrics 231

Technology Tidbits 238

Computer Setting Adjustments You Can Make 238

Managing Technology for Special Needs Students 246

Getting Parents Involved 251

Answer Key 254

CD-ROM Index 255

How to Use This Book

Introduction

Where do you fall on the technological continuum?

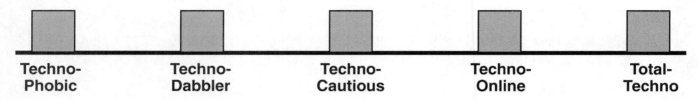

| Techno-
Phobic | Techno-
Dabbler | Techno-
Cautious | Techno-
Online | Total-
Techno |

Welcome to the wonderful world of educational technology! For some teachers, discovering the realm of superhighways, Power PCs, multimedia, and virtual reality will be one terrific adventure. For others, this experience will be similar to paying taxes. Wherever you may find yourself on the technological continuum, teachers all over the globe recognize that technology in the classroom is here and will be around for a long time.

For those folks who consider themselves Techno-Phobics, a common lament might be, *Whatever happened to the good old days? Nothing to plug in, nothing to logon—just books, the chalkboard, and thou.* A short walk down the halls of teaching history offers an interesting object lesson. During the 1840s, schoolhouses across the nation were being equipped with the latest item in educational technology. This piece of equipment was supposed to bring about mass educational reform, changing the face of learning forever. What was this revolutionary piece of hardware? Nothing other than the chalkboard!

Surprising to the reformers was the fact that teachers simply did not use the chalkboard. They did not know how, nor were they comfortable integrating this new piece of equipment into their one-room schoolhouses. Consequently, the "chalkboard reformers" wrote manuals for teachers, offering tips on how to use the new piece of classroom equipment. Teachers, however, did not see a need to use a large display device with a class of as many as 12 different grade levels. Students were all using individual textbooks, slates, paper and pencil, etc. However, over the course of time, schools became more crowded, building needs changed, and students were then grouped by ages. With this shift to group learning, the chalkboard became a perfect tool for the teacher and was eventually embraced as the mainstay of the model classroom lesson.

Any time history is reflected upon (or repeated), there are many lessons available for learning. The story of the chalkboard generates several thoughts, perhaps the most prominent being that some things never change. Those early American teachers were not about to use any new technology unless there was an actual reason for them to use it. The new technology seemed to be a hindrance, so teachers were not willing to put forth the effort to think of new ways to use the chalkboard. As the classroom changed, the needs of the teacher and students changed as well, creating a new set of problems needing solutions.

As classrooms across the country begin the twenty-first century, student and teacher needs are changing again. Access to information, information management, multicultures and languages, the global economy, and a rapidly changing world in which students are growing up all make for new and challenging demands upon the classroom teacher. One of these demands, of course, is how to successfully integrate and manage technology in the classroom program.

How to Use This Book *(cont.)*

Perhaps those on the opposite end of the technological continuum, Total-Technos, are so eager to learn more and teach more that they try the latest innovations and forget which drives which, the technology or the curriculum.

The fundamental question asked by teachers over the centuries has always been, "How do I excite my students about learning?" Educators are constantly asking themselves, "What goals do I want my students to achieve, and how do I help them obtain these goals?" Regarding the question of using technology in the classroom, the question should not be, "How do I use technology in this lesson?" but rather, "What tools can I use to help make this a more successful and meaningful lesson?" As Dr. David Dockterman of Tom Snyder Productions says, *You would never sit down and construct a lesson thinking, Now what can I do that will use the chalkboard?* The same holds true for technology tools.

As educators begin cruising the information highway and moving along that technological continuum, it is important to keep in mind that good, solid teaching will always be curriculum driven, not technology driven. So, welcome to those of you just now climbing aboard the tech train. And to the passengers already riding, hold on as this locomotive evolves from a steam engine to a high speed bullet train! But above all, remember that curriculum is the engine; technology is but one of the wheels.

Managing Technology in the Classroom is designed to be an easy-to-use reference for your educational technology needs. Depending upon the level of your technology expertise, you may refer to this book often or just on occasion for a technology-related lesson idea. Whatever the case may be, it is available as a resource to you as you integrate technology into your classroom plan.

The book is divided up into ten general sections:

- **How to Use This Book**
- **Introduction to Computers**
- **Your Computer System**
- **Purchasing Educational Software**
- **Getting Started with Software**
- **Installing Software**
- **Managing Your Classroom Software Library**
- **Managing Your Computer Placement**
- **Teaching with Technology**
- **Technology Tidbits**

If you consider yourself a "Techno-Phobic" or "Techno-Dabbler," you may want to start out by reading the *Introduction to Computers* and *Your Computer System* sections first. These will give you a working knowledge of basic technologies, what they are, and what they do. If you are a "Techno-Cautious" or "Techno-Online," your needs might take you first to the *Getting Started with Software* section for lesson ideas on how to integrate technology into the curriculum. For those of you who have worked hard and reached "Total-Techno" status—congratulations! You probably find yourself as the resident resource at your school with other teachers coming to you for help and ideas. *Managing Technology in the Classroom* can be your assistant when you are helping other colleagues to become more technologically literate.

Your commitment to integrating technology into your curriculum is to be applauded. As teachers, one of our most important responsibilities is to prepare students for the future workplace. By overcoming whatever insecurities we may have about technology, we can feel positive that we are meeting the needs of our students. Good luck and have fun!

About the CD-ROM

If you turn to the back of this book, you will find a CD-ROM. It contains the following types of files for your use:

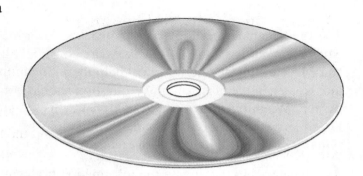

- student tracking sheets
- student learning activities
- visual learning diagrams
- self-evaluation forms
- student template files

Although the CD-ROM files are mentioned throughout the text, for a complete listing of every file on the CD-ROM, turn to the *CD-ROM Index* found on pages 255–256 of this book.

The CD-ROM files were created using the following software applications:

- *Microsoft Word*
- *Microsoft Excel*
- *Microsoft PowerPoint*
- *Inspiration*
- *Kidspiration*
- *Kid Pix Deluxe*
- *HyperStudio*

Please note that the CD-ROM does not contain any of the software applications listed above. You must have (or obtain and install a legal copy of) the software application associated with each CD-ROM file you plan to open and use with your students. For example, if you plan to open and use the Student Keyboarding Tracking Sheet for Kid Keys, you must have Microsoft Word installed on your computer system, because that is the software application in which it was created. (The CD-ROM Index lists the software application associated with each file.)

The CD-ROM files can be opened on both the PC and Macintosh platforms. To access the files, carefully remove the CD-ROM from the back of this book and place it in the CD-ROM drive of your computer system. Since the process for opening files is different for each platform, on page 7 you will find separate instructions for opening files on the PC and for opening files on the Mac.

About the CD-ROM *(cont.)*

Opening the CD-ROM Files on a PC

If you are using a PC, double-click on the **My Computer** icon on your desktop. At the **My Computer** window, double-click on the icon representing the CD-ROM drive, such as D:, E:, or F:. (You may also see the name of the CD, tcm_3500, right next to the CD drive label.) At the tcm_3500 window, you will see a list of all the files on the CD. Just scroll down until you find the file you want and double-click on the file to open it. If you have the software application in which the file was created on your computer system, Windows will automatically launch the software application that is associated with the file.

Opening CD-ROM Files on a Macintosh

If you are using a Macintosh system, double-click on the CD icon that is on your desktop. Scroll down until you find the file you want and double-click on the file to open it. The system will automatically launch the application that is associated with the file.

How to Save a File from the CD-ROM onto Your Computer System

CD-ROM means compact disk read-only memory. In a nutshell, that means that you can open a file from the CD and use it. However, you cannot save the file back to the CD, as it is able to be read only. When you are finished with a file you have opened from the CD, you have two options:

1. Close the file and lose any changes you made to it.

2. Use the **Save As** function to save the file to a new location on your computer system so that the changes you made will remain intact.

To Close a CD-ROM File

To close a CD file, click **File** on the menu bar. Then click **Close**.

To Save a CD-ROM File

Most computer applications allow you to click **File** on the menu bar and select **Save As**. At the **Save As** window, navigate to the folder where you would like to save your file. Rename the file, if you want. Then click the **Save** button.

Your Circle of Support

"Nothing makes one feel so strong as a call for help."

George MacDonald

No one on this planet has ever achieved greatness alone. There are always family members, friends, teachers, colleagues, and others who have contributed to his or her success along the way.

If you ask a successful computer-using educator how he or she managed to learn so much and do so well with technology, the answer will inevitably include a circle of support that not only formed the foundation but also paved the way for his or her accomplishments.

A dear friend of mine, Ariel Marks, first introduced me to the computer in the mid 1980s. He had an old Apple II system set up in the garage of his aunt's home in Los Angeles. We played for hours with the computer, trying to complete an educational project. It seemed that every command demanded a different diskette, so we spent as much time swapping 5 1/4 inch floppy diskettes as we did actually working on the project. Even though Ariel was a relatively new computer user, I quickly realized I would have been entirely lost without his help. He became the first member in my circle of support.

My first official computer classes were taken at Irvine College of Business in Irvine, California. They included an integrated accounting class, a word processing class, and a spreadsheet class. Admittedly, I didn't understand much of what I was doing, but I could follow directions, and that seemed to get me through. Shirley Chastain was my instructor and the second member of my circle of support. We became good friends—partly because I asked her so many questions in class and partly because I called her at home so often, asking for help with problems related to my newly acquired computer system. In fact, we became such good friends she was the maid of honor at my wedding!

Through "holding my hand" and explaining things about computer systems and software applications that I didn't understand, Ariel and Shirley helped me build a foundation of technology skills that have blossomed over the years. I am truly grateful for their help and the help of so many others, like the "guys" at The Computer Store in Long Beach, where I bought my first two computers and my professors at U.S.I.U. in San Diego, where I took every computer-related course offered in the College of Education.

So, forming your circle of support for building a foundation of technology skills that can blossom over the years is very important and very worthwhile. Maybe, when you take a few moments to think about it, you already have a circle of support in place—or at least well underway. If so, that's great! If not, get started forming your circle of support right now. You will feel more comfortable knowing that you have people who are willing to help you accomplish your educational technology endeavors.

Your Circle of Support *(cont.)*

To form your circle of support, list five to ten people you know who are available to help you with your computer systems and software applications. It may be the computer lab attendant who loads your educational software, the teacher next door who always finds your missing files, or your teenage son (or daughter) who keeps your computer system at home up and running with the latest "bells and whistles."

Whoever the people are in your circle of support, list their names, your relationship to them, the type of support they provide, and their contact information. Let these people know that they have been recognized as official members of your circle of support and that you appreciate their help very much!

My Circle of Support

	Person	Relationship	Type of Support	Contact Information
1				
2				
3				
4				
5				
6				
7				
8				
9				
10				

Keep this information handy. You never know when you will have to contact a member of your circle of support!

What is a Computer?

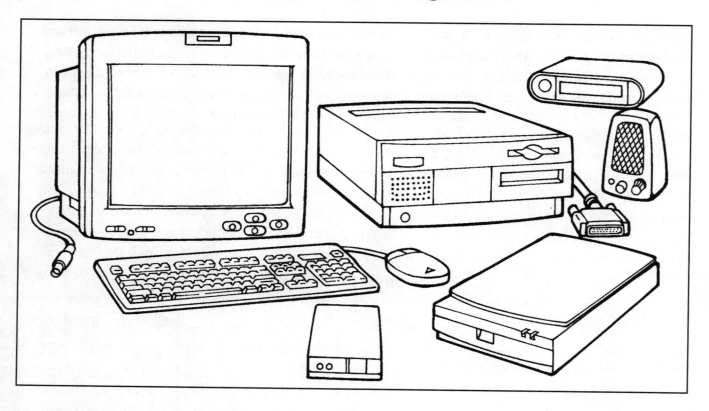

The computer that sits in your classroom is an amazing and mysterious machine. The computer, as a system, includes both hardware components and software applications that allow you to input, process, and output data for a multitude of purposes.

Computers are machines that process data. Computers take information that you input using a device such as the keyboard and process it. The processed data is output from the computer and sent back to you to be used in a variety of ways. Data can be viewed on the computer screen, transferred to paper through the printer (a hard copy), or stored on a disk to be kept in a safe place for future use. The central processing unit (CPU) is the computer's brain. The CPU interprets the data that it receives, carries out the instructions, and sends it back and forth between the computer's components. What makes computers so useful is their ability to process immense amounts of information very quickly.

Although computers come in all shapes and sizes, they look basically the same in that they are recognizable as "computers." When computers were first invented, they were so large that a single unit would take up an entire room. With technological advances and the invention of microprocessors, computers can now be small enough to fit on your lap or in the palm of your hand. Personal computers (the kind that schools use) are also known as microcomputers.

Depending on one's perspective, the computer can make life easier or much more complicated. Computers are designed to save time, create more efficiency, and allow the users to do and experience things that they would not be able to do with a two-dimensional medium, like paper and pencil.

Types of Computers

The two most common types of computers found in educational settings are the Apple Macintosh and the IBM® (Compatible) PCs. Although they use different operating systems, they are similar in the way you use them. When you use Microsoft® Windows or Macintosh OS, you will be using a menu-driven operating system in which you make choices from pull-down menus by clicking with a mouse. Both systems allow you to work on different programs simultaneously, easily exchanging text, graphics, and numbers from one program to another.

Most of the activities and lessons in this book are designed to be used with programs that are available for both the IBM Compatible and Macintosh computers. It actually doesn't matter if you have exactly the same programs that are named. Most software applications offer similar capabilities, even though the command names and functions may differ slightly. With a little experimentation and adjustment, you'll find that the lessons work well with the software of your choice. Many schools have different models of computers in the lab, in the media center, and in the classroom. Students often use one type of computer at home and another at school. They have become experts in using software on both platforms and will make almost seamless transitions from one application to the next.

IBM® (Compatible) Computers

In the past fifteen years, International Business Machines, Inc. (IBM) has made strides to capture a portion of the educational market. Although many schools still prefer the Macintosh platform, IBM and compatible computers are making their ways into the schools more and more. The price and performance of IBM and compatibles make them an attractive alternative to Macintosh computers.

Unlike Apple, IBM sold the right to manufacture computers that use the IBM technology. This opened the personal computer market to "clones" and "compatibles." The added competition has driven down the price and increased the performance and quality of personal computers. There are a host of companies who have marketed their own version of the IBM technology. Companies like Dell, AT&T, Packard Bell, Hewlett Packard, and Compaq compete with one another for their share of your computer-buying dollar. Each machine may have different "bells and whistles," but they all use the same basic technology.

All IBM and compatible computers need a Disk Operating System (DOS) to run software. It is, for lack of a better analogy, the computer's maid. DOS allows you to tell the computer where to store and retrieve things, how to organize itself, and how to clean up messes. It is a program that helps you run your other programs.

Windows provides IBM and compatible users with an operating system that is menu driven, with choices made by pointing and clicking a mouse. This operating system also allows the user to work on different programs simultaneously, easily exchanging text, graphics, and numbers from one application program to another.

Types of Computers *(cont.)*

Apple Macintosh Computers

Due to the positive and ongoing relationship between Apple computers and the American educational system, many schools use Apple computer products. There are a variety of different Apple computers available, and with so many to choose from, it is quite easy to become confused. Technology is constantly evolving. While these advances are exciting, keeping up with the rapid growth of technology can be challenging, especially for schools on limited budgets. That is one reason it is important to be sure that the system you purchase has upgrading capabilities. Fortunately, most computer and software companies recognize the economic realities of schools and create compatible systems, maintain outdated software for extended periods of time, and offer discounts.

Like IBM and compatible computers, Macintosh computers need an Operating System (OS) to run software. Once again, this operating system permits you to tell the computer where to store and retrieve things, how to organize itself, and how to clean up messes. It is a program that helps you to communicate with your other programs.

Hardware vs. Software

With all the equipment and technological jargon floating around these days, even the Total-Techno can become confused. One way to help a tech user understand all of the technology out there is to break it down into two categories. These categories are known as hardware and software.

Hardware

Hardware consists of all the electronic components and equipment that make up the computer. These parts include the CPU (central processing unit, the actual computing part), keyboard, printer, MODEM, monitor, scanner, and other peripheral equipment. Think of hardware as the technology parts that you can bump into. (See pages 13–22 for further information on the various hardware components of your computer system.)

Software

Software is the language and instructions needed to make the computer do what you want it to do. These instructions are usually stored on a small floppy disk or CD-ROM that is loaded into the computer. One example of software is the word processing program contained in Microsoft Works®. When you purchase this software program, you get a kit that includes a thick manual and several disks. On the disks you will find the encoded language that tells the computer what to do. Sets of instructions that allow the user to perform certain tasks are known as applications. By using a different type of software, a computer can do a number of varied tasks ranging from balancing your checkbook to showing a movie or even creating a Rolodex® file.

Your Computer System

Technically speaking, what you are looking at in your classroom is actually a computer system. The computer is merely part of that system—the part that processes data. The computer—as a system—consists of input devices, processing devices, output devices, and storage devices.

An Amazing, Mysterious Machine

The computer is amazing because it can perform so many incredible feats! It can calculate your grades in a snap. It can deliver great educational software programs that motivate your students to learn. It can take you to the Internet instantly—one of the greatest educational resources of our time. Via e-mail, it can help you communicate with just about anyone anywhere in the world at any time.

The computer is mysterious because it performs so many incredible feats (with a few flashes and maybe a groan or two) like magic-right before your eyes. If you are like most people, you probably don't really understand all the intricacies of how the computer performs. And, again, if you are like most people, you probably don't want to know either! You just expect the computer to work each and every time you turn it on.

The Components of Your Computer System

Can you name all the components of the computer system that sits in your classroom? Go ahead. Try listing the major pieces and parts below. Then we'll see how you did!

The Components of My Computer System

1. _____
2. _____
3. _____
4. _____
5. _____
6. _____
7. _____
8. _____
9. _____
10. _____
11. _____
12. _____

Input Devices

Input devices are hardware components used to enter data into the computer system or peripherals that assist in the process of getting data into a computer. Some of the most commonly used input devices are described below and on the following pages.

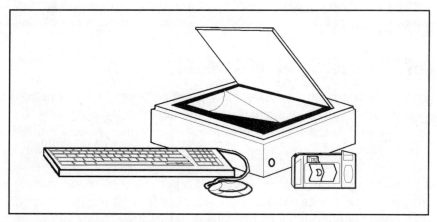

Keyboard

The keyboard is the primary device for entering data into a computer system. The keyboard contains a panel of buttons (or keys) that display the alphabet, numbers, and symbols. There is a wide range of keyboards in the marketplace today—from "split" natural keyboards to Internet keyboards with extra keys for quick accessibility options.

The keys have words or symbols on them and perform special tasks.

- The return or enter key which, when pressed, tells the computer to carry out an instruction.

- The shift, control, and option keys which, when pressed in combination with other keys, tell the computer to perform certain functions. For example, in many programs pressing the control key and the "s" key together tells the computer to save the file.

- The page up and page down keys let you move the document up and down from page to page.

- The caps lock and the insert keys are toggle keys. They are pressed to apply a certain formatting, and then pressed again to return to the previous formatting.

- The function keys on the keyboard are programmed by various software programs to do special tasks.

- The cursor keys, sometimes called the arrow keys, control the movement of the cursor up and down and side to side.

- Numeric keypads on some keyboards serve as calculators.

Mouse

The mouse is a small, hand-operated input device which moves across a mouse pad to manipulate the cursor or pointer on the screen. Clicking or double-clicking on a mouse button selects most menu items in a Windows or Macintosh environment. You can also use the mouse to draw on the screen and manipulate graphics objects. When you hold down the mouse button as you move the mouse, you are performing a common mouse action known as clicking and dragging. You perform this action to highlight blocks of text that you want to copy, edit, or spell check. There is a wide range of mice in the marketplace today, including optical and cordless mice.

Input Devices *(cont.)*

Remote Mouse

When you are using a large display device (television, LCD panel, or projector) while presenting to your class or other group of people (parents, the PTA, the school board, etc.), it is helpful to have the flexibility of standing in front of your desk, walking among the audience, or moving close to the displays you are talking about. This is nearly impossible to do if you have to remain close enough to your computer system to click the mouse whenever you want to change the display. So, don't be "tied" to your computer system! You can use a remote mouse to control your presentation from anywhere in the room.

A remote mouse is a small hand-held device, similar to a desktop mouse. You can program the remote mouse to take over the work of your regular mouse whenever your computer system "sees" that it is plugged in.

The remote mouse works with a little receiver, which you point to as you input a command, such as clicking to move to the next slide in your presentation. The tiny receiver is usually placed close to the display, as this is where you have a natural tendency to look and point.

CD-ROM Drive

A CD-ROM drive is a device used to play CD-ROMs. CD-ROM stands for compact disk read-only memory. CD-ROMs store information digitally. A great deal of information can be stored on a CD-ROM (just over 600 MB). This drive is known as a read-only disk drive, which means that it will only read the information and will not allow any more information to be added or recorded onto the CD-ROM.

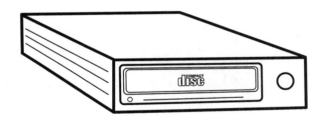

Touch Screen or Touch Window

Have you ever withdrawn money from an ATM? If so, you are probably already familiar with a touch screen. Using your fingers, you touch the screen displayed to input information into the bank computer system, like how much money you would like to deposit or withdraw. The monitor within your classroom computer system (which is typically considered an output device) can be converted to an input device with the addition of a touch screen or touch window and some special software.

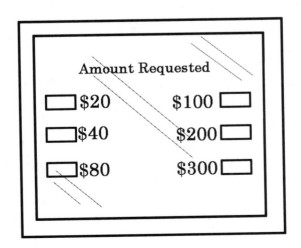

Input Devices *(cont.)*

Scanner

A scanner is used to transfer outside text, photos, or illustrations to the computer. It does this by taking a picture of the object. The picture is digitized (broken up into tiny dots). A special software program that is included with the purchase of the scanner controls its operation. Once the image is scanned it can be sent to the printer, imported into your favorite productivity software, or e-mailed via a modem.

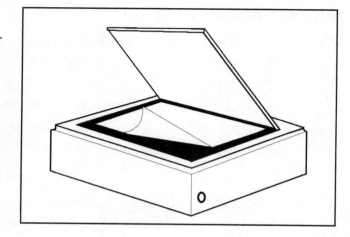

There are currently three types of scanners that are used in classrooms. The first is a flatbed scanner that works somewhat like a photocopy machine. To use the flatbed scanner, you insert the original document face down onto a glass plate for it to be scanned. The second, a handheld scanner, works as you roll it slowly across the paper (or image) to be scanned. The third is the portable drum or desktop scanner. To use this scanner, you insert the paper onto the top of the scanner. It passes around a drum and emerges out from another slot. Its main advantage is that it takes up very little desk space and that it often doubles as a FAX machine for transmitting brochures and correspondence. Its main disadvantage is that you can't scan from inside of a book. You can only use it to scan individual sheets of bendable paper.

Both students and teachers can benefit from using a scanner. Student projects are greatly enhanced because special images, photos, objects, artwork, drawings, and student writing can be scanned into any given project or document. Perhaps a student is writing a book report about *Charlotte's Web* on the computer and wants to include original illustrations from the story. These drawings can be scanned into the report and then sized up or down to fit the student's needs. Scanned photos can turn student-created autobiographies into treasured keepsakes for parents and family, and placing student work in full color on a school website is a breeze. As more and more teachers employ computerized portfolio management systems, the scanner's role becomes even greater. Using this device, the teacher can scan student projects that may be too large or unrealistic to keep in a traditional portfolio container, and import the images onto students' portfolio disks.

Digital Video Camera

Digital video cameras are used to take and to input moving pictures directly to the computer or to high capacity floppy disks. They can input both full motion video, which is high quality video, and freeze-frame video, which is poorer quality but requires less space and memory requirement than full motion video.

The uses and advantages of utilizing a digital video camera in a classroom are many. It can be used for video conferencing or teleconferencing between classes in different schools, states, and even countries over the Internet. It can be used to record field trips and selections from school performances and import them into multimedia presentations that can be shared with other classes and with parents.

Input Devices *(cont.)*

Digital Still Camera

A digital camera is similar to a regular 35mm camera. The main difference is that it outputs images in digital form instead of on photographic film. Much like a scanner, the digital camera transfers images into digital numbers that the computer can understand. A digital camera can be plugged into a PC or Macintosh in order to see the image on the screen. The digital images can be transferred directly to the computer or stored on a floppy disk.

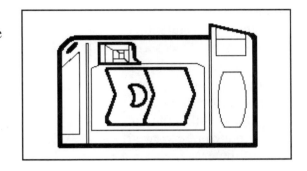

A digital camera acts like any camera in that it can take pictures of anything or anyone. Once a picture has been taken, it is stored inside the camera like traditional film. When the user is ready to retrieve the picture, the image is then transferred to the computer. Once downloaded to the computer, the image can then be screened, cropped, scaled, rotated, and incorporated into the proper medium.

The uses and advantages of utilizing a digital camera in the classroom are many. Student projects become more authentic and meaningful as personal touches are added. Perhaps a group of students is conducting a science experiment to observe bacterial growth over a period of a few days. Each day, the students would be able to take a picture of the petri dish and then record their observations in the computer. Writing activities, reports of all kinds, interviews, and art projects are just a few areas where a digital camera can be of assistance.

Laserdisc Player

A laserdisc player, also known as a videodisc player, is a piece of equipment that plays laserdiscs. Most laserdisc players come with remote controls, similar to a stereo, TV, or VCR. Just like your stereo, TV, or VCR remote, the laserdisc remote control allows the user to give commands to the machine from a distance. A bar code reader is another option you can get with a laserdisc player. Many educational laserdisc programs are formatted with a bar code design. By using the bar code reader, information can quickly be accessed with a swipe of the wand.

Processing Devices

Processing devices are hardware components that process the information that you enter into the computer system, preparing the data for output. You can't see the processing unit (or the processor) that is within your computer system since it is carefully mounted within the case. However, many manufacturers of computer systems proudly declare (or advertise) which type of processor they installed by placing a sticker representing the processor on the case. Do you see a sticker, such as Intel Inside! Pentium III, somewhere on the front of your computer case? If not, don't worry. You will learn how to tell which type of processor is within your case in the section entitled, *Purchasing Educational Software* (pages 23–38).

Output Devices

Output devices are hardware components that display or help store the resultant output of your processed input. In other words, the information that has been processed from the computer is called output. The output can be viewed on a computer screen, on a projection device, or it can be printed on paper.

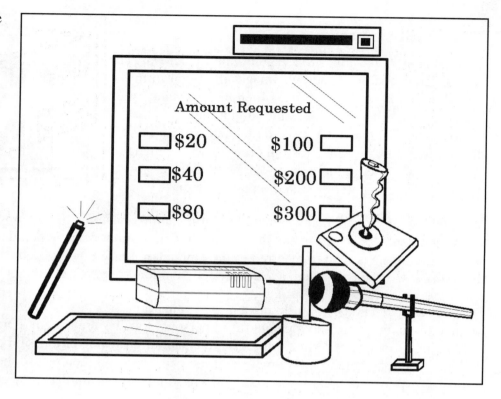

Monitor

Monitor is another name for a computer screen. Once the data has been processed, it is displayed on the computer monitor. Most monitors work the same way as your television set. A CRT (cathode ray tube) converts images to the screen when it receives electric signals from your computer. The electrons strike a dot on your monitor, which is called a pixel. The stronger the electron, the stronger the color that is given out. To create the different colors, each beam's strength is varied. For example, a strong red beam and a weak blue beam will create a medium brown pixel. The beam of electrons sweeps over the beam so quickly that your eyes see the completed picture even though the computer is only lighting up one pixel at a time.

The monitor is the primary output device used for multimedia presentation and Internet correspondence. Often three output devices—the monitor, an LCD, and a printer—are used to present a completed project.

CD R/RW Drive

The CD-ROM drive within your computer system is always considered an input device. However, if you have a CD-ROM drive that is not just readable (R), but also writeable (RW), then it is considered an output device as well.

The CD R/RW drive works with writeable CDs and special RW software. You place a writeable CD into the CD R/RW drive of your computer system. When the CD-ROM drive starts to "read" the CD, it recognizes that it is writeable and automatically launches the special RW software. The RW software application prompts you through the process of identifying the data you want stored onto the CD, such as project files. Once the files are identified, RW software "burns" them onto the CD for you.

Output Devices *(cont.)*

Printers

Data that is output from your computer is known as hard copy. Students love to print their finished work and hold it in their hands. Printed material also improves parent communication, reinforces learning, and is the basis for bulletin boards, books, displays, and class publications. Since there are usually many more computers than printers in the classroom, it is a good idea to discuss some criteria for printing. Teachers often request that students ask before they print and select only their best work to print. There are many types of printers used in schools. The two most commonly used are the ink-jet printer and laser printer.

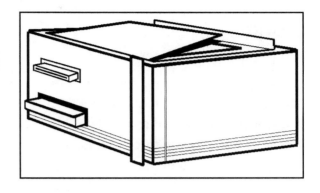

Ink-Jet Printers

Because ink-jet printers are inexpensive and can print in beautiful color, they are quickly becoming the dominant classroom printer. They use fine ink jets that are squirted from tiny nozzles onto the paper to print pictures or characters. Many ink-jet printers use cartridges containing four colors of ink as well as a separate black cartridge allowing hundreds of different colors to be created by mixing them together for printing. These cartridges are expensive and get used up quickly, so the teacher and students need to decided when and which work will be printed in color.

Laser Printers

Laser printers are more expensive than ink-jet printers. They are much faster and print much sharper images than ink-jet printers. They use a laser beam to convert binary data into print. The ink they use is in toners. Hundreds of documents can be printed using the same toner cartridge, which makes laser printers more economical to use than ink-jet printers. The ideal situation is for a classroom to have both laser and ink-jet printers. The bulk of the printing would be done on the laser printers and special art projects and presentations would use the ink jets.

There are several terms unique to computer printing. Some of the most common are listed below:

- **cps (characters per second)**—This describes the speed of the computer printing. When comparing computers to purchase for a classroom, this is a very important item to consider.
- **ppm (pages per minute)**—This describes how fast the computer will print the pages in a document. The computers which produce the most ppm are laser printers.
- **dpi (dots per inch)**—The more dots that make up an inch of a printed image, the sharper the image will be.
- **Consumables**—These are things that get used up and need to be replaced, such as paper, toner, and cartridges.
- **Memory buffer**—This is the part of the computer's RAM that stores data waiting to be printed.
- **Image quality**—This refers to the sharpness of the printout measured in dpi. Letter quality and near-letter quality printing are very sharp. Draft quality is not as sharp and is used when printouts do not need to look as good.

Output Devices *(cont.)*

Television

The television in your classroom can become an output device for your computer system. That way, everyone in the class can see what you have displayed on your computer screen. If you have a digital television, you simply have to hook it up to your computer. All you need is the appropriate cable. If you have the traditional analog television set, you will need to add a digital-analog converter when you hook the television up to your computer. The digital analog converter switches the digital signal from your computer system to an analog signal that the television can display.

LCD Panel

The LCD (liquid crystal display) projects what is being output by the monitor to a larger screen so that it can be viewed by several students who are sitting at a distance from the computer monitor. Everyday items such as the lighted panel on your digital alarm clock, the message light that blinks on your digital answering machine, and portable computer screens all use LCD technology. The screen on an LCD is filled with molecules of liquid that reflect light. When the computer scans the screen, some molecules work to shut the light out. These "off" molecules turn a pixel dark to form a part of the image.

Most LCDs work in conjunction with overhead projectors. When you place the LCD on your overhead projector and then connect the LCD panel to your computer, whatever you see on the screen will be projected onto a larger screen. This includes movies, animation, and multimedia presentations.

The Digital Analog Converter

The digital analog converter enables you to project what is normally displayed on your monitor onto the television screen in your classroom for all your students to view. As mentioned earlier in this section, the digital analog converter switches the digital signal from your computer system to an analog signal that the television can display. This small device comes with a remote that allows you to make several adjustments to the display on the television screen.

Storage Devices

If the output of your processing is something that you want to keep, you will need to store it. You have several options for storage, including the floppy disk, the hard disk (memory), the CD R/RW, the Zip disk, and the network folder.

Floppy Diskette

Floppy disks are not a permanent part of the computer. Your computer system has a floppy diskette drive into which you can place floppy diskettes for saving and storing your work. You put disks into the disk drive when you want to save data and remove them and keep them outside of the computer for future use. Floppy disks can also be used to keep backups of your data and to move data from one computer to another. For example, maybe you have a few minutes to begin creating a field trip announcement and permission form on your computer system at school. Of course, you don't have time to finish it. So, you save the field trip file to a floppy disk to finish on your computer system at home.

Hard Disk

Your computer system has a hard disk hidden within its case. It has a very large storage capacity (usually measured in gigabytes) and is the most convenient way for you to save your work. When you click File on the menu bar and then Save in any software application you are using, your computer system automatically assumes you are saving to your hard disk.

The place where the computer stores information is called its memory. Every computer has two types of memory, ROM (read-only memory) and RAM (random-access memory).

ROM holds lots of programs that tell the computer how to work. When you "boot up" (turn on) the computer, the ROM instructions tell it how to get going. The information stored in the ROM memory also contains instructions for running the input and output devices. ROM programs are read only; they can't be changed or deleted. The information that the computer keeps in its ROM memory remains in the computer whether it is turned on or turned off.

RAM stores information temporarily while the computer is turned on. When the computer is shut off, the information that has been stored in RAM is lost. If you want to keep the information that is in RAM, you will need to save it onto a disk.

Zip Disk

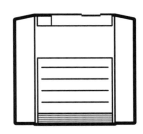

Zip disks provide 100 megabyte or 250 megabyte storage capacity. These disks are great for project files that need to move from one place to another while in progress. These disks are very similar to floppy diskettes, except that they are able to holder larger files. You must have a Zip drive connected to your computer in order to use these disks.

Storage Devices *(cont.)*

CD R/RWs

If you and your students create multimedia presentations with all the bells and whistles (clip art, pictures, movies, sound, and animation), the files may be too large to save onto floppy diskettes or Zip disks. One solution is to save large files to a CD. You can do this if you have a CD-ROM drive and CDs that are readable (R) and readable/writeable (R/W). This means that the CDs are just like your readable CDs; however, you can also write files to the CD. Once your project files are written to a CD; however, they cannot be rewritten. So, it is best to wait until the project files are in their final form before using the CD method of storage. You must have a CD-ROM R/W drive in order to write files from your computer to the CD.

Network Folders

The computer in your classroom is most likely connected to the school network. If so, your network administrator may designate a network folder where you can save your large project files or files you want to share with others. If you and your students are able to access the school network, you'll find it much easier for students to complete their classroom projects. They are then able to work on the project on a computer in the lab, save it to the network, and then return to the classroom and complete the project.

Know Your Computer System

Wow! You just received some money from the PTA. It is designated for purchasing educational software for your classroom. Although you are excited about the opportunity to buy a few new programs, you are also anxious about how to do so. This section will help relieve some of your anxiety by guiding you through the process of purchasing educational software for you and your students.

The educational software that you purchase must be able to run on the computer system that you have in your classroom. So, the first step in purchasing educational software is to know your computer system. When you know all about your computer system, you will be able to see if your system specifications meet the educational software application requirements.

Even if you don't know the first thing about your computer system other than how to turn it on, you can still learn what you need to know. Answer the following questions to learn a lot about your computer system. (Don't forget to ask members of your circle of support to help you with this, if you need assistance.)

1. **What type of computer system are you using? (In other words, what platform are you using?) Is it a Macintosh or a PC? Is it IBM compatible or an IBM clone? (If you have heard your computer system called either of the latter names, it's a PC.)**

Although most educational software programs are "hybrid" (which means they can run on both the Macintosh and the PC platforms), there are still many that are not. It is tremendously expensive for an educational software developer—especially a start-up company—to produce a program on both platforms. So, frequently a new program is produced on one platform first with plans to produce a hybrid version as soon as sales provide the opportunity for more development revenue.

When you are shopping for educational software and know your platform, you can quickly read the requirements and see if the program was designed to run on your computer system.

I have a Compaq® system, which is a PC. I also have a Macintosh system. So I can run most educational software on one of my computers.

Know Your Computer System *(cont.)*

2. What type of processor is within your computer? Is it a Pentium III, a Pentium IV, a Macintosh G4, or something else?

The processor is the "heart" of the computer system. Computer processors just keep getting better and better all the time. Many educational software developers draw the line with processors and only develop programs that run on newer systems. (They can't make everybody happy!) Therefore, if you have an older computer, knowing the type of processor you have is vital to making sure the educational software program you want to purchase can run on your system.

Here's how you can tell what processor you have in your PC computer.

- Place the mouse over the **My Computer** icon on the desktop.

- Click the right mouse button and a pop-up menu will appear.

- Select **Properties**.

- At the **System Properties** window, click the **General** tab to bring it to the forefront.

- I saw that I have a Pentium III processor!

Here's how you can tell what processor you have in your Macintosh computer.

- Click on the **Apple Menu** icon in the upper-left corner of your screen.

- Pull down to and click on **Apple System Profiler**.

- When the window opens, click to bring the **System Profile** tab to the front.

- Below the **Hardware Overview** you will see what processor your computer is using.

- I saw that I have a PowerPC G3 processor!

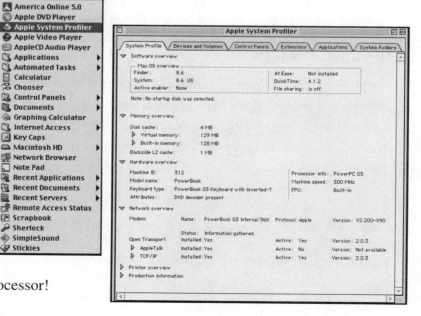

Know Your Computer System *(cont.)*

3. What type of operating system is installed on your computer? Is it Windows '98, Windows 2000, Windows ME, Windows XP, Mac OS X (10), or something else?

The educational software program that you purchase will only be able to run on select operating systems. Many educational software developers draw the line with operating systems—just like with processors—and only develop programs that run on newer systems. Therefore, if you have an older computer, knowing the type of operating system you have is vital to making sure the educational software program you want to purchase meets the operating system requirements.

Here's how you can tell what operating system you have in your PC computer.

- Click **Start** on the task bar.

- Running along the left-hand side of the **Start** pop-up menu is the operating system, such as Windows ME Millennium Edition.

- You can also go through the same steps you used to determine the type of processor that was on your system.

    - Place the mouse over the **My Computer** icon on the desktop.

    - Click the right mouse button and a pop-up menu will appear.

    - Select **Properties**.

    - At the **System Properties** window, click the **General** tab to bring it to the forefront.

- I saw that Microsoft Windows Millennium Edition was my operating system. The version number was 4.90.300.

- Finally, you can also restart your computer system and watch for the name of the operating system as it flashes across the screen at start-up.

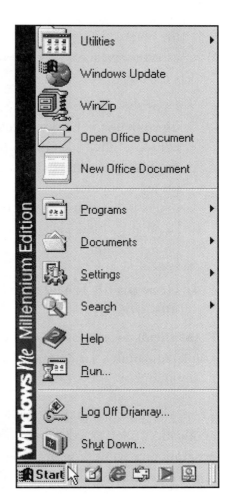

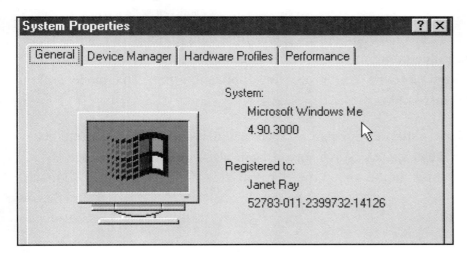

Know Your Computer System *(cont.)*

Here's how you can tell what operating system you have in your Macintosh computer.

- Click on the **Apple Menu** icon in the upper-left corner of your screen.

- Pull down to and click on **About This Computer**. If you do not see that as an option, be sure that you are at your Finder rather than within one of the programs on your computer.

- When the window opens, you will see what operating system (OS) your computer is using.

- You can also restart your computer system and watch for the name of the operating system as it flashes across the screen at start-up.

- I saw that I have Mac OS 8.6. Since that is not the most current edition of the Mac OS, there may be some programs I cannot run on my computer. I would want to check the software carefully to see that it could successfully run on my system.

4. How much RAM does your computer have? 128 MB, 255 MB, or some other amount?

RAM stands for random-access memory. It is also sometimes called desktop memory. The more RAM you have within your computer system, the more software applications you can have open and running at any one time.

There was a time—in the stone age of personal computing—when you could only run one software application, such as your word processing program, at a time. If you wanted to use a spreadsheet program or a paint program, you had to close the word processing application first. That made working among multiple applications nearly impossible.

Now you can multi-task. You can have multiple applications open that allow you to surf the Internet, answer your e-mail, write a letter, make calculations in a spreadsheet, play games (when no one is looking), and doodle in a paint program all at the same time. That makes using the computer so much more fun and productive!

Know Your Computer System *(cont.)*

Each application you open requires a certain amount of RAM. So the more RAM you have, the more applications you can run at one time. Some software applications, such as games or educational programs require tremendous amounts of RAM because they include spectacular graphics, animation, sound, and lots of interactivity.

Therefore, you need to know how much RAM is within your computer system to make sure the educational software program you want to purchase meets the RAM specifications.

Here's how you can tell how many megabytes of RAM you have in your PC computer.

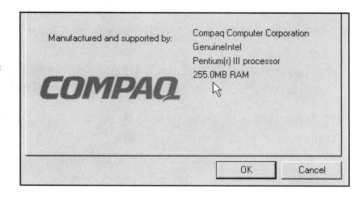

- Go through the same steps you used to determine the type of processor and the type of operating system that is on your computer.

- Place the mouse over the **My Computer** icon on the desktop.

- Click the right mouse button and a pop-up menu will appear.

- Select **Properties**.

- At the **System Properties** window, click the **General** tab to bring it to the forefront.

- I saw that I had 255 megabytes of RAM within my computer system.

Here's how you can tell how many megabytes of RAM you have in your Macintosh computer.

- Go through the same steps you used to determine the type of operating system that was on your computer.

- Click on the **Apple Menu** icon in the upper-left corner of your screen.

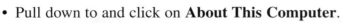

- Pull down to and click on **About This Computer**. If you do not see that as an option, be sure that you are at your Finder rather than within one of the programs on your computer.

- When the window opens, you will see how much built-in memory is on your computer.

- I have 128 megabytes of built-in memory within my computer system.

Know Your Computer System *(cont.)*

5. How large is your hard disk drive? Is it 10 gigabytes, 20 gigabytes, or some other amount?

The more hard disk drive space you have, the more educational software applications can be installed on your computer system. Some educational software applications, such as *SiteCentral*, require a specific amount of hard disk drive space (60 megabytes). Other educational software applications, such as *Kidspiration*, require a range of hard disk drive space, depending upon which features of the program you install (5 megabytes to 20 megabytes).

Knowing how much hard disk drive space is on your computer system is only the first step. The second step is determining how much of that hard disk drive space is still free.

6. How much hard disk drive space is free on your computer system? Is it 10 gigabytes, 25 gigabytes, or some other amount?

The more hard disk drive space you have free, the more educational software applications can be installed onto your computer system. When you are shopping for educational software, it is easier to make careful, calculated decisions about what programs to purchase when you know how much hard disk drive space is available on your computer.

Here's how you can tell how much hard disk space you have on your PC computer.

- Double-click on the **My Computer** icon on the desktop.

- At the **My Computer** window, click once on the hard disk drive. (In my case it was labeled Local Disk (C:).)

- The capacity of the hard disk drive, the amount used, and the amount free, as well as a pie chart representing the data, will be immediately displayed on the lower left-hand side of the window.

- I have a 34.5-gigabyte hard disk drive on my Compaq computer system. Of that, 26.5 gigabytes are free. I concluded that I had plenty of room for more educational software. Yeah!

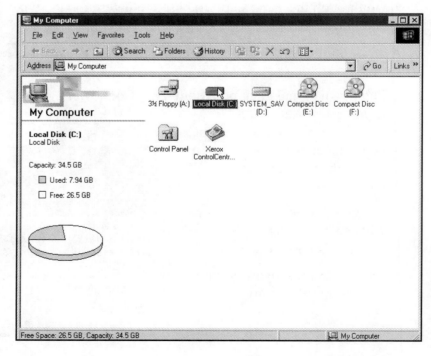

Know Your Computer System *(cont.)*

Here's how you can tell how much hard disk space you have on your Macintosh computer.

- Click one time on your hard drive icon. (In my case, the hard drive is labeled Macintosh HD.)

- Click on **File**, pull down to **Get Info**, and pull over **General Information**. You can also use the keyboard shortcut (Command key + I) to open the information window.

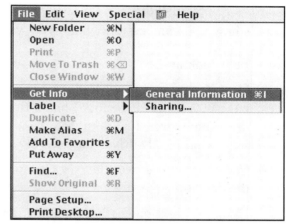

- When the **Macintosh HD Info** window opens, you can find out the capacity of your hard drive and the available space.

- I have a 7.6 gigabyte hard disk drive on my Macintosh. Of that, 5.8 gigabytes are free.

7. What other drives are available on your computer system? Do you have a floppy disk drive, a CD-ROM drive, a CD-R/RW drive, a DVD drive, or some other type of drive?

Look at your computer system (the hardware components like the picture below). Make a list of the drives that you see. You will probably have one floppy disk drive and a CD-ROM drive. You may also have a CD-R/RW drive, a DVD-ROM drive, a tape back-up drive, and more.

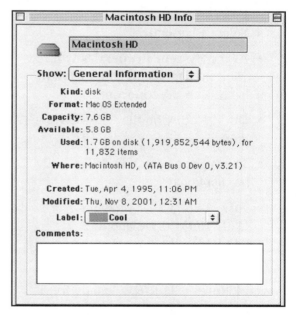

Most educational software applications come on CD-ROMs now. So, the developers require you to use a CD-ROM drive, with a specified minimum speed, for installation of their programs. Some educational software companies still provide their programs on floppy disks, just in case you don't have a CD-ROM drive. You will have to check their product box or written system requirements carefully, however, to see if floppy disks are enclosed or if you can purchase the CD-ROM version and send away for the installation floppy disks later.

If you have a CD-ROM drive, you will also want to determine its speed. Many educational software applications require a minimum speed, so that the software runs smoothly when the CD is accessed.

Know Your Computer System *(cont.)*

Matching the specifications for the drives that you have with the system requirements listed on a product box or spec sheet is the first step in assuring that you can successfully install and run the educational software application you want to purchase. So the time you take to gather this information is well worth it.

I have a floppy disk drive, a DVD-ROM drive, and a CD-R/RW drive on my Compaq computer system. Here's how you can can tell what drives you have on your PC system.

- First look at the front of your computer system (the hardware components).

- Look for the various drives that you might have. (See the picture on page 29.) I could see that I had a floppy disk drive and two CD drives; however, I couldn't tell from the front what kind of CD drives they were.

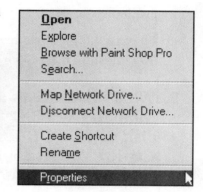

- Place the mouse over the **My Computer** icon on the desktop.

- Click the right mouse button and a pop-up menu will appear.

- Select **Properties**.

- At the **System Properties** window, click the **Device Manager** tab to bring it to the forefront.

- Double-click on the CD-ROM icon.

- The types of any CD drives will be displayed.

- Now, I know that I have a DVD-ROM drive and a CD R/RW drive. It also lists that its speed is 4x4x24.

Special Note: CD R/RW stands for Compact Disk with Recordable capabilities and Read/Write capabilities. That means that this CD drive acts as both a normal CD-ROM drive and as a writeable CD-ROM drive, where I can actually make my own CDs.

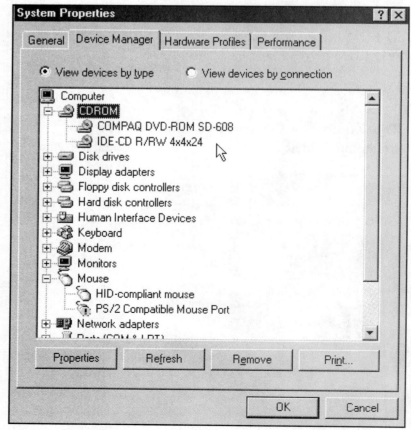

Know Your Computer System *(cont.)*

Here's how you can tell what drives you have on your Macintosh system.

- Click on the **Apple Menu** icon in the upper-left corner of your screen.

- Pull down to and click on **Apple System Profiler**.

- When the window opens, click to bring the **Devices and Volumes** tab to the front.

- The drives that you have will be listed in the window. I saw that I have a CD drive and a DVD-ROM drive.

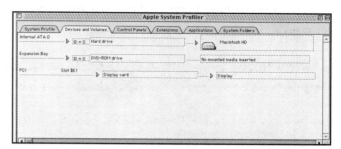

8. What other multimedia components does your computer system have? Do you have a soundcard, speakers, a microphone, or other multimedia components?

Due to the multimedia capabilities of many educational software applications, you will frequently find system requirements that include a soundcard, speakers, and a microphone. If you have a newer computer system, you probably have all of the aforementioned components—even if you don't know where the microphone is right now. (Look carefully at your monitor. It might be built in.) However, if you have an older system, you may need to have a sound card installed to enjoy the full benefit of the educational software program you want to purchase.

If you have speakers attached to your computer system, it's a sure sign that you have a sound card. That's pretty much all you need to know.

9. What are the display settings for your monitor? Is your monitor set at 16 colors, 256 colors, 16 bit, or 24 bit? Is your screen display set at 640 x 480 pixels, 800 x 600 pixels, 1024 x 768 pixels, 1152 x 864 pixels, 1280 x 1024 pixels, or 1500 x 1200 pixels?

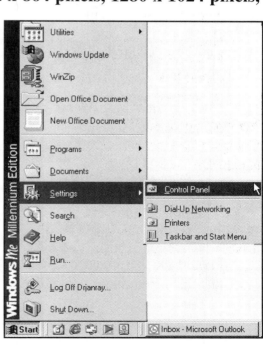

Many educational software applications list system requirements for the monitor settings as well. For example, *Kidspiration* system display requirements are 640 x 480 pixels and 256 colors. So, if your monitor display settings are equal to or greater than 640 x 480 pixels and 256 colors, you meet or exceed the *Kidspiration* system display requirements.

Here's how you can tell what the display settings on your PC computer are.

- Click **Start** on the task bar.

- Click **Settings**.

- Then, click **Control Panel**.

Know Your Computer System *(cont.)*

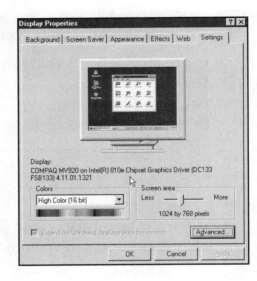

- At the **Control Panel** window, double-click on **Display**.

- At the **Display Properties** window, click on the **Settings** tab to bring it to the forefront.

- I could see that I have a Compaq MV920 monitor that displayed 16-bit color. My screen area was set at 1024 x 768 pixels.

My PC monitor display settings are 1024 x 768 pixels with 16-bit color. So, I would have no problem using *Kidspiration* on my system.

Here's how you can tell what the display settings on your Macintosh computer are.

- Click on the **Apple Menu** icon in the upper-left corner of your screen.

- Pull down to and click on **Control Panels**.

- Pull over and down to **Monitors & Sound**.

- When the window opens, click on the **Monitor** tab to bring it to the forefront.

- I could see that I have a Color LCD monitor that displayed thousands of colors. My screen area was set at 1024 x 768 pixels.

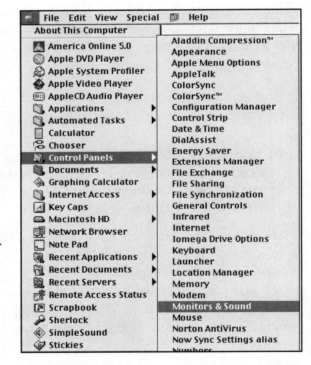

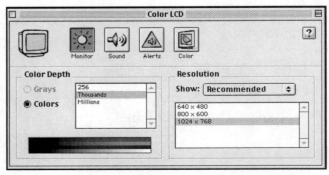

Know Your Computer System *(cont.)*

10. What types of peripheral devices are attached to your computer system? Do you have a printer, a scanner, or some other device?

Many educational software applications list optional system requirements, such as printers. In other words, you really don't need to have a printer to run the program; however, if you want to take full advantage of the educational software application, a printer (or other peripheral device) is recommended.

11. Do you have Internet access? If so, what browser are you using? What version?

Some educational software developers have integrated the use of the Internet in their products. If the Internet is an integral component of the software application, such as a program that helps you build classroom websites, then an Internet connection may be a system requirement. A specific version of the browser may be required as well. For example, *SiteCentral* is a software application that helps you create classroom websites. It requires you to have *Microsoft Internet Explorer 4.0*, *Netscape Navigator 4.7*, or a newer version on your computer system.

If the Internet is an optional feature of the software application, such as a program that allows you to access their technical support online, then an Internet connection may be an option. For example, *Kidspiration* is a visual learning software application that allows you to create live hyperlinks from *Kidspiration* projects to Internet sites. It also allows you instant access to their home page and online technical support. However, you don't need an Internet connection to create projects, so an Internet browser is listed as an optional system requirement.

Now that you have found the answers to all the questions about your computer system, enter them in the *My Computer System* information sheet on the following page. The *My Computer System* information sheet is also available on the CD-ROM [filename: system.doc].

Be sure to have the *My Computer System* information sheet handy when you begin to shop for your educational software. Then you can rest assured that the software you select will run on your computer system.

My Computer System

Questions	Answers	Special Notes
1. What type of computer system are you using?		
2. What type of processor is within your computer?		
3. What type of operating system is installed on your computer?		
4. How much RAM does your computer have?		
5. How large is your hard disk drive?		
6. How much hard disk drive space is free on your computer system?		
7. What other drives are available on your computer system?		
8. What other multimedia components does your computer system have?		
9. What are the display settings for your monitor?		
10. What types of peripheral devices are attached to your computer system?		
11. Do you have Internet access? If so, what browser are you using? What version?		

Know What You Want

"Well, let me see," you sigh. "I want a lot of things in an educational software application. I want one that reinforces what I just taught about compound words. I want one that provides my students with a fun way to practice their addition and subtraction facts. I want one that has lots of pictures of dinosaurs. I want one that helps them write little stories. I want one that allows them to draw and illustrate concepts. I want . . ."

Perfect! It sounds like you have already thought of several ways the computer can support your instruction and motivate your students to learn. The best part is that there are educational software applications that can provide everything you want—just maybe not all in one program.

There are thousands of educational software applications on the market today. So, how do you begin to make the right selection?

- First, think of educational software as a tool you can use to help you achieve your instructional goals and motivate your students to learn (rather than just one more thing you have to do).

- Second, with that in mind, identify the instructional goals you wish to achieve with your students.

- Third, use an evaluation instrument like the one on the following pages to evaluate your software options and choose the best educational software for your needs.

Software Evaluation Instrument
Developed by Children's Software Revue

Reviewers and testers associated with the Children's Software Revue use the following definitions and key considerations in evaluating software titles.

Key	Definition
A	Always
SE	To some extent
N	Never
NA	Not applicable

I. Packaging Integrity—*(Does the box accurately represent the software?)*

_____ Clearly states educational objectives and age appropriateness

_____ Describes specific learning skills addressed by software content

_____ Uses true screen shots to illustrate content features

II. Ease of Use—*(Can a child use it with minimal help?)*

_____ Skills needed to operate the program are in developmental range of the child

_____ Children can use the program independently after the first use

_____ Accessing key menus is straightforward

_____ Reading ability is not prerequisite to using the program

_____ Graphics make sense to the intended user

_____ Printing routines are simple

_____ It is easy to get in or out of any activity at any point

_____ Getting to the first menu is quick and easy

_____ Controls are responsive to the touch

_____ Written materials are helpful

_____ Program instructions can be reviewed on the screen, if necessary

_____ Children know if they make mistakes

_____ Icons are large and easy to select with a moving cursor

_____ Installation procedure is straightforward and easy to do

Software Evaluation Instrument *(cont.)*

III. Childproof—*(Is it designed with "child-reality" in mind?)*

_____ Survives the "pound on the keyboard" test

_____ Offers quick, clear, obvious response to a child's action

_____ The child has control over the rate of display

_____ The child has control over exiting at any time

_____ The child has control over the order of the display

_____ Title screen sequence is brief or can be bypassed

_____ When a child holds a key down, only one input is sent to the computer

_____ Files not intended for children are safe

_____ Children understand feedback and know when they have made a mistake

_____ This program would operate smoothly and bug-free in a classroom setting

IV. Educational—*(What can a child learn from this program?)*

_____ The program offers good presentation of one or more content areas

_____ The graphics do not detract from the educational intentions of the program

_____ Feedback employs meaningful graphic and sound capabilities

_____ Speech is used

_____ The presentation is novel with each use

_____ Offers a nice challenge range and this program will grow with the child

_____ Feedback reinforces content and embedded reinforcements are used

_____ Program elements match direct experiences

_____ Content is free from gender bias

_____ Content is free from ethnic bias

_____ A child's ideas can be incorporated into the program

_____ The program comes with strategies to extend the learning

_____ There is sufficient amount of content

Software Evaluation Instrument *(cont.)*

V. Entertaining—*(Is this program fun to use?)*

_____ The program is enjoyable to use

_____ Graphics are meaningful and enjoyed by children

_____ The program is appealing to a wide audience

_____ Children return to this program time after time

_____ Random generation techniques are employed in the design

_____ Speech and sounds are meaningful to children

_____ Challenge level is fluid or child can select from a range of difficulty levels

_____ The program is responsive to a child's actions

_____ The theme of the program is meaningful to children

VI. Design Features—*(How "smart" is this program?)*

_____ The program has speech capacity

_____ The program has printing capacity

_____ The program keeps records of each child's work

_____ The program "branches" automatically and the challenge level is fluid

_____ A child's ideas can be incorporated into the program design in some way

_____ Sound can be toggled or adjusted

_____ Feedback is customized in some way to the individual child

_____ The program keeps a history of each child's use over a period of time

_____ Teacher/parent options are easy to find and use

VII. Value—*(How much does the program cost versus what it does? Is it worth it?)*

Considering the factors rated above and the retail price of software, rate this program's relative value in the current software market. Consider also any extra hardware attachments required to get full potential of the programming, such as a sound card, CD-ROM, etc.

Poor									Good
1	2	3	4	5	6	7	8	9	10

Paint, Draw, and Graphics Software

Paint, draw, and graphics software, or creativity software, is designed to let students create a variety of artwork and illustrations and to modify photos and existing graphics. Among the things these tools allow your students to do is create lines, shapes, and free-hand sketches; edit existing images one pixel at a time; and add special effects such as shadows, perspective, and distortion to artwork. The finished products can be saved and printed directly or saved and imported into your favorite word processing, desktop publishing, multimedia, Web creation, and other productivity and creativity software. Among the many projects students can create using paint, draw, and graphics programs are the following:

- stationery logos
- illustrations for newspaper articles and reports
- painted images
- school artwork
- diagrams and maps
- original illustrations and designs

Below are some of the most common tools included in paint programs:

- **Paint Can**—Students use this tool to fill designs with both solid colors and patterns.

- **Undo**—Selecting this tool will allow a student to undo his/her last action.

- **Eraser**—A student uses this tool to erase something he/she has drawn.

- **Pencil**—This is used much like the pencils in your classroom in creating illustrations. Different size points are available with which to draw.

- **Brush**—This is used to paint illustrations. Students are able to select the thickness of the brushes they use in creating their artwork.

- **Line**—Nothing can produce straight lines better than this tool. A drawing and painting program allows the student to select the thickness of lines he or she wants to use.

- **Oval & Rectangles**—Use these tools to create rectangles, squares, circles, and ovals. These shape tools are easy for students to use as they compose their drawings.

- **Stamps**—In addition to graphics, which are imported one at a time, some paint programs also include stamps. When you choose a stamp, it becomes attached to the cursor and will repeat until you deselect it. By using stamps, you can create lines and borders or maybe just fill a sky.

- **Eyedropper**—This tool lets you pick up the color in one area of the picture and make it the selected color in your palette.

- **Spray Can**—The spray can sprays the selected color or shade from the color palette in the fill patterns. It is different from the paintbrush or bucket because the spray does not have a distinct line, thereby creating a softer look.

Paint, Draw, and Graphics Software *(cont.)*

The paint, draw, and graphics program most referred to in this book is *AppleWorks (ClarisWorks)*. *AppleWorks (ClarisWorks)* is an easy, fun-to-use drawing program that contains two modules: Paint and Draw. The Paint module allows students to use some very engaging art tools to illustrate whatever their imaginations can conjure. The Draw module allows students to design more complex graphic representations. *AppleWorks (ClarisWorks)* also allows students to pull several of their illustrations into a sequential presentation where they can add narration, sounds, and transitions between slides.

The heart of the program is the tools described below:

- **Pencil**—There are multiple sets of pencil options, giving you square-, circle-, or line-shaped pencil points. You can also choose the width and pattern for your **Pencil** lines.

- **Line**—Choose the **Line** tool to draw straight lines. There are options for the line widths and patterns. Hold the shift key down to draw straight lines.

- **Rectangle**—Choose the **Rectangle** tool to draw rectangles with various patterns. Hold the shift key down to draw perfect squares.

- **Oval**—Choose the **Oval** tool to draw ovals in various patterns. Hold the shift key down to draw perfect circles.

- **Paintbrush**—The **Paintbrush** tool option offers you choices for painting spirals, bugs, or pyramids, to name just a few.

- **Paint Can**—The **Paint Can** tool fills all or part of your picture with glorious colors and fun patterns.

- **Eraser**—Click with the mouse to erase a part or all of your picture.

- **Text Tool**—The **Text Tool** lets you type fonts of different styles onto your picture.

Various Programs

Most paint, draw, and graphics activities can be used with a variety of draw and paint programs. Some of the commands and procedures may differ slightly from program to program, but the basic operations are pretty much the same. Below is a list of popular software.

Corel Draw—Grades 5–12—Corel

Kid Pix—Grades K–8—The Learning Company

Painter—Grades K–12—MetaCreations

AppleWorks (ClarisWorks)—paint and draw modules

This software is like having all of your art supplies inside your computer!

A Cartoon Story

InfoNet

A popular form of storytelling is through the use of cartoons as the storytelling medium. In cartoons, characters are drawn in a humorous fashion. Cartoon strips are found in newspapers and magazines throughout the world.

This Project

You are going to make, write, or retell a story in cartoon fashion. For this particular project, we will retell the story of Aladdin. There is a planning sheet for you to use. It makes your work easier if you preplan what you are going to create on the computer.

1. Choose a story that you want to tell. Use the *Cartoon Strip Planning Sheet* (page 42) to list your characters, objects, and story plot.

2. Select the Rectangle tool and make a large rectangle across the screen. Make another one directly underneath.

3. To divide the rectangles into sections, select the Straight Line tool and hold down the Shift key as you draw dividing lines for four sections on each strip.

4. Draw a picture in the very first section. If available, use stamp options to add to the picture.

5. To fill in color for the background, select the Paint Can tool and choose a color and texture option.

6. If you need a speech bubble for your strip, draw in the speech bubbles. Some programs have choices from which you can choose a bubble to put in your cartoon strip.

7. Continue designing each of the sections. Use text boxes or the Typewriter tool if you need any writing in your strip.

What Else Can I Do?

Think of all the stories you can tell in this cartoon strip form. You can adapt stories you already know or create your own original stories to be shown in the cartoon strip form. Perhaps you and a friend can write a strip together.

1. Write and draw a cartoon that tells about a relationship between two animal enemies.

2. Can you write a cartoon strip that uses all of your spelling words for the week?

3. Write and draw your autobiography in cartoon strip form.

Cartoon Strip Planning Sheet

Title

Characters in story
- •
- •
- •
- •

Important locations
- •
- •
- •
- •

Important objects
- •
- •
- •
- •

Story Plot for the Cartoon Strip

Your story plot will be used for eight sections of a cartoon strip. If you want the story and the strip to be longer, save the screen and start over on a new screen. Be sure to save the screens so that you know what is on them—Cartoon set 1, Cartoon set 2, etc.

The Tale of Aladdin

Aladdin, a poor young boy, was looking for work in the marketplace. There, he met a stranger who claimed to be his uncle. "Come with me," he said, "and I will take you to a fabulous treasure." Now Aladdin did not trust this man, but he liked an adventure, so off he went.

What Aladdin did not know was that the stranger was really a greedy magician who wanted to use Aladdin because the boy had the courage of a lion. The magician led Aladdin far out into the desert and then up into the mountains. It was very cold that night, so the magician commanded Aladdin to build a fire. The magician threw some magic powder into the fire, and a cave in the side of the mountain was revealed. He gave Aladdin a ring. "Within this cave is a magical lamp. Bring me this lamp. The ring will protect you from the terrors within," he said to Aladdin. But he had an evil heart. He had given Aladdin a ring that would turn the boy into a stone statue if he carried it back out of the cave.

Aladdin found the lamp very quickly, but he was afraid the magician would try to hurt him once he left the cave. He searched around the cave and found a bag full of gold coins. He dumped out the coins and put a large, golden cup inside. He also took off the ring the magician had given him and placed it in the cup. He then tied up the bag and went back to the entrance of the cave.

"Oh, uncle, I have returned with the lamp. Let me throw it out to you." Saying this, he threw the bag out near the fire. When the magician saw this, he quickly put out the fire. The secret entrance to the cave disappeared! Aladdin was trapped. The magician picked up the bag and started down the mountain.

Poor Aladdin! He sat down in the pile of gold and rubbed his hands together for warmth. He was still holding the lamp. As he rubbed his hands back and forth, he was also rubbing the lamp. Suddenly, a genie appeared out of the lamp.

"What is your wish, Aladdin?"

Aladdin's reply was instant. "Oh, genie of the magic lamp, take me and all of the treasures in this cave to my poor mother's hut."

The genie snapped his fingers. Aladdin was standing in the middle of his mother's very small hut, which now seemed even smaller because of all the gold, silver, and precious jewels piled high in the house. Aladdin wished for a feast for his family and all of his friends.

They all lived very happily ever after, except for that wicked magician. Unable to wait until he returned to his magic shop, he put his hand into the bag and felt around for the magic lamp. Quite by accident, the magic ring slipped onto his finger, and he was turned into a stone statue. And he is still there to this day, if he hasn't been covered by a sandstorm.

Aladdin Planning Sheet Example

Characters in story

- Aladdin—young, poor boy with a lot of courage
- Magician—evil-hearted man who tries to trick Aladdin
- Mother—poor woman who lives in a hut
- Genie—comes from the magic lamp and saves Aladdin

Important locations

- outside where Aladdin meets uncle
- cave where Aladdin finds lamp

Important objects

- magic lamp
- magic ring
- gold pieces

Story Plot for the Cartoon Strip

Aladdin is playing ball.	Aladdin meets the magician Magician: Hi! I'm your Uncle.	The magician drops the magic powder into the fire.	Aladdin finds the lamp and tricks the Magician.
The Genie: What can I do for you?	Aladdin: Get me out of here!	Aladdin's mother: Give me food.	Happy! Happy! Happy!

A Cartoon Story Sample

This sample is on the CD-ROM as cartoon.kpx (cartoon.bmp) in the *Paint Draw Lesson* folder.

Word Processing Software

Word processing is one of the most important computer applications in schools. It helps students with the writing process and allows them to create documents such as letters, stories, and reports on the computer. The power of a word processing program is in its ability to manipulate, store, and retrieve text. This can simply be to add a sentence to the middle of a paragraph, or it can be to move large blocks of text within a document to another document all together. It has many functions that make writing easier. Students can edit their documents as much as they like during the writing process. Below are some definitions of the most common things a word processor can do:

- **Word Wrap**—moves a word automatically to the line below when the end of a line is reached.

- **Page Layout**—arranges text on the page. The student can set margins at the top, bottom, right, and left of the page, and place headers and footers at the top and bottom of the page.

- **Cut and Paste**—moves text from one part of the document to another.

- **Copy**—duplicates text from one part of the document to another.

- **Format Text**—changes the appearance of text. Common formats are bold, italic, and underline.

- **Font**—changes the type style. There are thousands of different fonts to choose from when writing a document.

- **Size**—adjusts the height of the type.

- **Spell Check**—checks the spelling of a word, phrase, or the entire document, and suggests replacement words.

- **Find and Replace**—searches for a word (for example—a name) and changes it into another word throughout the text.

When to Use Word Processing Software

Have your students use word processing documents when they want to write and format text. Some documents that your students can create with a word processor include:

- letters and memos

- personal journals

- stories

- lists and outlines

- research papers and reports

- copy for newsletters, brochures, and announcements

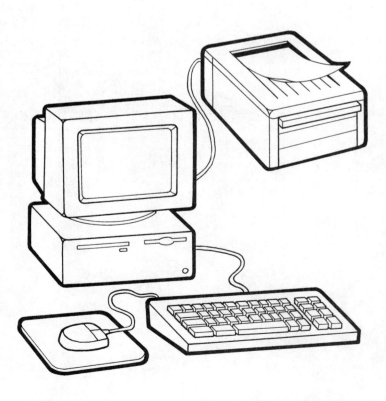

Word Processing Software *(cont.)*

Word Processing Software Programs

The two word processing programs that are the most popular integrated software packages used in schools today are *AppleWorks (ClarisWorks)* and *Microsoft Works*. Each of these programs is described below.

AppleWorks (ClarisWorks)

AppleWorks is the newest release of *ClarisWorks*. If you are buying a new computer or ordering new software from Apple, the integrated software package you purchase will be titled *AppleWorks*. All previously owned and installed packages are titled *ClarisWorks*.

AppleWorks (ClarisWorks) is an all-in-one productivity application that includes word processing, spreadsheet, database, painting, and graphics modules. It includes an extensive clip art library and several templates to help with the most common writing tasks. It is a cross-platform product which means it is available for both PCs and Macintosh computers, but it is most often used on Macintosh computers.

Microsoft Works

This is by far the most popular integrated software product which is used in schools that have *Microsoft Windows*. Its integrated package includes a word processor, a spreadsheet program, a database program, a drawing tool, and communication tools. Included in its package is an extensive clip art gallery and several templates to help students get started with the most common writing tasks.

Although some word processing activities may refer to specific software, they can be used with a variety of word processors. Some of the commands and procedures may differ slightly from program to program, but the basic operations are pretty much the same. Below is a list of other popular word processing software.

Recommended Word Processing Software Programs

Corel Word Perfect Suite 8 by Corel

Microsoft Word by Microsoft

Student Writing Center by The Learning Company

The Amazing Writing Machine by The Learning Company

The Writing Center by The Learning Company (Macintosh or Windows)

It's Negotiable
A Conflict Resolution Activity

This Project

In this project your students will write about resolving a conflict. They will identify the groups in the conflict and list each group's interests. They will evaluate possible resolutions. The conflict might be real or imaginary, from history or an actual conflict that they or their classmates are confronting.

Note: If you use the template provided on the CD-ROM (filename: conflict.doc in the *Word Processing Lesson* folder), direct your students to follow the prompts in the document.

Computer Skills

- word processing
- creating a table
- using the bullets and numbering tool
- using different font styles

Before Beginning

- Identify a conflict, the groups in the conflict, and each group's interests. Discuss conflict resolution and how to try to meet the needs of each group. Students can use the Planning Sheet/Template on Page 50.

Quick Steps

- Open a new word processing document.
- Type "**A Conflict Resolution**" as your title.
- Write a paragraph about a problem or conflict.
- Create a table of two columns and two rows.
- Type the names of the two groups in the first row.
- List each group's interests in the second row.
- Below the table, write about what might happen if the conflict is not resolved.
- List several resolutions to the conflict.
- Write about the best resolution and explain why.
- Save and print your document.

It's Negotiable
A Conflict Resolution Activity *(cont.)*

Step 1　Open a new word processing document.

Step 2　Click on the **Center** button on the Formatting tool bar. Set the font size to 24 or 36 points. Type **A Conflict Resolution**.

Step 3　Reset the font size to **12** points. Press the **Enter** or **Return** key twice. Click on the **Align Left** button. Type a paragraph about a conflict or problem. Press the **Enter** or **Return** key twice.

Step 4　Insert a table with 2 columns and 2 rows.

Step 5　Click at the top of the first column. Type **Group 1:** and the name of the first group in the conflict. Press the **Enter** or **Return** key.

Step 6　In the second row of the column, type the first group's interests in list format.

Step 7　Click at the top of the second column. Type **Group 2:** and the name of the second group in the conflict. Press the **Enter** or **Return** key.

Step 8　Type the second group's interests in the second row of the column.

Step 9　Click under the table. Press the **Enter** or **Return** key.
Click on the **Bold** button on the Formatting tool bar.
Type **What will happen if the conflict isn't resolved?**
Press the **Enter** or **Return** key. Click on the **Bold** button again to deactivate the function.
Type your answer to the question. Press the **Enter** or **Return** key twice.

Step 10　Click on the **Bold** button. Type **Possible conflict resolutions:** Press the **Enter** or **Return** key. Click on the **Bold** button again to deactivate the function. List several possible ways to resolve the conflict. You can number this list if you think that would make it easier to read. Press the **Enter** or **Return** key at the end of each resolution.

Step 11　Click on the **Bold** button. Type **What is the best resolution and why?** Press the **Enter** or **Return** key. Click on the **Bold** button again to deactivate the function. Type what you think is the best resolution and explain why.

Step 12　Save and print the document.

It's Negotiable
A Conflict Resolution Activity *(cont.)*

Planning Sheet/Template

Problem:

Group 1:	Group 2:
Interests:	Interests:

What will happen if the conflict isn't resolved?

_____

_____

Possible conflict resolutions:

_____

_____

_____

What is the best resolution and why?

_____

_____

_____

It's Negotiable
A Conflict Resolution Activity *(cont.)*

Sample

Problem: There is only one computer at the back of the room. Though the students in Mr. Garcia's fourth-grade class usually have specific assignments, this week they are allowed "free time," or an activity of their choice, during their center rotation time. The only requirement is that they work in pairs.

Hector and Seth can't agree on what to do. They only have 20 minutes.

Group 1: Hector	**Group 2:** Seth
Interests: play football math game	**Interests:** draw with *Kid Pix*

What will happen if the conflict isn't resolved?

Neither Hector nor Seth will do what they want to do at the computer. Maybe neither will use the computer at all, or one will have to do what the other wants.

Possible conflict resolutions:

- Hector agrees to do what Seth wants.
- Seth agrees to do what Hector wants.
- Hector plays his game for 10 minutes. Seth draws for 10 minutes.
- Seth and Hector decide to stay at their seats and not use the computer.
- Seth does what he wants this week. Hector gets his way next time there is free time, or vice versa.

What is the best resolution and why?

Number 3 is the best resolution because then both Hector and Seth do what they each want to do for an allotted time. Since they don't get free time each week, resolution 5 might not work. In resolutions 1 and 2, someone is not getting to do what he wants. Therefore, resolution 3 seems the fairest. It meets both groups' interests.

This sample is provided on the CD-ROM as sample.doc in the *Word Processing Lesson* folder.

Spreadsheet Software

A spreadsheet program is used for financial and other number-related information processing. Spreadsheet data is arranged on a grid that is composed of rows and columns, with individual boxes called cells. The cells inside of each row or column hold the information. Spreadsheets can be used to store and organize all kinds of numerical information. For example, your students can use a spreadsheet to calculate how much time they spend on daily activities such as eating, recreation, homework, television, school, and other classes, and then produce graphs to display this information.

There are a number of opportunities to use spreadsheets in all subjects and in all grade levels. Below are ideas for spreadsheet topics in the content areas.

- **Science**
  - Enter the number of hours of sunlight at various places around the world in four different months on a spreadsheet. Graph the data.
  - Use the spreadsheet grid to create a graph of how long sunlight hits different parts of the world.

- **Social Studies**
  - Take a survey of the places where each student was born. Show this information on a graph.
  - Plan a five-day trip. Calculate your daily expenses. Include room, transportation, sightseeing, meals, etc.

- **Mathematics**
  - Create magic squares by arranging numbers so that every row and column adds up to the same predetermined sum.
  - Keep track of magazine or candy drive sales.

- **Language Arts**
  - Keep a reading log. Include the title/author, start date, finish date, type of book, and its rating on a scale of 1–5.
  - Create a school subject attitude spreadsheet to discover and graph student preferences in percentage of students who like or dislike math, reading, social studies, physical education, writing, art, and music.

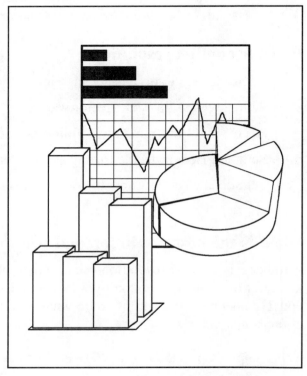

Spreadsheet Software *(cont.)*

Spreadsheet Software Programs

The spreadsheet programs most referred to are *Microsoft Excel* and the integrated programs *Microsoft Works* and *AppleWorks (ClarisWorks)*. *Microsoft Excel,* which is designed specifically for the purpose of creating a spreadsheet and has many more features for doing so, is somewhat more difficult to use than *Microsoft Works* and *AppleWorks (ClarisWorks)*. So, it is an excellent teacher tool and may be a good purchase for middle school or high school classrooms that are not using one of the integrated programs for word processing or database management and wish to invest in one good spreadsheet program for use by both the teacher and the students.

AppleWorks (ClarisWorks)

AppleWorks is the newest release of *ClarisWorks*. If you are buying a new computer or ordering new software from Apple, the integrated software package you purchase will be titled *AppleWorks*. However, all previously owned and installed packages are titled *ClarisWorks*.

AppleWorks (ClarisWorks) is an all-in-one productivity application that includes word processing, spreadsheet, database, painting, and graphics modules. It includes an extensive clip art library and several templates to help with the most common spreadsheet tasks. It is a cross-platform product, which means it is available for both PCs and Macintosh computers, but it is most often used on Macintosh computers.

Microsoft Works

This is by far the most popular integrated software product that is used in schools that use *Microsoft Windows*. Its integrated package includes a word processor, a spreadsheet program, a database program, a drawing tool, and communication tools. Included in its package is an extensive Clip Art Gallery and several templates to help students get started with the most common spreadsheet tasks.

Microsoft Excel

Excel is a complete spreadsheet program that brings powerful spreadsheet operations, formula creation, printing, formatting, and charting to the surface to make it easier than ever to analyze, report, and share your spreadsheet data. Interactive help is available as you work with the Office Assistant program.

Spreadsheet Software *(cont.)*

Spreadsheet Software Programs *(cont.)*

Although some spreadsheet lesson plans refer to specific software, they can be used with a variety of spreadsheet programs. Below are some factors to consider when selecting a spreadsheet program for your classroom.

- **Is the spreadsheet application easy to learn and user-friendly?**

  It is important for students and teachers to focus on the tasks they are trying to accomplish rather than on how to use the spreadsheet software and access the information. Spreadsheet programs that allow your students to begin working with data from a file within a few minutes after you introduce a program allow them to focus their time on completing the tasks they wish to accomplish.

- **Is it easy to design a file in the spreadsheet program?**

  It is important that teachers and students have experience with many different types of data files designed for many different purposes. The program should be flexible enough to allow for experimentation.

- **Does the spreadsheet program have presentation possibilities?**

  Users should be able to prepare and present information clearly. The program must be capable of printing selected information in a variety of forms, including lists, tables, graphs, or charts, as well as able to sort numerically, alphabetically, and chronologically.

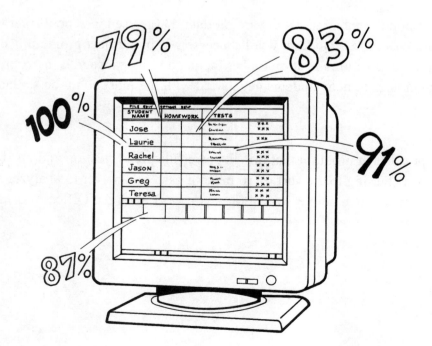

Righty or Lefty?
An Introduction to Charting

How many of your students are left-handed? How many are right-handed? This is a fun activity in which the students survey their classmates to find the proportion of right- and left-handed students in the class. This is a nice activity to introduce yourself and/or your students to the charting capability of your spreadsheet program.

Grade Level: Third to Fifth

Materials

- Printout of *Righty or Lefty Survey Form* (page 63) for students to compile data
- *Righty or Lefty Microsoft Excel* template on the CD-ROM (filename: righty.xls in the *Spreadsheet Lesson* folder)

Before the Computer

- Pass out the survey form for compiling data on left- and right-handedness. You can either copy it from page 63 or on the CD-ROM (filename: survey.doc in the *Spreadsheet Lesson* folder).
- Ask the students to make some predictions. Will there be more right-handed or left-handed students? What do they think is the reason for this?
- Get the students thinking about what it is like to be left-handed in a right-handed world. Ask them questions such as:
  - Do you think it is easier to be right-handed or left-handed? Why?
  - What are some things in our classroom that are easier for right-handers than left-handers to work with? (scissors, wall-mounted pencil sharpener, modular desks—desk attached to right side of chair)
  - What is more awkward about writing left-handed than right-handed? (When writing left-handed, your hand covers up the writing as soon as you write it—another artifact of our right-handed world. If we wrote from right to left, the advantage would be with the left-handers!)
- Allow the students to come up with different ways of collecting the data. The class may choose to collect the data all at once with a simple show of hands, or by taking a few minutes to move about the classroom and tally the results by questioning their classmates.

On the Computer

- Open the *Righty or Lefty Microsoft Excel* template on the CD-ROM (filename: righty.xls).
- Enter the information from your prediction in cells **C10** and **C11**.
- Enter your collected data in cells **D10** and **D11**.
- Select cells **B9** through **D11**, and create a chart for your data.

Extensions

- Have students collect left-handed and right-handed data for all the students in their grade level or school, and compare it to the data they collected for just the class. Is the classroom data a good predictor for the larger group?
- Nationally, the percentage of left-handed people is about 13%. Have the students compare this data to their classroom data.
- Have the students collect data on foot dominance. Is hand dominance a good predictor of foot dominance?

Righty or Lefty?
An Introduction to Charting *(cont.)*

Extensions *(cont.)*

- What about eye dominance? To determine which eye is dominant, have the student hold his/her finger at arm's length and line it up with a distant object (at least three feet away) with both eyes open. Instruct the student to close one eye at a time—the eye that sees the finger and distant object in alignment is the dominant eye.

- Have the students collect handedness data on their parents and display the results collectively. How does it compare to the student data? Do you think that if your mom or dad is left-handed, your chances of being left-handed are greater?

Righty or Lefty? Example (filename: example.xls in *Spreadsheet Lesson* folder)

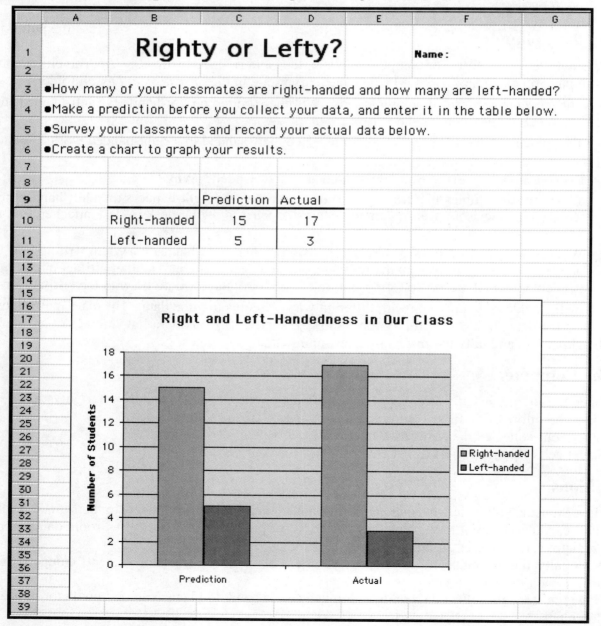

Righty or Lefty?
An Introduction to Charting *(cont.)*

Step-by-Step Instructions

Note: If you are using the *Righty or Lefty* template from the CD-ROM, begin with Step 15. These directions are specifically designed for *Microsoft Excel,* but will also work for other spreadsheet programs. Some of the specific directions may be slightly different.

Step 1

Open a new spreadsheet document.

Step 2

Click in cell **C1** once to highlight the cell and change the font to 24 point. You can use the pull-down font menu on the formatting tool bar.

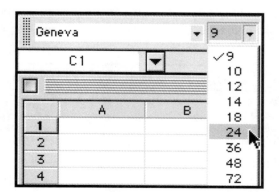

Step 3

Now let's apply bold text style to the cell. Click on the **Bold** icon in the formatting tool bar. Alternatively, you can pull down the **FORMAT** menu and select *Font*, and choose bold in the dialog

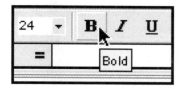

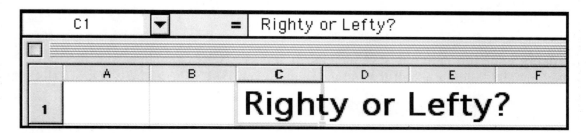

Righty or Lefty?
An Introduction to Charting *(cont.)*

Step 5

Let's center the text we just typed in cell **C1**. First we need to reselect the cell. To do this, click in any other cell, then click once back in cell **C1**. Now click on the **Center Alignment** button on the formatting tool bar.

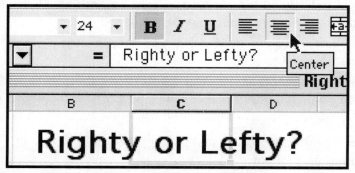

Step 6

Now let's make cell **C1** taller so the larger font fits better. Double-click on the gridline between rows one and two to make it fit the text you just typed. (In *Excel*, you can use the Format, Row—Height function and make the height 40.)

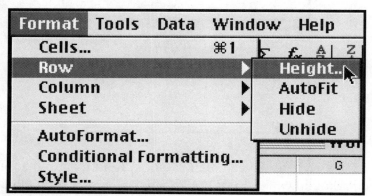

Step 7

Now click in cell **F1** and type your name. You can make the font bold if you like. See if you can make it a different color while you're at it!

Step 8

Click in cell **B10** and type **Right-handed**, and click in cell **B11** and type **Left-handed**.

Step 9

Click in cell **C9** and type **Prediction**, and click in cell **D9** and type in **Actual**.

Step 10

Now let's apply some formatting to several cells all at once. Select the block of cells from **B9** through **D11** by clicking and holding in cell **B9** and dragging to cell **D11**. The entire block of cells should now be selected.

Righty or Lefty?
An Introduction to Charting *(cont.)*

Step 11

Change the font size to 12 point (see step 2). The columns are now running together, but don't panic! We will fix this in the next step.

Step 12

In *Microsoft Excel*, with the block of cells still selected, pull down the **FORMAT** menu and select *Columns—AutoFit Selection*. Your columns will automatically adjust to fit your new font size. Do the same thing for the row height by pulling down the **FORMAT** menu and selecting *Rows—AutoFit*. The AutoFit feature is a very handy way to adjust cell size to fit your data! With most spreadsheet programs, you can simply double-click on the gridlines separating the rows or columns to autofit the words within the cell.

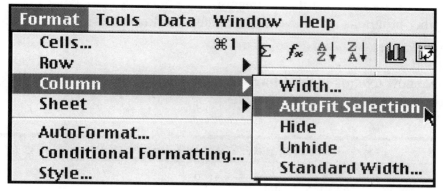

Step 13

Let's apply some borders to our data table to make it easier to read. Highlight cells **B9** through **D9**. Using the **Border** button on the formatting tool bar, apply a dark lower border to these cells.

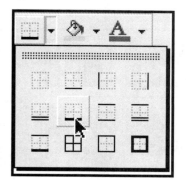

	Prediction	Actual
Right-handed	17	21
Left-handed	6	2

Step 14

Cells **B9** through **B11** could use a light right border. Select these cells and apply the border using the **Border** button.

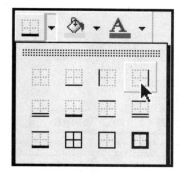

	Prediction	Actual
Right-handed	17	21
Left-handed	6	2

Righty or Lefty?
An Introduction to Charting *(cont.)*

Step 15

Now let's enter our data from the survey of our classmates. Click in cell **C10** and type in your prediction for how many right-handed students are in your class. Enter your data in cells **C11**, **D10**, and **D11** the same way.

Step 16

We are ready to create our chart! For this lesson, we will create a simple bar graph. Before creating a chart, you must always select the data you wish the chart to be based on. Select cells **B9** through **D11** by clicking, holding, and dragging from cell **B9** to cell **D11**. Pull down the **INSERT** menu and select *Chart*. (Please note that these directions are specifically for *Microsoft Excel* and other programs may have different steps in this process.

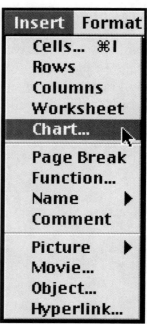

Step 17

You are now looking at the **Chart Wizard** window. For this graph, let's use **Column** for chart type. Click on **Next.**

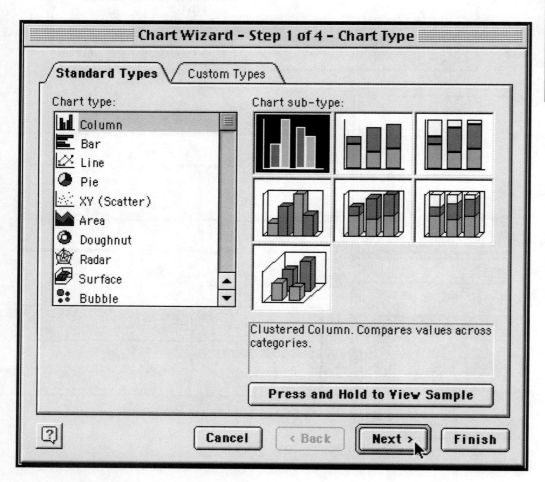

Righty or Lefty?
An Introduction to Charting *(cont.)*

Step 18

Note that you are now on Step 2 of the **Chart Wizard**. Click on **Next** again.

Step 19

Now you are on Step 3 of the **Chart Wizard**. You can type in a chart title and an Y-axis title. What would be a good title for the graph? Also think of an appropriate title for the Y-axis. Click on **Next.**

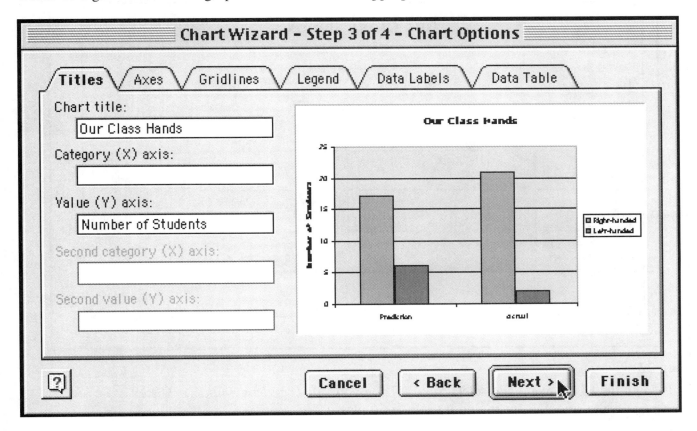

Step 20

This is Step 4 of the **Chart Wizard**—the last step. Make sure **As object in** is checked. This will place your graph in the same sheet as your data table in your *Microsoft Excel* worksheet. Click on **Finish.**

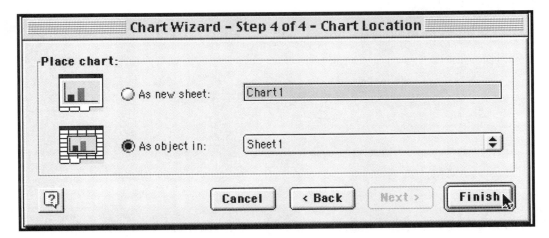

Righty or Lefty?
An Introduction to Charting *(cont.)*

Step 21

Congratulations! You have created your first chart. You can move it wherever you wish in your document by clicking, holding, and dragging it to its new location. (You have to click and hold on white space in the chart window, not on the chart itself.)

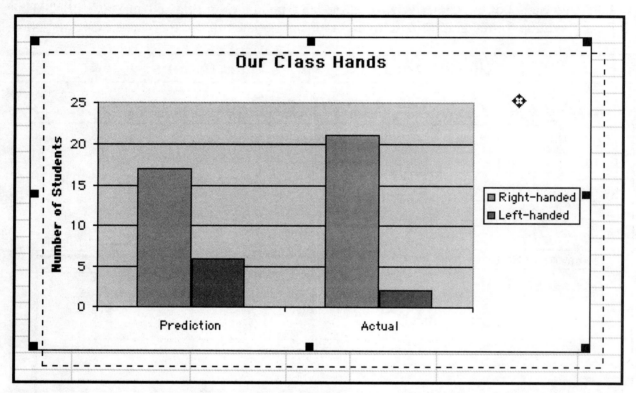

Step 22

Pull down the **FILE** menu and select *Save*. Name your file *(handyourinitials)*. Check with your teacher to make sure you are saving it to the right place.

Step 23

If you want to print your document, pull down the **FILE** menu and select *Print*.

Righty or Lefty?
An Introduction to Charting *(cont.)*

Righty or Lefty? Survey Form

Use this form to collect data on your classmates to determine how many are left-handed and how many are right-handed.

1. First make a prediction of how many students in your class you think are left-handed and right-handed. Record your information in the data table below.

2. Now poll your classmates for left and right-handers. Then record the information in the data table.

3. Before going to the computer to create your chart, draw your bar graph with pencil on the axes below.

	Prediction	Actual
Right-handed		
Left-handed		

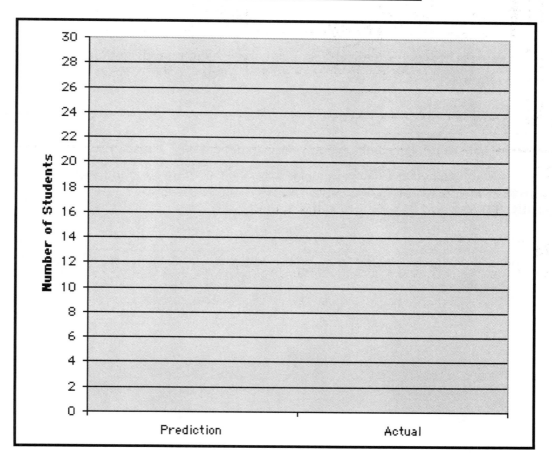

Database Software

A database is a way of storing and managing information on any particular area of interest or subject, electronically. The completed database is a collection of related information that you and your students can sort, search through, and print as needed. Each type of data is called a field. Examples of fields are names, addresses, phone numbers, and so forth. A single piece of information, such as the name George Washington, is called an entry. Below are ideas for database topics along with suggested fields in the content areas.

Science

- The Planets: name of planet, size, density, distance from the sun, rotation time, revolution time, number of moons, makeup of atmosphere
- Healthy Menus and Recipes: breakfast menus, lunch menus, dinner menus, appetizers, soups, salads, breads, meats & poultry, side dishes, desserts
- Famous inventors: inventor, invention, year, country, description, impact, current applications

Social Studies

- Presidents: name, party, term, year, state, background, major contributions
- States: name, capital, governor, bird, flower, flag, facts, tourism, population, famous residents, chief industries
- Native Peoples of North America: name of tribe, location, food, clothing, housing, modes of transportation, tools, ceremonies

Mathematics

- History of Measurement: unit, event, year, person, country, impact, use today
- Famous Mathematicians: name, country, year, theory, application, impact

Language Arts

- Caldecott Award Winners: year awarded, title of book, author, illustrator, publisher, brief synopsis
- Authors and Addresses: author's last name, author's first name, street address, city, state, zip code, most popular books
- Reading Record: title of book, author/illustrator, start date, finish date, type, how shared, rating

Database Software *(cont.)*

Database Software Programs

The two database programs most referred to are those included in the integrated programs *Microsoft Works* and *AppleWorks (ClarisWorks)*. Two other popular and widely used database programs are *FileMaker Pro* and *Microsoft Access,* which are designed specifically for the purpose of creating a database and have many more features for doing so. These two programs are somewhat more difficult to use than *Microsoft Works* and *AppleWorks (ClarisWorks)*, but the extra features could be useful to students in middle school or high school. It is an excellent teaching tool and may be a good purchase for classrooms that are not using one of the integrated programs for word processing or spreadsheets and wish to invest in one good database program for both the teacher and the students.

AppleWorks (ClarisWorks)

AppleWorks is the newest release of *ClarisWorks*. If you are buying a new computer or ordering new software from Apple, the integrated software package you purchase will be titled *AppleWorks*. However, all previously owned and installed packages are titled *ClarisWorks*.

AppleWorks (ClarisWorks) is an all-in-one productivity application that includes word processing, spreadsheet, database, painting, drawing, and graphics modules. It includes an extensive clip art library and several templates to help with the most common database tasks. It is a cross-platform product, which means it is available for both PCs and Macintosh computers, but it is most often used on Macintosh computers.

Microsoft Works

This is by far the most popular integrated software product that is used in schools that use *Microsoft Windows*. Its integrated package includes a word processor, a spreadsheet program, a database program, painting and drawing tools, and communication tools. Included in its package is an extensive clip art gallery and several templates to help students get started with the most common database tasks.

FileMaker Pro

This software from FileMaker, Inc. gives you and your students the power to organize, share, and gain value from their information—from the desktop to the Web. If you or your students use *Microsoft Excel*, which is included in the *Microsoft Office* products, the files can be dragged and dropped into *FileMaker Pro* databases.

Microsoft Access

This software from Microsoft helps you and your students organize, analyze, and share information. Data can be easily interchanged between *Access* and *Microsoft Excel*.

Database Software *(cont.)*

Database Software Programs *(cont.)*

Although some database lessons refer to specific software, they can be used with a variety of database programs. Below are some factors to consider when selecting a database program for your classroom.

- **Ease of Learning**—It is important for students and teachers to focus on the task they are trying to accomplish rather than focus on how to use the database software and how to access database information. Programs that allow you and your students to begin file retrieval within a few minutes after you introduce a program allow students to spend time completing the task they wish to accomplish.

- **Ease of Use**—The program should be easily entered and operated and not be bogged down by a multitude of obscure commands and complicated menu formats.

- **Ease of File Design**—The program you select should be capable of a wide range of formats without limitations on the length, number of entries, or design of entry.

- **Ease and Flexibility in Naming Data Items**—When designing and interpreting data files, students need to work with headings that are clearly and accurately labeled. Avoid selecting programs in which headings need to be represented in code, symbol, or obscurely abbreviated form.

- **Ease of Search and Retrieval**—Criteria for the search and retrieval of appropriate information should be easy for students and teachers. In addition, students and teachers should be able to search more than one field or item, such as people who have October birthdays who are relatives.

- **Ease and Flexibility in Printing Reports**—This is inherent in integrated programs. Both *Microsoft Works* and *AppleWorks (ClarisWorks)* have the feature of mail merge that is used to print letters or labels.

	Last Name	First Name	Street Address	City	State	Zip Code	Telephone Number
1	Bell	Frank	108 Bearch Road	Brooklyn	NY	11457	555-9876
2	Bronza	Rosanne	67 Rodeo Street	Houston	TX	10990	555-9886
3	Dolton	Maureen	5 Hallow Lane	Tampa	FL	14457	555-7364
4	Guero	Celia	4 Andrew Lane	Marysville	CA	10678	555-9784
5	Harry	Tom	64 Hanes St.	Ann Arbor	MI	12990	555-8765
6	Pero	John	74 Buswel Street	Boston	MA	16784	555-0953
7	Rusin	Julia	17 Angel Place	Rome	VA	11974	555-8573
8	Ryan	Al	6 Conway Court	Roanoke	VA	15678	555-7538
9	Smith	John	78 Spring Circle	Hollywood	FL	14497	555-8907
10	Zimman	Annmarie	8 Kinder Lane	Macon	GA	12876	555-6428

Animal Classification

This Project

In this project your students will create a database of the various types of animals. This information system can be used to compare vertebrates and invertebrates. Once all of the facts have been recorded, students will be able to classify and categorize animals based on their body structures, habitats, and special features.

Computer Skills

- database
- entering data
- finding information
- sorting data

Before Beginning

- Your students should be familiar with the differences between vertebrates and invertebrates. They should also be able to identify the different body structures that diverse invertebrates have.

- Assign students various animals to research. They should be able to locate the information that is requested on page 70. Student will use the completed database to complete the planning sheet on page 71.

- Prepare an Animal Classification database using the Teacher Task card on page 69.

Quick Steps

- Open the *AppleWorks* template from the CD-ROM (filename: animal.cwk in the *Database Lesson* folder).
- Go to the Browse mode.
- Create a new record.
- Enter the information for your animal.
- Save the database with the same file name.
- Use the Find feature to answer the questions on the planning sheet on page 71.
- Use the Sort feature to categorize animals according to these characteristics: Where they live, Vertebrate/Invertebrate, and Group/Type.
- Print a listing of all of the animals that fit into the same category for one characteristic.

Note: The directions on the following page assume you are using the *AppleWorks* template from the CD-ROM. So, these directions are specifically designed for AppleWorks, but the activity can also be completed in other database programs with some changes in the directions.

Animal Classification *(cont.)*

Step 1 Open *AppleWorks*. Click on the **Cancel** button to close the opening window.

Step 2 Pull down the **FILE** menu and select *Open*. Find the file on the CD-ROM called animal.cwk and click on it. Click on the **Open** button.

Step 3 Pull down the **LAYOUT** menu and select *Browse*.

Step 4 Pull down the **EDIT** menu and select *New Record*.

Step 5 Type the name of the animal that you researched for this project into the first field. Press the tab key to move to the next field.

Step 6 Use the information that you gathered on the planning page sheet on page 71 to fill in the data for this record.

 Press the tab key to move from field to field. You can also change fields by moving the mouse and clicking in the field where you want to enter information.

Step 7 Pull down the **EDIT** menu and select *Save As*. Keep the same file name. Click on the **Save** button. Yes, you do want to replace the original file with this new one.

How to Find Information

Step 8 Open *AppleWorks*. Click on the **Cancel** button to close the opening window.

Step 9 Pull down the **FILE** menu and select *Open*. Find the file on the CD-ROM called animal.cwk and click on it. Click on the *Open* button.

Step 10 Pull down the **LAYOUT** menu and select *Find*. You will see a blank form for this database.

Step 11 Move the mouse until you are pointing to the field you want to use. For example, if you are looking for all of the fish in the database, move the pointer to the field called Group/Type. Click the mouse button to place the cursor in that field.

Step 12 Enter the word or words that you want the computer to find. In our example, you would type *fish*. Click in the **Find** button at the left side of the screen. All records that have the word fish in the Group/Type category will be shown on the screen.

Step 13 Repeat Steps 3 to 5 to answer the questions on the planning page on page 71.

Sorting Information

Step 14 Pull down the **ORGANIZE** menu and choose *Sort Records*.

Step 15 Click on the category that you want to sort by. Click on the **Move** button. Click on the **OK** button. Categorize the animals by these characteristics: Where they live, Vertebrate/Invertebrate, Group/Type.

Step 16 Pull down the **FILE** menu and select *Print*. Click on the **Print** button to print a copy of each of your sorted lists.

Animal Classification *(cont.)*

Teacher Task Card

Follow these directions to set up a template of the Animal Classification database for your students to use as they complete this activity.

- Open a new *AppleWorks* document. At the opening window, select **Database**, and then click on the **OK** button.

- Enter the following field names in the define fields window:

    Animal Name, Vertebrate/Invertebrate, Group/Type, Special features: Body structure, Where found

- Click on the **Done** button when you have entered all of the field names.

 Remember to click on the **Create** button after you have typed each field name.

- Pull down the **LAYOUT** menu and select *Layout*.

- Click on the frame next to the field Animal Name to select it. Pull down the **FORMAT** menu and choose *Size*. Make this text *14 points*. Pull down the **STYLE** menu and select *Bold*. This will make the name of the animal larger and bolder than the rest of the information.

- Pull down the **EDIT** menu and choose *Select All*. Place the pointer arrow in the middle of the selected objects and drag them down the screen about one inch (2.5 cm).

- Move the pointer arrow until it is on the gray line that says *Body*. When the pointer becomes a double arrow, drag the gray line down until all of the field names are above it.

- Adjust the size of all of the frames so that the words fit neatly.

- Choose the *text* tool from the tool bar. Drag the mouse to make text field at the top of the screen. Type the title of this database, *Animal Classification*.

- Drag the mouse over the words to highlight them. Pull down the **SIZE** menu and select *18 points*. Pull down the **STYLE** menu and choose *Bold*.

- Select the *rounded rectangle* tool from the tool bar. Hold the mouse button down as you drag the mouse across the title. Choose a *six-point* line, transparent fill pattern, and a line pattern of your own choice.

- Pull down the **FILE** menu and choose *Save As*. Give the file the name *animal*. Click on the **Save** button.

- Pull down the **FILE** menu and choose *Quit*.

Animal Classification *(cont.)*

Planning Sheet

You will need to know the following information in order to complete this database.

Animal Name—This is the name of the animal that you will be adding to the database.

Vertebrate or Invertebrate—Which category does your animal belong to?

Group/Type—Is your animal a fish, amphibian, reptile, bird, mammal, sponge, hollow-bodied, flatworm, roundworm, segmented worm, mollusk, spiny-skinned, or anthropod?

Special Features: Body Structure—In this field include items such as the way the body looks, the way the body feels, segmented body, legs, skeleton, exoskeleton, warm blooded, cold blooded, type of eggs, lungs, or gills.

Where Found—In this field, tell where the animal lives, for example, in fresh water, in salt water, on land, inside other animals or plants, or in the soil.

Enter the information for your animal on this form. Then, use the Animal Classification database to help you find the answers to questions on the following page.

Animal Classification

Animal Name	
Vertebrate • **Invertebrate**	
Group/Type	
Special features • **Body structure**	
Where found	

Animal Classification *(cont.)*

Planning Sheet *(cont.)*

Which animals live in water? _____

Which animals are invertebrates?_____

Which animals have segmented bodies? _____

Which animals are mammals? _____

Which animals are found in salt water? _____

Which animals live in fresh water? _____

Which animals are amphibians?_____

Which animals are warm blooded? _____

Which animals are cold blooded?_____

Which animals have an exoskeleton?_____

Which animals are birds? _____

Which animals lay eggs? _____

Which animals are mollusks?_____

Which animals are anthropods? _____

Which animals have hair or fur? _____

Presentation Software

Presentation programs create dynamic multimedia projects. Students use a combination of video, sound, text, and graphics. Multimedia projects, reports, and presentations turn students into directors as they create interactive presentations. Among the many projects students can create using multimedia and presentation software are the following:

- school projects
- multimedia portfolios
- family projects
- interactive games
- slide shows
- stories

Multimedia Presentation Software Programs

The multimedia presentation programs most referred to are *HyperStudio* by Knowledge Adventure, *PowerPoint* by Microsoft, and *Kid Pix Studio* by The Learning Company.

- *HyperStudio* is an easy-to-use program designed to allow teachers and students to prepare multimedia documents complete with text, graphics, animation, and video. Below are the basic elements of *HyperStudio*.

  - **Cards**—A card is similar to an index card. It can contain text, graphics, and buttons. At the click of a button, music may be heard or a short *QuickTime* video may be seen.

  - **Stacks**—A stack is a number of cards that are grouped together. The cards in the stack usually revolve around a common theme such as space, poetry, or information on a given country.

  - **Home Stack**—Home is the central stack. It is usually used as the base of operations and it can contain buttons to open other stacks.

  - **Buttons**—Buttons enable the user to move from one place to another within a stack. Buttons may also be used in a single-card *HyperStudio* presentation to play a sound, a movie, display text, or create a visual effect. Clicking on buttons is a convenient way to explore a stack.

  - **Fields**—Fields are the boxes on each card where text can be typed. It is possible to have more than one field on a card.

  - **Linking**—It is possible to link a button from one card to another. Buttons allow students to link pieces of information together. For example, a button on the first card of a stack can be linked to another card in the stack, no matter how many cards are in the stack. It is possible to select where the button is to go and what action it is to perform. A button can link a card to another card, another stack, and even to another program. Some actions it can perform are to play a sound, to play a movie, and to play a video.

Presentation Software *(cont.)*

Multimedia Presentation Software Programs *(cont.)*

- *PowerPoint* by Microsoft is an easy-to-use presentation program for students in grades 4 and up. Although it runs on both Windows and Microsoft platforms, it is primarily used in classrooms that use *Microsoft Windows* on their PCs. *PowerPoint* is an excellent tool for cooperative learning. Students work together to collect data, graphics, and illustrations for a topic relating to seasonal activities, social studies, science, language arts, or mathematics and place them into a *PowerPoint* presentation. Some of the features that add impact to these multimedia reports include the following:

  - **Charting Tools**—allow students to represent data on a variety of innovative charts.

  - **Multimedia Clip Gallery**—stores clip art, sounds, movies and pictures in a common location.

  - **Action Buttons**—allow students to add hyperlinks to other slides, files and even to the Internet using a set of predefined buttons.

  - **Drawing Tools**—this OfficeArt collection includes drawing tools, flowchart symbols, curves, textures, and 3-D text effects.

  - **Hyperlinks**—allow you to insert invisible links to other pages in your presentation, other presentations, or the Internet.

- *Kid Pix Studio* is a simple program that allows students of all levels to add all or some of the following elements: pictures, animations, digital movies, special transitions, and sound effects to create a slide show. To do this, students do the following:

  - Select an image for each of the slides and place them one at a time, each in a separate moving van, in the order they want to present them.

  - If his/her picture does not already have a sound recording attached to it, select the musical note to bring up the Pick a Sound! screen. Select a sound from *SlideShow's* ready-made set of sound effects and music.

  - Select the **Transition** button and choose a transition effect to take the show from one slide to the next. Click on the **Preview** button to see the transition selected.

  - Use the **Time Slider** to control the length of time they want each slide to play.

Most activities can be used with a variety of multimedia and presentation software. Some of the commands and procedures may differ slightly from program to program, but the basic operations are pretty much the same.

Nutrition

This Project

In this project, your students will use a slide show format to document the types of foods they eat and to demonstrate whether they are meeting their basic daily nutritional requirements.

Computer Skills

- Adding graphics
- Adding text boxes
- Using and adding bullets
- Creating a complete slide show presentation

Before Beginning

- Review the Food Pyramid on page 77 with your students.
- Review portions and servings with your students.
- Have students use the Student Planning Sheets on pages 78–79 to record the food they eat in a single day.
- Show students how to locate the template for this project.

Quick Steps

- Open the template from the CD-ROM (filename: pyramid.ppt in the *PowerPoint Lesson* folder).
- Insert a text box listing all the foods you ate at breakfast.
- Insert graphics of some of the foods you ate at breakfast.
- Scroll to the next slide, *Lunch*.
- Insert a text box listing all the foods you ate at lunch.
- Insert graphics of some of the foods you ate at lunch.
- Scroll to the next slide, *Dinner*.
- Insert a text box listing all the foods that you ate at dinner.
- Insert graphics of some of the foods you ate at dinner.
- Scroll to the next slide, *Snacks*.
- Insert a text box listing all the snacks you ate throughout the day.
- Insert graphics of some of the snacks you ate.
- Scroll down the next slide, *My Nutrition*.
- Click on the text box that asks for the number of servings you ate in each category.
- Fill in the number of servings that you ate for each of the categories.
- Click on the question at the bottom of the page.
- Answer whether or not you ate foods that match the nutritional requirements on the food pyramid.
- Resize the text boxes as needed.
- Save and print.

Nutrition *(cont.)*

Procedure

Step 1   Open *PowerPoint* and select **Open an existing presentation**. Click **OK**. Select the *pyramid* template from the CD-ROM and click **Open**.

Step 2   The first slide of the presentation is *Breakfast*. Pull down the **INSERT** menu and select *Text Box*.

Step 3   Move your mouse to place the arrow where you want the text box to be on your slide.

Step 4   Click the **Bullets** icon to make a list of all the foods you ate at breakfast.

Step 5   Pull down the **INSERT** menu and select *Picture*.

Step 6   Select *Clip Art*. Select a type of food you want to put on your slide and click **Insert**.

Step 7   Select the graphic and grab one of the handles with the mouse to resize as needed.

Step 8   Move your mouse to the scroll bar at the right of the screen, and scroll down to the next slide, *Lunch*.

Step 9   Pull down the **INSERT** menu and select *Text Box*.

Step 10   Move your mouse to place the arrow where you want your text box to be on your slide.

Step 11   Click the **Bullets** icon to make a list of all the foods you ate at lunch.

Step 12   Pull down the **INSERT** menu and select *Picture*.

Step 13   Select *Clip Art*. Select a type of food you want to put on your slide and click **Insert**.

Step 14   Select the graphic and grab one of the handles with the mouse to resize as needed.

Step 15   Move your mouse to the scroll bar at the right of the screen, and scroll down to the next slide, *Dinner*.

Step 16   Pull down the **INSERT** menu and select *Text Box*.

Step 17   Move your mouse to place the arrow where you want your text box to be on your slide.

Step 18   Click the **Bullets** icon to make a list of all the foods you ate at dinner.

Step 19   Pull down the **INSERT** menu and select *Picture*.

Step 20   Select *Clip Art*. Select a type of food you want to put on your slide and click **Insert**.

Step 21   Select the graphic and grab one of the handles with the mouse to resize as needed.

Step 22   Move your mouse to the scroll bar at the right of the screen, and scroll down to the next slide, *Snacks*.

Step 23   Pull down the **INSERT** menu and select *Text Box*.

Step 24   Move your mouse to place the arrow where you want your text box to be on your slide.

Step 25   Click the **Bullets** icon to make a list of all of the snack foods that you ate throughout the entire day. Be sure to include snacks that you ate between breakfast and lunch, lunch and dinner, and dinner and bedtime.

Nutrition *(cont.)*

Step 26   Pull down the **INSERT** menu, select *Picture* and then *Clip Art*.

Step 27   Locate clip art for snack food you ate that day, and click **Insert** to add to your slide.

Step 28   Move your mouse to the scroll bar at the right of the screen, and scroll down to the next slide, *My Nutrition*.

Step 29   Move your mouse over the number of servings of each of the food groups, and click once to access the text box.

Step 30   Add up the number of servings you ate in a single day of each of the food groups, and enter them into the text box.

Step 31   Move your mouse over the questions at the bottom of the page and click once to access the text box.

Step 32   Answer the questions in the text box.

Step 33   Use the handles to resize the text boxes as needed.

Step 34   Pull down the **FILE** menu and select *Save As*. Give your file the name (*Nutrition your initials*).

Step 35   Pull down the **FILE** menu and select *Print*. Click **OK** (PC) or **Print** (Mac).

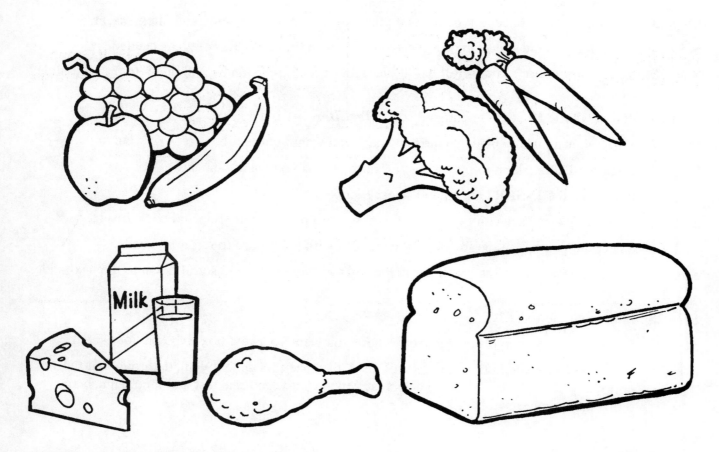

Nutrition *(cont.)*

Food Pyramid

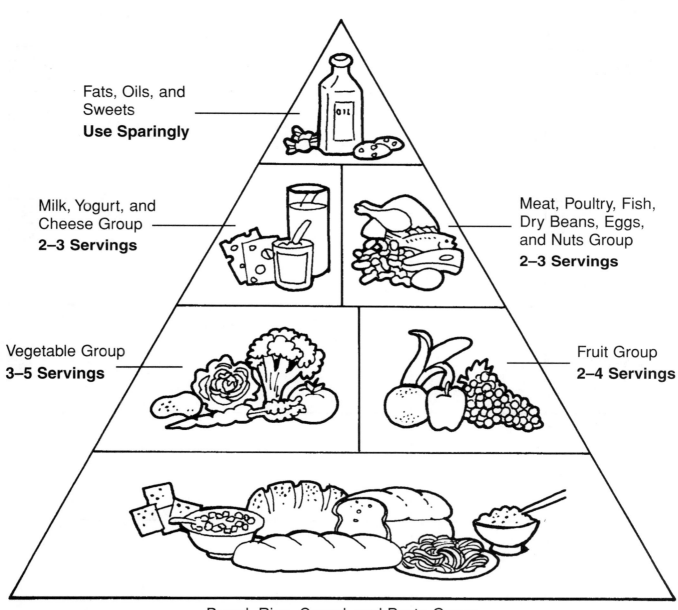

Fats, Oils, and Sweets
Use Sparingly

Milk, Yogurt, and Cheese Group
2–3 Servings

Meat, Poultry, Fish, Dry Beans, Eggs, and Nuts Group
2–3 Servings

Vegetable Group
3–5 Servings

Fruit Group
2–4 Servings

Bread, Rice, Cereal, and Pasta Group
6–11 Servings

Name:_____

Nutrition *(cont.)*

Student Planning Sheet

Directions: Today you are going to keep track of everything you eat. You need to record all the food you eat at breakfast, lunch, and dinner. You also need to write down all the snacks and treats you eat throughout the day. Under each category, list the food you ate beside the food group it belongs to.

Food Groups	Breakfast	Lunch	Dinner	Snack
Bread				
Fruits				
Vegetables				
Dairy				
Meat				
Fats/Sugars				

Name:_____

Nutrition *(cont.)*

Student Planning Sheet *(cont.)*

Directions: Use your food record to complete the graph below.

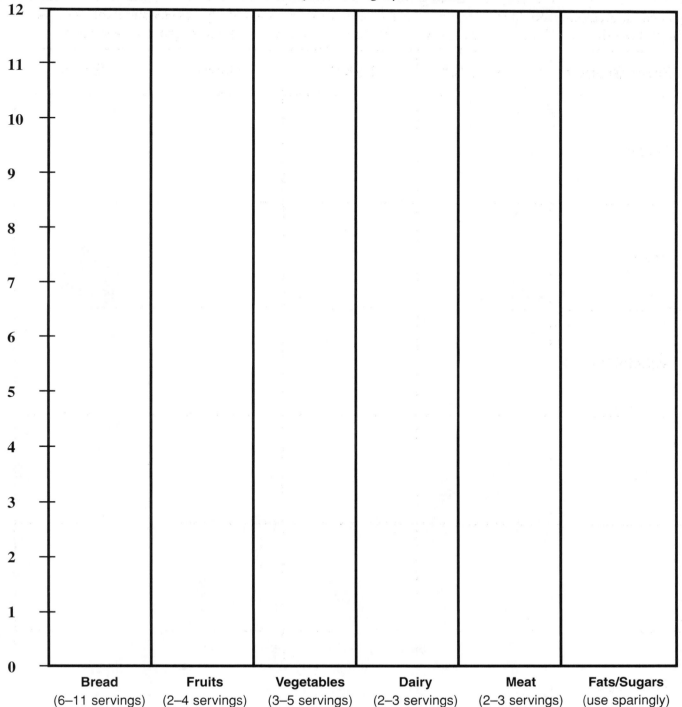

The Apple Doesn't Fall Far from the Tree

Creating a Picture-Perfect Family Tree Using the Cookie Cutter

Overview

The cookie cutter is *HyperStudio*'s built-in framing capability, enabling you to use selections as stencils to mat images with. This project introduces a simple way to use apples on a family tree as mats for scanned photographs which, in turn, could be included as part of a family heritage stack.

Hardware/Software Needed

- *HyperStudio* for Macintosh or Windows
- Scanner

Subject: Social Studies

Before Using the Computer: Gathering Information

On the Resource CD-ROM (included with *HyperStudio*) is an example of a family tree. This project presents the basic steps your students can follow to create similar family trees of their very own.

Creating an accurate family tree first begins with research. Included on pages 90–91 are two planning sheets you may wish to have your students use in getting started on this project. The *HyperStudio* Heritage Project Guidelines (page 87) and Evaluation Form (pages 88–89) will also be helpful resources for this project.

The Apple Doesn't Fall Far from the Tree *(cont.)*

The *Family Tree Planning Sheet Guide* (page 90) provides a handy reference showing where to place the names of various relatives, which can then be recorded on the *Family Tree Planning Sheet Template* (page 91).

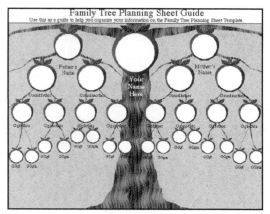

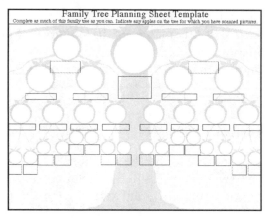

Students should be encouraged to find as much information as they can. For some, that may only be possible for a few generations. Other students may be able to go back even further than the tree allows. There are remedies for either situation. Included on the CD-ROM with this book is a readymade card of *Apples* in various sizes, depending on which version of the tree is used (which will be covered later). These apples can be copied and pasted into any positions for which a student does not have photographs. Students who have names and/or photographs going back beyond the tree might consider extending the project to a second tree. For example, the tree only provides room for the student, his or her parents, grandparents, great-grandparents, and great-great grandparents (five generations in all). If a student has names and/or photographs beyond this, he or she could place those individuals in a second tree.

Students who are adopted or who have stepparents need not be concerned about doing this project since the family tree does not have to be based solely on biological heritage. At the conclusion of this write-up, a sample heritage project introduction has been included so that it can be discussed with students and sent home to parents.

Using the Computer:
Scanning Photographs and Determining Stack Resolution

Students will need to bring in photographs to be scanned for use in their family trees. It is not essential that the photographs be individual portraits. Using the cookie cutter, it is quite easy to crop faces from group pictures. What *is* important is the quality of the original photograph, which, in turn, will determine how well it can be scanned and its final appearance in the tree. A good choice for the student's picture in the top center apple is a recent school photograph.

It is recommended that you create family tree stacks using at least 256-color resolution. If possible, you should work in thousands or millions of colors. At the time the family tree for the Resource CD (included with this book) was created, *HyperStudio* only supported up to 256 colors.

The Apple Doesn't Fall Far from the Tree *(cont.)*

While the results are satisfactory, you will notice a graininess to the images. This results when an image contains more colors than the resolution will allow for. To compensate for this, the software mixes pixels to simulate those colors as best it can—a process known as *dithering*. At higher resolutions, this becomes less of a problem. The drawback to increasing the number of colors, however, is that this increases the memory required for saving stacks. You will want to make a determination on this matter beforehand, based on the resolutions supported by your computer(s) and the amount of memory you can work at easily.

Using the Computer: Determining Card Size

Another consideration is the card size you wish to use for this project. The CD-ROM included with this book includes three different sizes of *Family Tree* readymade cards:

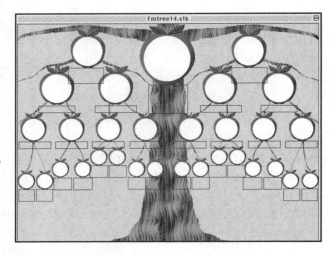

512 x 342 pixels—*HyperStudio's* standard card size, suitable for 9" monitors

512 x 384 pixels—suitable for 12" monitors

640 x 480 pixels—suitable for 14" monitors

Obviously, the major determining factor will be the size of your computer monitor(s). There are two other factors to consider, however. Card size affects stack memory. The larger the tree you use, the more memory the stack will require. The other factor has to do with the size of the photographs. To place images in the apples, some scaling will be necessary. But images placed in the 9" version of the family tree will need to be scaled to a greater degree than if they were placed in the 14" version. Again, you will want to weigh these factors carefully beforehand.

Using the Computer: Scaling Photographs for the Tree

As your students create their family trees, they will probably need to have at least three cards as they work: the actual family tree, a card of apples, and a scratch card. The scratch card will serve as the place for importing images, scaling them, and applying the cookie cutter.

It is suggested that students bring their scanned photographs in as clip art. That way, the photographs can be more easily scaled. Scaling photographs to the proper sizes will take a lot of trial and error. You can reduce the amount of errors if you stress to your students that continued scaling of an image lessens its quality. So, if a student brings in a scanned photograph, scales it to a certain percentage using **Scale…** (if lassoed) or **Scale & Rotate…** (if selected with the rectangle selector) in the **Effects** portion of the **Edit** menu) and finds that is not the right size, he or she should

The Apple Doesn't Fall Far
from the Tree *(cont.)*

immediately undo it by selecting **Undo** in the **Edit** menu (or by simply pressing **cmd-Z** on a Macintosh, **ctrl-Z** on a Windows machine). The image will return to its original size and remain selected, and the student is then free to try a different percentage. Students will be much more pleased with their results if they use this method.

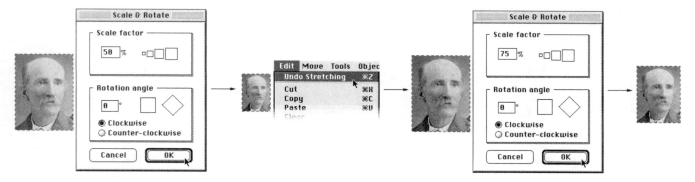

Using the Computer:
Putting Photographs into the Apples

Placing a scanned photograph inside an apple can be accomplished in eight easy steps.

STEP 1: Determine into which apple in the tree the photograph will be placed.

STEP 2: On a scratch card, bring in a portion of the photograph as clip art.

STEP 3: On the tree card, get the lasso tool from the tools palette.

STEP 4: Place the lasso inside the cutout area of the apple. While holding down the **option** key (Mac) or **control** key (Win) on the keyboard, click the mouse one time. This causes the lasso to expand outward to fill up the entire cutout area. While the area is still selected, select **Copy** from the **Edit** menu (**cmd-C** Mac, **ctrl-C** Win).

STEP 5: Move to the scratch card and select **Paste** from the **Edit** menu (**cmd-V** Mac, **ctrl-V** Win). **With the area still selected**, click inside of it and drag it on top of the photograph. Get it positioned where you want it before moving on to the next step.

The Apple Doesn't Fall Far
from the Tree *(cont.)*

STEP 6: **With the area still selected**, choose **Cookie Cutter** from the **Effects** portion of the **Edit** menu. (With Mac, you can also use the keyboard shortcut **cmd-option-C.**) This allows the photograph to show through the cutout, as if being soaked up. **With the area still selected**, Copy it. (If you used the Mac cookie cutter keyboard shortcut, then you do not need to copy the selection.)

STEP 7: Move back to the first card and **Paste** the selection. With the area still selected, click inside of it and drag it over to the apple into which you want it placed.

STEP 8: When the photograph is in position, click outside of it. Your photograph will be matted!

Using the Computer:
Entering Names on the Tree

The *Family Tree* is a readymade card with text fields already in position. Students may want to tweak the sizes of some of the fields and/or use different fonts than those that are preset. Because the text fields are transparent, they have been given frames to make it easier for students to work with them. However, students may want to turn off the frame option and/or the transparent feature. That is a matter of personal choice. And just as full apples can be placed in those positions for which students do not have pictures, text fields can be left blank or deleted as necessary.

Using the Computer:
Transforming the Tree into a Menu

Students may wish to add special biographical cards to their family tree stacks. They can then place invisible buttons over key individuals in the tree. In the *Fleck Family Tree,* the creator simply placed an invisible button over Jacob Fleck's picture, which links to a stack about his life.

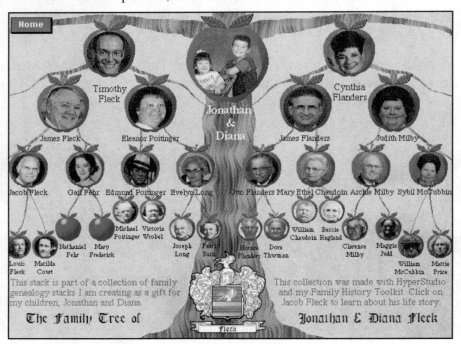

The Apple Doesn't Fall Far from the Tree *(cont.)*

Using the Computer: Embellishing the Tree

Students may also wish to place additional items on their trees to give them extra distinction. The example includes an image of the *Fleck Coat of Arms* to the base of the family tree.

Going Beyond

The *Family Tree* and *Apples* on the CD-ROM included with this book are actually just a small portion of a much larger genealogy product called the *Family History Toolkit.* FHT is a collection of original artwork and tutorials designed to help you create your own multimedia family genealogical record.

The following pieces make up the artwork included in FHT:

- *Family Album*
  (shown in two positions—open and closed)

- *Three Picture Frames*
  (one gold, one marbled, and one wooden)

- *Extra apples and cutouts*
  (for use with the family tree or mat, just in case you need them)

- *Keepsake Box*

- *An open drawer, drawer front, and open lid*

- *Letter*

- *Blue Wall background*
  (great for using with the wooden frame)

- *Wood Surface background*
  (great for using with the family album and letter)

- *Blue Wall & Wood Surface background*
  (great for using with the gold frame, marbled frame, and/or keepsake box)

- *Family Tree*
  (allows you to show up to five generations at one time and includes transparent text fields so that you can easily input relatives' names)

Family Album (Closed)   Family Album (Open)   Letter

Family Tree   Keepsake Box   Keepsake Lid & Drawer

Gold Frame   Wood Frame   Marble Frame/Apples/Cutouts

Blue Wall   Wood Surface   Blue Wall & Wood Surface

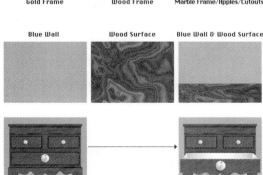

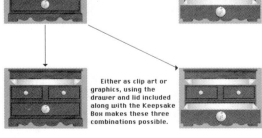

Either as clip art or graphics, using the drawer and lid included along with the Keepsake Box makes these three combinations possible.

The Apple Doesn't Fall Far from the Tree *(cont.)*

FHT also includes two tutorials:

- The *Picture Frame Tutorial* demonstrates how to use the cookie cutter to transfer family photos to the picture frames included in the toolkit.

- The *Keepsake Box Tutorial* demonstrates how to use *HyperStudio's* digitizing, paint, and graphics capabilities to add personal items to the keepsake boxes included in the toolkit.

The *Family Tree* and *Apples* on the CD-ROM included with this book will work with both *HyperStudio* platforms.

Online Research

A number of Internet sites are available to help students find information concerning their heritage. A good place to begin searching through records and data is **The Family Forum for Genealogists** at

http://www.gengateway.com/queries.htm

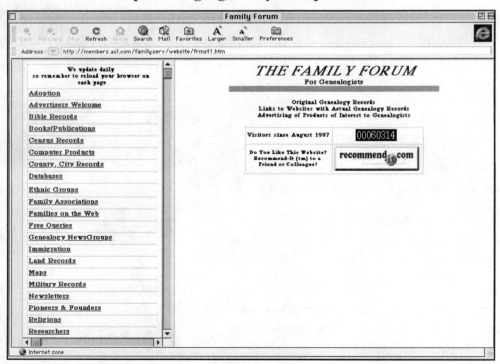

Name_____

The Apple Doesn't Fall Far
from the Tree *(cont.)*

You have a special family history which, together with those of Americans past and present, make up America's "family history." The *HyperStudio* Heritage Project is an opportunity for you to become better acquainted with and appreciative of the history behind your family, to put together a record of that history, and to present this to your fellow classmates.

You will create a four-card stack for our study of family heritage. Your stack will have the following requirements:

1. a **title card** which will introduce your family heritage stack

2. a **family tree card** which will include scanned pictures of you and your direct ancestors (parents, grandparents, etc.) (You will use the cookie cutter to place these into a Family Tree readymade card.)

3. a **biography card** (This card will focus on at least one older relative and will present information and stories that have been passed on to you.)

4. a **family "coat of arms"** card (On this card you will create an original family coat of arms using the HyperStudio paint tools. Your family coat of arms is to be different from ones that may already exist for your family/family name. The coat of arms is to represent positive events and/or interests of the members of your family.)

You will be given special planning sheets to help you gather and prepare your information. These must be completed satisfactorily **before** you will be permitted to go to the computer and are to be kept in a special family heritage folder.

You will present your project to the class and be videotaped. Your videotape and stack will be special mementos you can treasure as part of your family history.

You will find a copy of the *HyperStudio Heritage Project Evaluation Form* attached to this letter. This is an exact copy of the sheet I will be using to evaluate your project. Knowing the specific requirements beforehand should help you in your preparations.

Some of you may be concerned that your grade will be based on HOW FAR BACK or HOW MANY GENERATIONS you are able to trace in your family histories. A quick look at the evaluation form will show you that this is something that will NOT be evaluated at all! Some of you will be able to easily trace your histories back several generations; others will not. And in the case of stepparents, etc., by all means include them and their family histories if you wish. This is a FAMILY history project designed to help you learn more about your family and its history.

HyperStudio Planning Sheets

The Apple Doesn't Fall Far from the Tree *(cont.)*

HyperStudio Heritage Project

Evaluation Form

Name _____   Date _____

Stack Component

The student's project includes a stack that has…	Not completed	Poor	Avg	Good	Excellent
1. **a title card**—This card shows originality and creativity. The student has included an interesting design that relates well to the theme. He or she has added a title for the stack, along with his or her name, both of which are clearly visible and easy to read.	0	3	5	7	10
2. **a family tree card**—This card features scanned photographs of the student and his or her direct ancestors, along with their names.	0	3	5	7	10
3. **a biography card**—This card focuses on at least one older relative, and presents information and stories that have been passed down. This material is presented in an interesting manner.	0	3	5	7	10
4. **a family "coat of arms" card**—The student has used this card to create an original coat of arms representing positive events and/or interests of the members of his or her family.	0	3	5	7	10
5. **proper spelling and grammar**—The student has used correct spelling, especially of key words and ideas, and has used complete sentences where appropriate and necessary.	0	3	5	7	10

POINTS EARNED x 2 = _____   LETTER GRADE = _____

HyperStudio Planning Sheets

The Apple Doesn't Fall Far
from the Tree *(cont.)*

Evaluation Form *(cont.)*

Planning Component (Folder)

The student's project includes a folder that has...	Not completed	Poor	Avg	Good	Excellent
1. *planning sheets*—The student has a planning sheet(s) for each card in his or her stack. Each sheet shows evidence of in-depth thought and is neatly and completely done.	0	3	5	7	10
2. *a table of contents*—It appears in the front, is neatly written or typed, and is detailed and specific. Papers in the folder are arranged in proper order to match the table of contents.	0	3	5	7	10
3. *proper maintenance*—The folder is in satisfactory condition. It is neatly arranged and is properly identified (the student's name and the title of the folder are neatly and clearly displayed on the front of the folder).	0	3	5	7	10

Planning Component (Presentation)

The student's project was presented in a manner that demonstrated...	Not completed	Poor	Avg	Good	Excellent
4. *preparedness*—The student was organized and prepared to share his or her project. He or she used time wisely and fulfilled project requirements in a timely manner.	0	3	5	7	10
5. *knowledge*—The student had a good understanding of the material he or she presented.	0	3	5	7	10

POINTS EARNED x 2 = _____   LETTER GRADE = _____

COMMENTS:

The Apple Doesn't Fall Far from the Tree *(cont.)*

Name _____

Family Tree Planning Sheet Guide

Directions: Use this as a guide to help you organize your information on the *Family Tree Planning Sheet Template.*

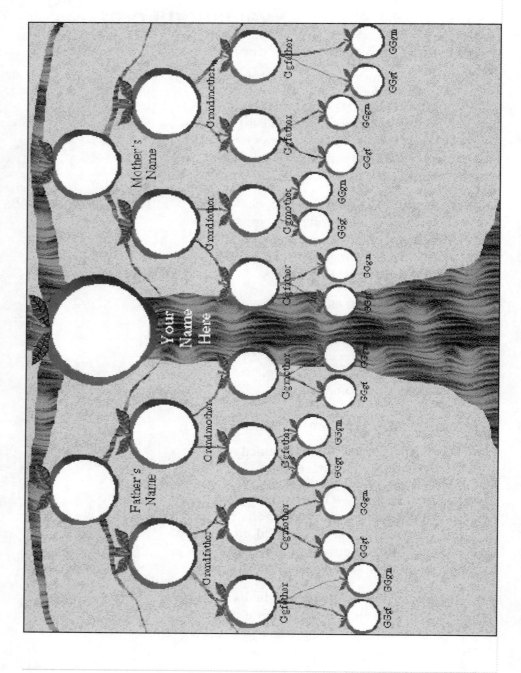

The Apple Doesn't Fall Far from the Tree *(cont.)*

Name _____   Date _____

Family Tree Planning Sheet Template

Directions: Complete as much of this family tree as you can. Indicate any apples on the tree for which you have scanned pictures.

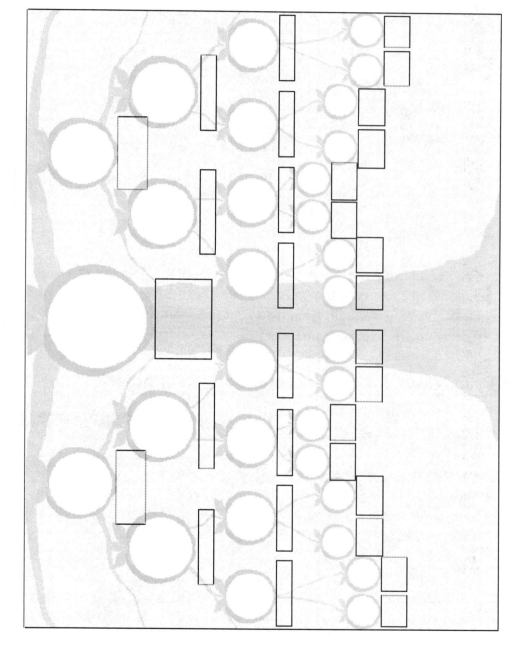

Visual Learning Software

Visual learning software, such as *Kidspiration* (designed for grades K–3) and *Inspiration* (designed for grades 4–12), help your students develop ideas and organize their thinking. You can use visual learning software for a variety of educational purposes, including the following.

- brainstorming
- planning
- diagramming
- outlining
- organizing
- concept mapping
- webbing
- categorizing
- storyboarding

If you don't have *Kidspiration* or *Inspiration* in your school or district and would like to "try before you buy," download a free trial version of either software application from the *Inspiration* website (**http://www.Inspiration.com**).

Using Visual Learning Software with Your Students

There are several ways to use visual learning software with your students. First, if you are just getting started with visual learning software, make it easy on yourself. Use one of the pre-existing activities or templates that come with the software application.

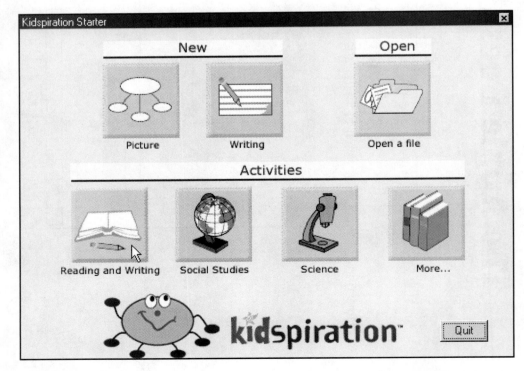

Visual Learning Software *(cont.)*

Using Pre-Existing Activities and Templates

If you are new to *Kidspiration*, select a Reading and Writing, Social Studies, Science, or More activity that aligns with the curriculum you are teaching. For example, select the Reading and Writing student-learning activity *Alphabets Examples* to create a picture alphabet with your students. In this activity, have a student click on an alphabet letter, such as the letter B, and navigate the symbol libraries to find a picture of something that begins with B, such as a bike. Have your student click on the picture to select it.

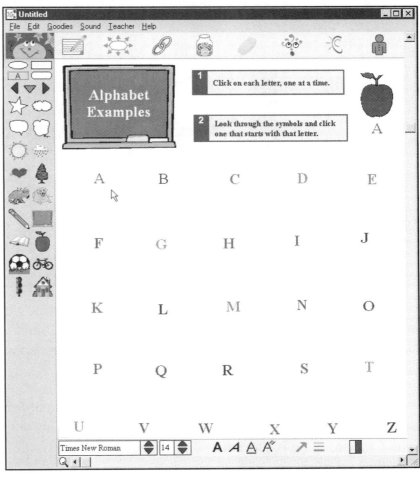

When finished, your class has created a picture alphabet. Print the picture alphabet and display your students' work.

Special Note: If your students are capable of navigating the symbol libraries on their own, you may opt to have pairs of students or each student create his or her own picture alphabet independently in a computer learning center in your classroom.

If you are new to *Inspiration*, select a template that aligns with the curriculum you are teaching. For example, select the Language Arts-Comparison template to list the similarities and differences between two objects, events, or people your students are reading about.

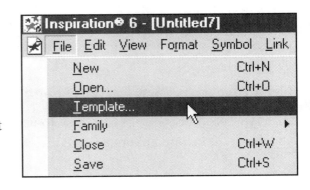

Visual Learning Software *(cont.)*

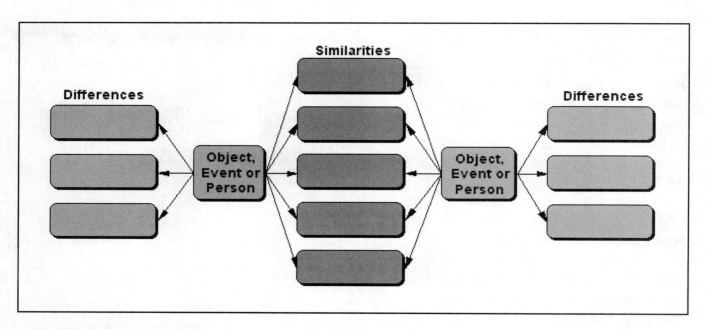

A Special Note About Template Files: All the pre-existing files you open within *Kidspiration* and *Inspiration* are template files. So what does that mean? Templates are files that have been specially designed to always stay intact, ready for you and your students to use again and again. They can never be replaced.

When you select an activity in *Kidspiration* or a template in *Inspiration*, it opens as an untitled file. So, when you are finished using the file, you and your students will be prompted to discard it or save it with a new name to the location of your choice. That way, the original file always remains clean and untainted, so to speak.

That is why one student in your classroom can open the *Alphabet Example* activity, create a picture alphabet, and close or save the file. Then a second student can open the same *Alphabet Example* activity and it is intact, free of the previous students' work.

Did you understand that? If so, can you see how valuable templates can be when working with students? You don't have to ever worry about your original files being replaced. "My original files?" you say. Well, yes, because you can create template files, too!

Creating Your Own Activities and Templates

Once you become familiar with how to use *Kidspiration* and *Inspiration* (and maybe you already are), you may feel inspired to create activities for your students that they can use again and again.

Using *Kidspiration*, you can open a new file in Picture View. Then add symbols, pictures, text, and even SuperGrouper boxes to create a student learning activity aligned to the curriculum you are teaching.

Visual Learning Software *(cont.)*

For example, the *My Money* student-learning activity displayed below includes a symbol, pictures, text, and three SuperGrouper boxes. In this activity, students click and drag the coins necessary to make ten cents three different ways. Notice that the symbol library with coins is displayed in the Symbol Palette, making it easy for students to click and drag the penny, nickel, and dime coins into the red, yellow, and blue SuperGrouper boxes.

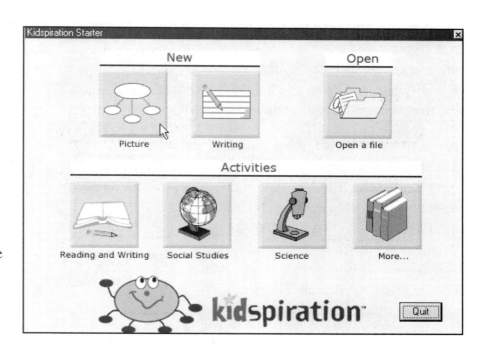

Special Note: The *My Money* student learning activity is available on the CD-ROM [filename: *money.kid*].

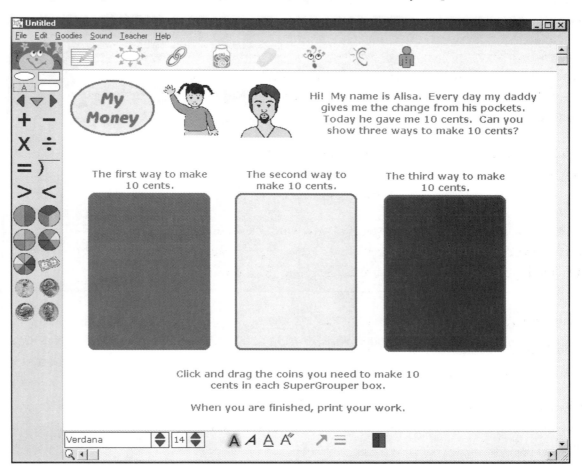

Visual Learning Software *(cont.)*

Once the learning activity you create looks just right, save it as a template file so that it can be used again and again by your students. In *Kidspiration*, you do so by clicking **Teacher** on the menu bar and selecting **Save As Activity**.

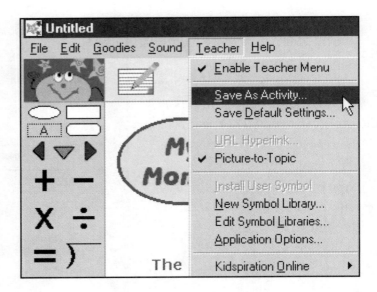

An **Activity Wizard** appears. Simply read the messages and instructions provided on each screen carefully. You may accept the default options or select the options you desire when prompted to do so. (When in doubt, accept the default options. Only change an option when you know exactly what you want, and it is different than the default option.)

The last screen you see will prompt you to select a category for the activity (Reading and Writing, Social Studies, Science, or More), name the activity, and provide a brief description for it. Then you are finished!

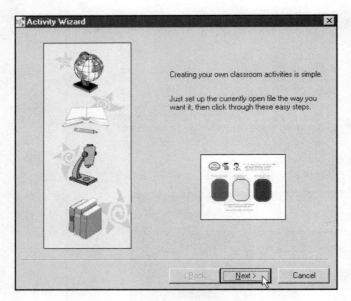

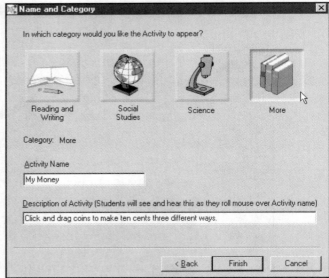

Your students can open the newly created *Kidspiration* activity by clicking on the category under which you saved it, such as More; navigating to the activity; clicking on the activity to select it; and clicking OK. The activity appears on the computer screen as an untitled file, ready for students to use and save under another filename.

Visual Learning Software *(cont.)*

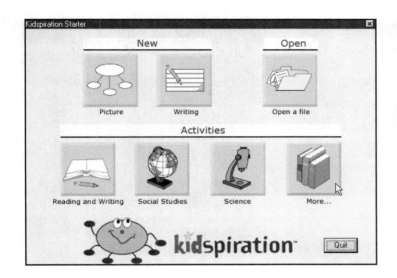

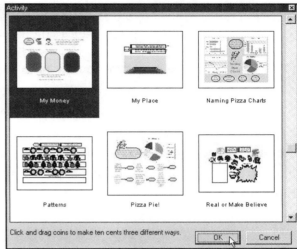

Using *Inspiration*, you can open a new file in Diagram View. Then add symbols, pictures, and text to create a student learning activity aligned to the curriculum you are teaching. For example, the *Classifying Rocks* student-learning activity displayed on this page includes symbols, pictures, and text. In this activity students type the names of igneous, metamorphic, and sedimentary rocks in the blue boxes.

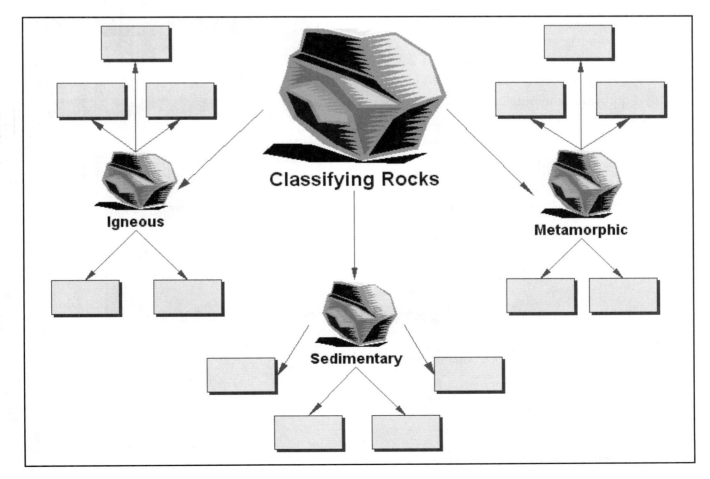

Visual Learning Software *(cont.)*

Special Note: The *Classifying Rocks* student learning activity is available on the CD-ROM [filename: *rocks.ins*].

Once the learning activity you create looks just right, save it as a template file so that it can be used again and again by your students. In *Inspiration*, you do so by clicking **File** on the menu bar and selecting **Save As Template**. At the **Save As Template** dialog box, simply type a name for the newly created activity in the **Save with what filename?** text box. Then click **Save**.

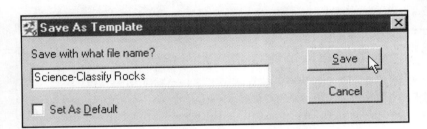

Your students can open the newly created *Inspiration* activity template by clicking **File** on the menu bar and selecting **Template**. At the Template dialog box, have students scroll until they find the activity template, click on it, and then click **Open**. The activity you created appears on the computer screen as an untitled file, ready for students to use.

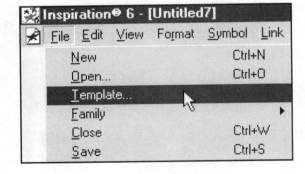

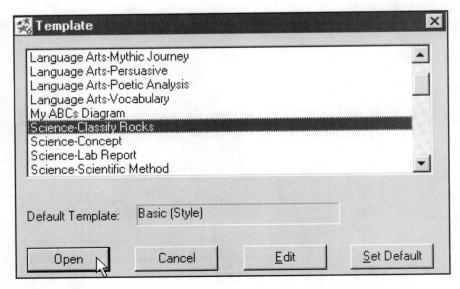

Visual Learning Software *(cont.)*

Using Visual Learning Software for Brainstorming

Using visual learning software, you can facilitate your students' brainstorming of ideas for projects, reports, and more. Open the visual learning software, enter the topic or project for brainstorming, and enter your students' ideas as they "shout 'em out." The ideas you enter will initially be displayed as text within symbols. To incorporate pictures, navigate the symbol libraries to find and select pictures that represent your students' ideas.

Using Visual Learning Software for Planning

Using visual learning software, you can facilitate your students' planning of projects, such as a classroom mural, columns for a class or school newspaper, and more. Open the visual learning software; brainstorm ideas, steps, or events; and then order them to make a plan. If your plan is text-oriented, you can switch from Picture View (in *Kidspiration*) or Diagram View (in *Inspiration*) to Writing View (in *Kidspiration*) or Outline View (in *Inspiration*) to see an ordered list of the plan. Print the ordered list to use as a checklist!

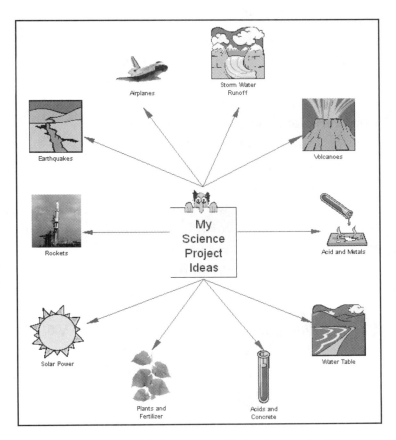

Visual Learning Software *(cont.)*

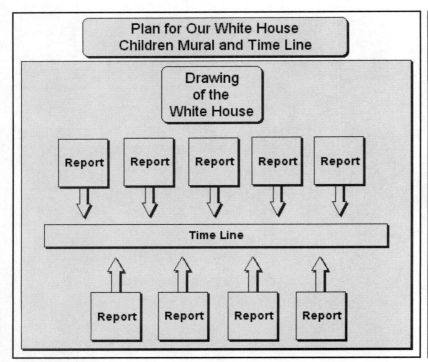

Using Visual Learning Software for Diagramming

Using visual learning software, you can facilitate your students' diagramming of cycles, processes, and procedures, such as the water cycle, the steps in an experiment, and more. Open the visual learning software and allow students to brainstorm all the steps in the cycle, process, or procedure you are diagramming. Then place the steps in their proper or logical order, using links to indicate the flow. If your diagram is text-oriented, you can switch from Picture View (in *Kidspiration*) or Diagram View (in *Inspiration*) to Writing View (in *Kidspiration*) or Outline View (in *Inspiration*) to see a step-by-step list of the cycle, process, or procedure. Print the cycle, process, or procedure to use as a checklist!

+ Our Music Column Ideas

    I. + September
       A. – Calling All Instruments!
    II. + October
       A. – Our Classroom Choir
    III. + November
       A. – Planning Songs for Our Thanksgiving Play
    IV. + December
       A. – Music Makes Christmas Merry!
    V. + January
       A. – Learning to Listen to Classical Music
    VI. + February
       A. – A Note About Notes
    VII. + March
       A. – Our Musical Parents
    VIII. + April
       A. – Our Schoolwide Spring Sing-a-Long
    IX. + May
       A. – Music We Will Remember

Visual Learning Software *(cont.)*

Using Visual Learning Software for Outlining

Using visual learning software, you can facilitate your students' outlining of a project, report, process, and more. Open the visual learning software in Writing View, if you are using *Kidspiration*. Open the visual learning software and change from Diagram View to Outline View, if you are using *Inspiration*.

Additional Resources for Visual Learning Software

Teacher Created Materials provides books that can help you learn *Kidspiration* and *Inspiration*, including *Kidspiration for Terrified Teachers* and *Inspiration for Terrified Teachers*. The first half of each book teaches you how to use the software application. The second half of each book provides you with project ideas for using *Kidspiration* or *Inspiration* with your students.

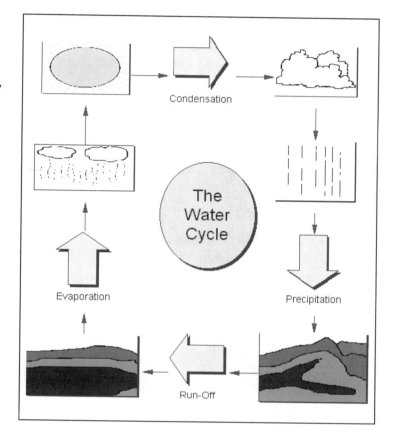

In addition, Teacher Created Materials provides Simple Projects books that contain project ideas related to specific content areas, such as language arts, mathematics, social studies, science, health/physical education, and the arts. Current titles include the following:

- *Inspiration Simple Projects: Primary* (designed for grades K–3)
- *Inspiration Simple Projects: Intermediate* (designed for grades 3–5)
- *Inspiration Simple Projects: Challenging* (designed for grades 5–8)

You can find these books at your local teacher supply store. They are also available on the Internet at the Teacher Created Materials website (**http://www.teachercreated.com**).

Teacher Created Materials has also developed a *TechTools Resource Kit* for *Inspiration*, which includes 100 How-to cards that provide illustrated step-by-step instructions, a Teacher's Resource Notebook with 60 problem-based lessons, and a multimedia CD-ROM.

Teacher Created Materials also provides a hands-on online course entitled, *Using Visual Learning Software in the Classroom: Inspiration,* where you can earn university credit while learning how to integrate *Inspiration* into language arts, mathematics, social studies, science, health/physical education, and the arts curricula.

Getting Set for Storytelling

Project Description

In this project, students get ready for storytelling by selecting stories they will enjoy telling; creating storyboards story webs, and outlines to help them learn their stories; and using their voices, faces, and bodies to make their stories come alive.

Hardware and Software Needed

For this project you will need your computer system and *Inspiration*. If you choose to record your students' storytelling, you will also want to obtain a tape recorder or video camera.

Materials Needed

You will need to collect a number of books from which your students can select stories. (You will find several such books listed in the Additional Resources section of this project.)

CD-ROM Files in the *Inspiration Lesson* folder

Name	Description	Filename
Types of Stories Template	concept map template	*typestem.ins*
Types of Stories	concept map	*typestor.ins*
Six Blind Boys and an Elephant	storyboard	*boysele.ins*
We Make Our Stories Come Alive!	idea map	*alivest.ins*
We Make Our Stories Come Alive! Template	idea map template	*alivetem.ins*

Stage 1—Introducing the Project

Provide students with a good selection of books from which they can select stories to tell. This activity provides a perfect opportunity to help students understand the different kinds of stories available to them.

A *Types of Stories Template* is provided on this page (Fig. 8) and is available on the CD-ROM for you to use to guide your discussion of story types, including folk tales, tall tales, myths, legends, fairy tales, fables, and literary stories [filename: *typestem.ins*]. A sample completed concept map of *Types of Stories* is provided on the following page (Fig. 9) and is also available on the CD-ROM [filename: *typestor.ins*].

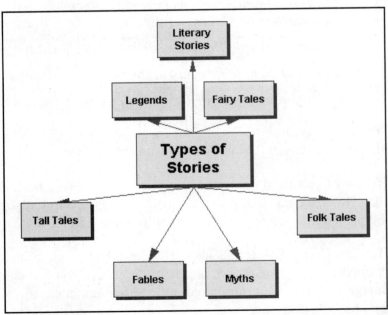

Fig. 8. *Types of Stories Template*

Getting Set for Storytelling *(cont.)*

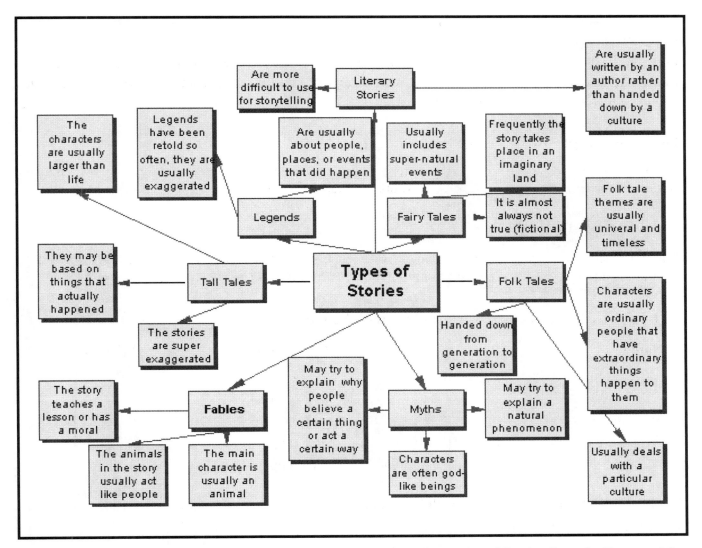

Fig. 9. *Types of Stories* Sample Concept Map

After helping your students find stories that they would really love to share with others, it's time to help them learn their stories. According to Martha Hamilton and Mitch Weiss, authors of *Stories in My Pocket—Tales Kids Can Tell* (Richard C. Owen Publishing, 1990), there are many different ways you can help students learn their stories in preparation for storytelling. They recommend making a written outline of the story, creating a storyboard of the story, or drawing a story web. Fortunately, you can do all three in *Inspiration*.

Launch *Inspiration* and demonstrate how to create a storyboard or story web of a sample story that can also be viewed as an outline. First, enter the title of a story. Then list and link each major event in the story—in the right order, of course. Then change from diagram view to outline view. In the outline view, you may find it necessary to move topics to the right or to the left to adjust the hierarchy of events. Just use the **Move Topic Left** and **Move Topic Right** buttons on the outline toolbar.

Getting Set for Storytelling *(cont.)*

A sample storyboard for *Six Blind Boys and an Elephant* is provided below (Fig. 10) and on the CD-ROM [filename: *boysele.in*s]. The outline for *Six Blind Boys and an Elephant* is provided on the following page (Fig. 11).

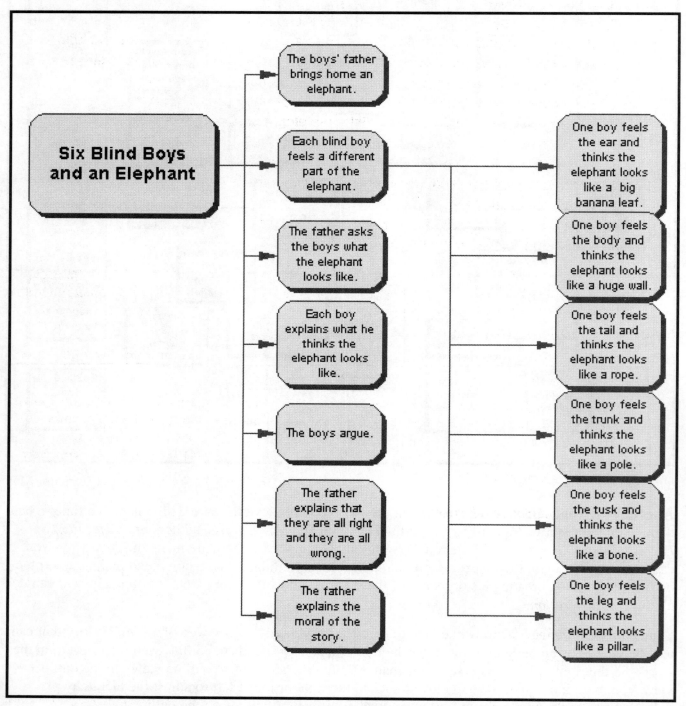

Fig. 10. *Six Blind Boys and an Elephant* Sample Storyboard

Getting Set for Storytelling *(cont.)*

⇔Six Blind Boys and an Elephant

   I. – The boys' father brings home an elephant.

   II. + Each blind boy feels a different part of the elephant.

      A. – One boy feels the ear and thinks the elephant looks like a big banana leaf.

      B. – One boy feels the body and thinks the elephant looks like a huge wall.

      C. – One boy feels the tail and thinks the elephant looks like a rope.

      D. – One boy feels the trunk and thinks the elephant looks like a pole.

      E. – One boy feels the tusk and thinks the elephant looks like a bone.

      F. – One boy feels the leg and thinks the elephant looks like a pillar.

   III. – The father asks the boys what the elephant looks like.

   IV. – Each boy explains what he thinks the elephant looks like.

   V. – The boys argue.

   VI. – The father explains that they are all right and they are all wrong.

   VII. – The father explains the moral of the story.

Fig. 11. *Six Blind Boys and an Elephant* Outline

Stage 2—Producing the Project

Of course, telling a story takes lots of practice, practice, practice. Practice is fun when students focus on making their stories come alive.

Brainstorm with students how they can achieve the storytelling goal of making their stories come alive by using their voices, their faces, and their bodies. A sample of an idea map for *Making Our Stories Come Alive!* is provided on the following page (Fig. 12) and on the CD-ROM [filename: *alivest.ins*]. A *Making Our Stories Come Alive! Template* is also provided on the CD-ROM for you to use with your students [filename: *alivetem.ins*].

Stage 3—Presenting the Project

Have students practice telling their stories in front of each other. You may also wish to use a tape recorder or video camera to record the stories, play them back for students, and provide constructive feedback for each teller. When students are ready, schedule a storytelling event and invite other classes, the entire school, or parents to attend.

Additional Project Ideas

- If your students are going to share their stories with others, have them create announcements or invitations to their storytelling event.

- Students can also create a program for their storytelling event! Brainstorm everything you want in your program, using *Inspiration*.

- If you have a video camera, make a videotape of your students' culminating storytelling event. It will become more precious with time.

Getting Set for Storytelling *(cont.)*

- If you have a digital video camera or the technical capabilities of transferring a video image to a digital image, video tape each student telling his or her story and place the files on your class or school website. That way your students can share their stories with family members and friends worldwide. If you do so, make sure that your video clips follows the guidelines for assuring your students' safety on the Internet explained in the *Kids' Rules for Online Safety* available at SafeKids.Com. The site address is **http://www.safekids.com**

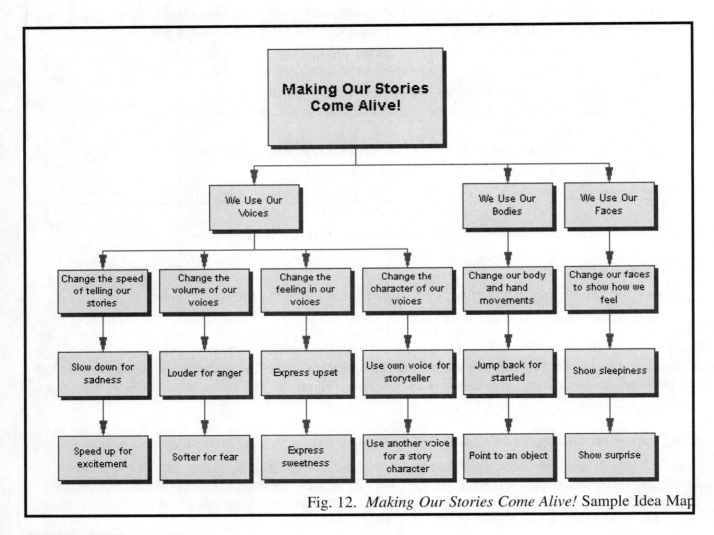

Fig. 12. *Making Our Stories Come Alive!* Sample Idea Map

Additional Resources

Here are some books that will help you and your students get ready for great storytelling:

- *Caroline Feller Bauer's Handbook for Storytellers* by Caroline Feller Bauer (American Library Association, 1993)

- *Easy-to-Tell Stories for Young Children* by Annette Harrison (Storytelling Foundation International, 1992)

Getting Set for Storytelling *(cont.)*

- *Children Tell Stories—A Teaching Guide* by Martha Hamilton and Mitch Weiss (Richard C. Owen Publishing, 1990)

- *Figures, Facts, and Fables—Telling Tales in Science and Math* by Barbara Lipke (Heinemann, 1996)

- *Joining In—An Anthology of Audience Participation Stories and How to Tell Them* by Teresa Miller, Anne Pellowski, and Norma Livo (Yellow Moon Press, 1988)

- *Just Enough to Make a Story—A Sourcebook for Storytellers* by Nancy Schimmel (Sister's Choice Press, 1992)

- *Once Upon a Time: A Storytelling Handbook* by Lucille Breneman and Bren Breneman (Burnham, Inc., 1993)

- *Stories in My Pocket—Tales Kids Can Tell* by Martha Hamilton and Mitch Weiss (Fulcrum Pub., 1997)

- *Telling Your Own Stories for Family and Classroom, Public Speaking, and Personal Journaling* by Donald Davis (August House Pub., 1993)

- *The Storyteller's Start-Up Book—Finding, Learning, Performing, and Using Folktales* by Margaret Read MacDonald (August House Pub. 1993)

- *Twenty Tellable Tales* by Margaret Read MacDonald (H. W. Wilson, 1986)

Here are some great storytelling websites.

- Visit the *Storytelling Foundation International* at the following Internet address:

  http://www.storytellingfoundation.net/

- The *National Storytelling Network* has a wealth of resources to support your storytelling instructions, such as a national storytelling directory, a storytelling magazine, a storytelling list serv, and lots more. The Internet address is as follows:

  http://www.storynet.org/index3.htm

- Learn more about the *Annual National Storytelling Festival* held in Jonesborough, Tennessee. The Internet address is as follows:

  http://www.storytellingfestival.net

Sorting Solid Shapes

Learning Activity Description

In this activity, students learn about solid shapes—the sphere, the cylinder, the cube, and the cone. Then students group common objects into the four shape categories using SuperGrouper in *Kidspiration*.

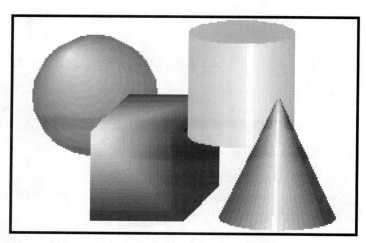

Hardware and Software Needed

For this activity, you will need your computer system and *Kidspiration*. If you plan to use the *Sphere, Cylinder, Cube,* or *Cone* resource files or the *Searching for Solid Shapes* student activity sheet provided in the **Additional Resources** section, you will also need the word processing software application *Microsoft Word* to open and print the activity sheet for your students. If you do not have *Word*, you can use the copies of the activity pages provided in this book. Consider using the copier to enlarge the pages so that students have sufficient writing space.

Materials Needed

For this activity, gather some common objects in the classroom that exemplify the four solid shapes.

CD-ROM Files in the *Kidspiration Lesson* folder

Name	Description	Filename
Sphere	resource file	sphere.doc
Cylinder	resource file	cylinder.doc
Cube	resource file	cube.doc
Cone	resource file	cone.doc
Sorting Solid Shapes	student learning activity	shapes1.kid
Searching for Solid Shapes	student activity sheet	shapes2.doc

File Preparation

For this activity, open and save the following file as a student learning activity so that you and your students can use it again and again.

- *Sorting Solid Shapes* [filename: shapes1.kid]

Open the resource files *Sphere, Cylinder, Cube,* and *Cone* that are shown on page 110 [filenames: sphere.doc, cylinder.doc, cube.doc, and cone.doc]. Print these shapes to share with your students and display on the bulletin board or a wall of your classroom.

Sorting Solid Shapes *(cont.)*

Introducing the Activity

Explain to students that they will be learning about solid shapes—the sphere, the cylinder, the cube, and the cone. Display the pictures of the solid shapes and discuss their names and characteristics with students. Display the common objects from the classroom that you gathered. Help students to identify the solid shapes exemplified by these objects.

Facilitating the Activity

Open and display the *Sorting Solid Shapes* student learning activity [filename: *shapes1.kid*] that is shown on page 111. Review the names of the solid shapes. Help students name the objects at the bottom of the screen. Demonstrate to students how to click and drag each object into the SuperGrouper representing its shape.

Provide students with the opportunity to complete the *Sorting Solid Shapes* student learning activity in pairs or individually in the computer-learning center in your classroom.

Additional Resources

The following Internet sites, books, and student activity will provide you with additional information and educational materials related to solid shapes.

Internet Sites

- Visit the **Draw and Color with Uncle Fred**® website. Your students will have fun drawing a dozen cartoons. Don't worry about your students' drawing skills. Uncle Fred provides step-by-step instructions for each drawing, using simple shapes. **http://www.unclefred.com/**

- Visit the **Enchanted Mind Tangrams** website. Your students can click and drag seven tangram pieces to make any of the120 different shapes available. **http://www.enchantedmind.com/tangram/tangram.htm**

Books

- *Cartooning with Letters, Numbers, and Shapes* by Bill Costello was published in 1995 by Thinkorporated [ISBN-1-89190-530-9].
- *Afro-Bets Book of Shapes* by Margery W. Brown was published in 2000 by Just Us Books [ISBN-0-94097-558-0].
- *Colors, Shapes, & Sizes* by Michelle Warrence was published in 2000 by Scholastic Trade [ISBN-0-43916-421-4].

Additional Student Learning Activity

- The *Searching for Solid Shapes* student activity sheet is shown on page 112. It is also available on the CD-ROM [filename: shapes2.doc]. Use this activity sheet for students as they find and record objects at school or at home that exemplify the solid shapes.

  Special Note: You will need the word processing program *Microsoft Word* to open this file.

Sorting Solid Shapes *(cont.)*

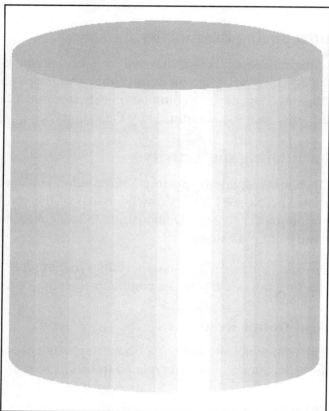

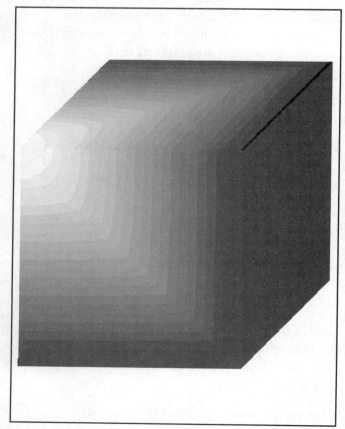

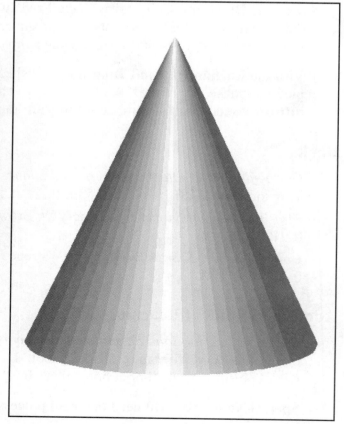

Sorting Solid Shapes *(cont.)*

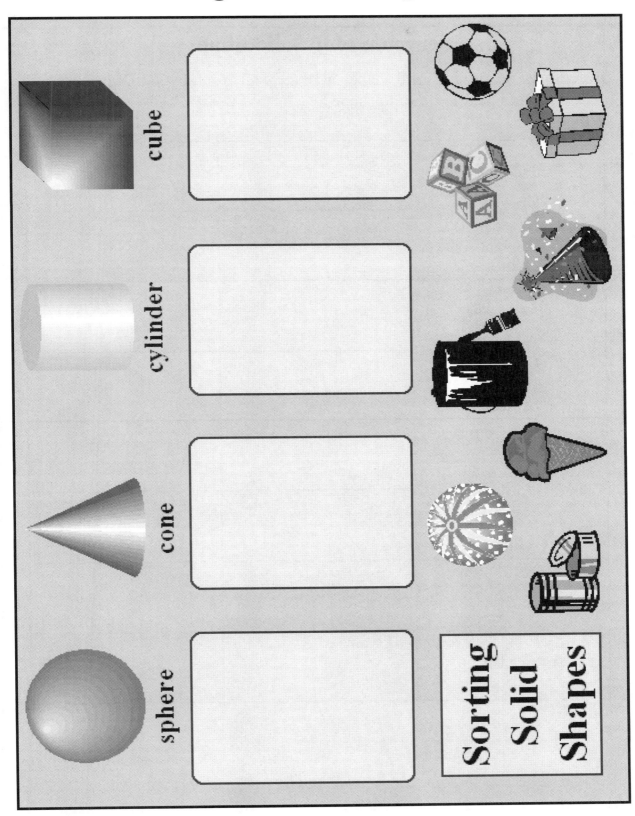

Sorting Solid Shapes Activity *(shapes1.kid)*

Sorting Solid Shapes *(cont.)*

Searching for Solid Shapes

Directions: Search for solid shapes in objects all around you. Draw each object you find next to its solid shape.

Cone		
Sphere		
Cylinder		
Cube		

Name_____

Searching for Solid Shapes Activity *(shapes2.doc)*

The Internet and E-mail

The Internet

The Internet is a network of computers composed of smaller networks that span the world. The World Wide Web is the place where millions of computers exchange information. To become members of this online world, the district, school, or classroom must select an Internet provider. Some of the widely used services are America Online and Earthlink. A browser, such as *Netscape Navigator* or *Microsoft Internet Explorer,* is also necessary.

The hardware that is needed to get online is a computer, phone or cable line, and a modem. The modem is a device that connects the computer to a telephone line and allows the computer data to be sent down the line to another computer. Your school may instead have a local-area network service that provides you with your Internet service. If this is the case, you do not need to have a modem because you use a cable to connect your computer to the wiring within your school's walls.

There are many ways for you to use the Internet with your students—for communication, e-mail pen pals, online research, publication of ideas and student work, and cooperative learning.

Communication

E-mail is the easiest and most common use of the Internet. Children have always loved sending and receiving mail. The immediacy of corresponding on the Internet, coupled with the quick exchange of mail from a foreign country, will motivate and excite your students.

The list below is designed to give you some correspondence and writing ideas for using e-mail with your students.

- Co-write a story.
- Connect your students with kids on the other side of the earth. Collect and exchange weather reports during the school year as the classes move through opposite seasons.
- Connect your students with students living in a different environment. For example, if your students are from a large city, connect them with a class from the country.
- Correspond in second languages.
- Give and request information on seasonal activities and celebrations.
- Describe some great places and things to do on a vacation in the area in which they live.
- Describe the things they are learning in the classroom.
- Find out what they have in common and how they are different.
- Exchange designs created on a paint/draw program or in *Logo*.
- Exchange scanned photos of themselves, classroom, family, and their community.

The Internet and E-mail *(cont.)*

E-mail Pen Pals

The pen-pal experience using the Internet is an excellent way to provide students with a cross-cultural learning experience. When students correspond with each other via e-mail, their exchanges tend to be much more frequent and less formal than when they use the post office. The ease and frequency of these exchanges generally means higher motivation.

It takes good coaching from you to maximize the benefit your students receive from the pen-pal experience. Help students to formulate good questions for their pen pals and encourage them to take the time to provide good answers to their pen pals' questions. Have students print and share e-mail correspondence in whole-group situations.

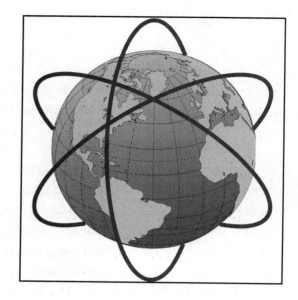

When possible, have the pen-pal experience include some collaborative project work. Some ideas for having the students work together include the following:

- compare favorite foods in each food group
- compare viewpoints on political situations around the word
- design a multi-cultural recipe book
- make maps of both of the pen pals' communities
- interview both of the pen pals' families and friends to ask them to describe their daily lives.

There are several websites to help you find pen pals for your class. Two of the largest and most well known are described below.

- ePALS Classroom Exchange—**http://www.epals.com**

  ePALS is the world's largest classroom pen pal network. It presently connects classrooms from 96 countries speaking 98 languages.

- Intercultural E-Mail Classroom Connections—**http://www.iecc.org**

  IECC is a free service to help teachers link with partners in other countries and cultures for classroom pen pal and project exchanges. It was established in 1992. At last count more than 7,100 teachers in 79 countries were participating in one or more of the IECC lists. The IECC mailing lists are hosted by St. Olaf College, which is a liberal arts college in Minnesota.

Websites change over time. If a resource listed is not available, use search engines such as *Yahoo*, *Lycos*, or *Excite* to find other sources of the information you are looking for.

The Internet and E-mail *(cont.)*

Online Research

Online research is an inexact art form rather than a precise science. When we consider the multitude of information available through the Internet, we must also consider the ramifications of such a collection on student research.

There are several schools of thought when considering online research for students. Of course, much of this depends on the age and ability levels of the students. While each individual situation should be considered, most schools feel safer with a blanket response or position. Let's take a look at the prevailing attitudes about online research for students.

Willie-Nilly: Some teachers allow their students to go online to do research without any parameters at all. Sadly, this policy is usually a result of the teacher's lack of knowledge, rather than as a conscious statement about online research. These teachers often rely on the knowledge levels of their students, often greater than their own, to make the decisions for them. While many teachers wind up with this kind of Internet use, many others create this approach purposefully. They view open use of the Internet as a positive thing. They recognize the fact that Internet use has permeated our society, and they want their students to be well versed in its use without restrictions. These students are growing up in a world where they have access to the Internet almost everywhere.

Don't Go Near It: Other teachers and schools feel that because of the sheer amount of information that is "out there," it is developmentally inappropriate for students to use any kind of search engine or tool. Teachers in this camp feel that it is their job to provide the students with a safe arena for their searches. As such, these teachers usually provide their students with small collections of three to six websites to use for each specific activity on which they're working. Generally, these teachers are not impressed with the hit-or-miss method of researching through search engines. They feel that it teaches better research skills when they provide the specific documents—documents they know contain the information the students need, documents they know to be accurate, and documents which support rather than detract from the learning objectives.

In Between: There is, as for most situations in life, a happy middle ground—an in-between which borrows from each end of the spectrum to create another choice. Many teachers find themselves operating in this middle ground. With some activities, these teachers might provide specific websites to be used, while with other projects they may allow their students to use kiddie search engines in order to train them in their use.

These teachers know that if the intent of going online is to collect information, their students should each have, at the bare minimum, a piece of paper and a pencil in hand when they go online. Better than this bare minimum, they know that their students need to have an activity specific note-taking form of some kind.

The Internet and E-mail *(cont.)*

Online Research *(cont.)*

In Between *(cont.)*: Teachers in this middle ground know that their students need to be trained in the use of search engines. So many of the engines have distracting links, advertising, and extraneous information, it's very easy for students (especially those who are easily distracted) to be drawn away from their purpose. Students need to be shown what to ignore and what to focus on while they're researching. They need to know how to properly word an Internet search, a skill which baffles many adults, let alone students. They need to have an understanding of the organization of the results which the search engines return. All of these needs can be met through simple practice. These teachers usually chose one or two kiddie engines to explore with their students, helping them become acclimated to the Internet environment.

Search Engines

There are a variety of search engines which are designed for school-aged children. Each one of these engines has specific details which you'll need to know about before taking children to them. I recommend that you go to these sites and literally play around on them. Do some searches of topics you're likely to ask your children to do. Get a feel for the return results. Look for organization and readability levels of the site. You know your learners best, so you'll be the best judge of which kiddie engines to use. The most important thing is that you feel comfortable with the process before taking your learners to it.

You might want to employ a few classroom procedures when using the search engines. Try these on for size:

- Have your students write their searching words on an index card and make sure they show it to you so that you can give them guidance and direction before they go online.

- Make a class rule that everyone pays attention to only the top three or four results. This can come in handy when the search engine brings back a list of hundreds!

- When you're first starting out, ask students to answer this question: How could I have made my search stronger? Keep a running list of answers on a poster in the room so that others can improve their skills too!

- Establish search partnerships which allow students to go online in pairs so that they can have two sets of eyes and two brains involved in their searching!

The Internet and E-mail *(cont.)*

Online Research *(cont.)*

Logging on to the information superhighway is the equivalent of having access to virtually every library and source of information in the world. No longer are students limited to encyclopedia, text, resource books, and the occasional letters requesting more information from a source. With this up-to-the-minute data, reports and research take on a whole new meaning.

Because the terrain is so vast and it is so easy for students to go down some inappropriate paths, teachers are advised to take time to perform a search of their own before they assign a theme or topic to students. By doing that, you will get a feel for how well your students might be able to perform their research. Many educators use the search engines listed below.

- *Excite*
- *Lycos*
- *Yahoo!* and its children's site, *Yahooligans!*
- *AltaVista*

There are many Internet sites that are ideally suited to research. Sites highly rated by educators include:

- ARTSEDGE—Linking the Arts and Education Through Technology
  Sponsored by the John F. Kennedy Center for the Performing Arts
  http://artsedge.kennedy-center.org/artsedge.html

- EdWeb—Online K–12 Education Resource Guide
  Sponsored by the Corporation for Public Broadcasting
  http://edweb.gsn.org

- Library of Congress
  http://www.loc.gov

- NASA K–12 Home Page
  Homepage of NASA's Award Winning Quest Team
  http://quest.arc.nasa.gov

- Scientific American
  http://www.sciam.com

- Kids' Web—Digital Learning Resource Library
  http://www.kidsvista.com/index.html

- AskERIC—Educational Resource Information Center
  http://ericir.syr.edu/

The Internet and E-mail *(cont.)*

Internet Safety

Certainly one of the main concerns of the "online teacher" is Internet safety. By this point in time, most school systems have created some provision, policy, or statement of philosophy regarding student use of the Internet. Fueled by concerns from parents and occasional bad press, Internet use has gotten a bad rap in some areas. I'd like to address the issue of Internet safety in hopes of providing some guidance to teachers who might be just starting out and affirmation to those who have been traveling the information superhighway safely for years. Teachers should always provide both a purposeful use and appropriate supervision to their online activities.

Purposeful Use: How is the Internet approached in your classroom? Is it treated as a toy or a tool? There is a dangerous message being sent in classrooms where children are rewarded for completed work and good behavior with extra time to "play" on the Internet. In classrooms where the Internet is treated like the powerful tool that it is, there is a greater likelihood that the Internet will be used appropriately. The core of this debate about approaches is summed up in one little word: *intent*.

How is the Internet used in your classroom? When you ask your learners to go online to find out something about whales, you're setting them up for a frustrating experience—"I might find something, I might not." We wouldn't dream of standing a fourth grader at the doors to the New York Public Library and shoving him gently into the abyss, saying to him, "Run in there and find out something about whales." As teachers, we'd go with him, guide him through the card catalog, bring him to the section on animals, point out the shelves where the books on whales are found, and help him find five books which might give him good information. We should treat the Internet the same way. We should tell our students to go to a class bookmarks page (a website collection of teacher-approved, content-specific sites) to find five facts about whales which we instruct them to write down on index cards. Then we've set them up for success!

Beyond the intent behind our use of the Internet is another word which comes in handy in this discussion: *direction*. It is imperative that we give our students a specific direction when they go online. They should go to some specific place and should do some specific thing when they get there. As we discussed in the section on online research, there is just too much information out there for students to manage alone. It is developmentally inappropriate to expect young students to be able to manage search results in excess of even 50 hits, let alone searches which bring back thousands of hits. Send your young students to a specific site or collection of sites which you've already approved. Be sure they know that they're expected to do something specific once they get there. Empower them with pre-printed Internet index cards. On one side print the word "Target" where they write the URL or page name of the website they're going to. The other side reads "Action" where they've written down what action they have to take once they have arrived at the site and read the content.

The Internet and E-mail *(cont.)*

Internet Safety *(cont.)*

Appropriate Supervision: The second Golden Rule of Internet safety is providing appropriate supervision. Much of this will depend on your school's philosophy about Internet use. Most schools have a requirement that students have some kind of supervision while they're online. That supervision might be peer supervision or adult supervision. Adult supervision allows for greater accountability.

Of course, age also plays a part here. We have different concerns about Internet safety when working with high school students than we do when working with elementary students. The adult supervision for elementary school students often has more to do with helping them with the technology than it does with protecting them from harm's way. The location of the computers has a lot to do with providing supervision. If the computers are in your classroom, then you have greater control of the situation. Make sure the computers are positioned so that you can see the screens from anywhere in the room. If the computers are located elsewhere, in a lab or in the media center, then make arrangements to have a staff member from the media center or a parent volunteer provide supervision.

Class Expectations: When considering Internet safety, it's important to make sure that we recognize the importance of having clear expectations of our students regarding their use of the Internet. Let them know what kind of task commitment you require, let them know what kind of behavior is appropriate, and let them know what the consequences are if they don't meet those expectations. Most schools or school systems require students to sign an Acceptable Use Policy (AUP) which outlines appropriate use of the Internet. One thing to be sure of with an AUP is that you want to make sure that it is written on a level the students can understand, rather than in legalese which amounts to a signature without understanding. We've included a copy of an AUP on page 230.

Time Constraints: One of the best strategies to use when you're attempting to ensure Internet safety is to place time constraints on your students' use of the Internet. If they know they have a limited amount of time to go online, they're more likely to use that time to accomplish their goals. Time constraints are often a naturally occurring factor, due to the ratio of students to computers, so this is a strategy which can be employed without much effort.

Filtering Software: Many school systems are using filtering software to help protect their children. The most important thing to consider here is that we should not allow the presence of a filtering program to lull us into a false sense of security. Filters or not, we should employ other safety strategies.

The bottom line with Internet Safety is this: If your students are trained to treat the Internet as a powerful tool, if they are supervised in their use, if they have specific purposes and objectives when they're online, and if they have a limited amount of time to be online, their online safety is much more secure.

The 5 W's of Website Evaluation

For the Teacher

Evaluation of Internet information takes a multi-tiered approach. At the simplest level, students can use a checklist to determine whether the information that they find is easy to use, authoritative, and applicable to their purpose. The following lesson can help teach students about the triggers they should be looking for when evaluating a website.

Objective

Students will become familiar with some of the aspects of evaluating websites.

Materials

- "The 5 W's of Website Evaluation" description sheets (pages 121–122)
- "The 5 W's for Evaluating Websites Information Sheet" (page 123 or in the *Internet Lesson* folder on the CD-ROM, filename: infosheet.pdf)
- Evaluation sheets for each student (elementary or middle) (pages 124–128 or in the *Internet Lesson* folder on the CD-ROM, filenames: elemetr.pdf and middle.pdf; an advanced evaluation is also provided, filename: advanced.pdf)
- Large screen projection device, computer, and Internet access

Procedures

1. The teacher will first share the description sheets and explain the rationale for each of the criteria of website evaluation to the students.

2. Together, the teacher will lead the class through a formal evaluation of a chosen website, talking about the various items to look for when evaluating a site and using the appropriately leveled student evaluation sheet.

3. Students will then complete evaluation sheets for each of the websites they will be using for their projects.

Evaluation

Students will complete an evaluation sheet for each one of the sites that they are using for their research. The teacher should review the evaluation sheets for complete answers and the summary paragraphs.

The 5 W's of Website Evaluation

The following are descriptions of the 5 W's of website evaluation to be shared with the students. Full-page copies of these slides are provided as PDF files and a *PowerPoint* presentation in the *Internet Lesson* folder on the CD-ROM (filename: 5wslides.pdf and 5wslide.ppt)

Who? What? When? Where? Why? 5 W's of Web Site Evaluation	Explain to students the importance of thinking carefully about the information that appears on a website. Let them know that the traditional who, what, when, where, and why questions will lead them to easily evaluate a site.
 Who wrote the pages and is he/she an expert? **Is a biography of the author of the site included?** **How can you find out more about the author?**	Explain that the authority of the author is always an important piece. If a biography of an author is included, this makes it easier, but there should also be a way to contact the author for further information whether by e-mail or regular mail. Searching the online library card catalogs and large bookstore offerings will also indicate if the author has written any published books on the topic.
 **What does the author say is the purpose of the site?** **What else might the author have in mind for the site?** **What makes this site easy to use?**	Every good website includes a rationale for why the site was created and why the author chose to include certain types of information. The navigation of the site is also an important aspect which aids the students with ease of use and should be addressed with them.

The 5 W's of Website Evaluation *(cont.)*

When?

When was the site created?

When was the site last updated?

All good websites include the date they were created and the date the site was last updated. This is very important in an area of frequent and rapid development, like cloning, the space program, or negotiations in the Middle East.

Students who are working on topics that change should be encouraged to visit these types of sites frequently to get the latest information.

Where?

Where does the information come from?

Where can I look to find out more about the producer of the page?

If a bibliography of sources used by the Web page author is included, students have an easy way to verify the information on their own.

However, if there are no citations, as stated before, students should have the information needed to contact the author and ask for further information.

Why?

Why is the information useful for my purpose?

Why should I use this information?

Why is this page better than another?

After examining the information they have found, students should assess whether the information is useful for the purpose of their research papers. They should also be able to justify why they are choosing one piece of information over another and using one particular page instead of another.

This can only be accomplished after acquiring a knowledge base on the topic at hand and widely investigating websites and print sources.

Name: _____

The 5 W's for Evaluating Websites

Information Sheet

Who	Who wrote the pages and is he/she an expert? Is a biography of the author included? How can you find out more about the author?
What	What does the author say is the purpose of the site? What else might the author have in mind for the site? What makes the site easy to use?
When	When was the site created? When was the site last updated?
Where	Where does the information come from? Where can I look to find out more about the producer of the page?
Why	Why is this information useful for my purpose? Why should I use this information? Why is this page better than another?

Name: _____

Critical Evaluation of a Website: Elementary School Level

Directions: Circle or write your response as appropriate.

1. How are you connected to the Internet?

   _____ Computer and modem   _____ Direct connection at school

2. If you are using a modem, what is the speed?

   2400   9600   14.4K   28.8K   33.6K   56K

3. What Web browser are you using? _____

4. What is the URL of the Web page you are looking at?

   http:// _____

5. What is the name of the site? _____

How Does It Look?

1. Does the page take a long time to load?   YES   NO

2. Are there big pictures on the page?   YES   NO

3. Is the spelling correct on the page?   YES   NO

4. Is the author's name and e-mail address on the page?   YES   NO

5. Is there a picture on the page that you can use to choose links? (Image map) YES   NO

6. Is information on the page in columns? (Table)   YES   NO

7. If you go to another page, is there a way to get back to the first page?   YES   NO

8. Is there a date that tells you when the page was made?   YES   NO

9. Do the photographs look real?   YES   NO   NO PHOTOGRAPHS

10. Do the sounds sound real?   YES   NO   NO SOUND

©1996 Kathleen Schrock (kschrock@capecod.net)

Kathy Schrock's Guide for Educators—http://discoveryschool.com/schrockguide/

Critical Evaluation of a Website: Elementary School Level *(cont.)*

What Did You Learn?

Directions: Circle the correct response.

1. Does the title of the page tell you what it is about?   YES   NO

2. Is there an introduction on the page that tells you what is included?   YES   NO

3. Are the facts on the page what you were looking for?   YES   NO

4. Would you have gotten more information from the encyclopedia?   YES   NO

5. Would the information have been better in the encyclopedia?   YES   NO

6. Does the author of the page say some things you disagree with?   YES   NO

7. Does the author of the page include information that you know is wrong?   YES   NO

8. Do the pictures and photographs on the page help you learn?   YES   NO   NO PICTURES

Summary

Looking at all of the questions and answers above, write a paragraph telling why this website is or is not helpful to you for your project.

_____

_____

_____

_____

_____

_____

_____

_____

_____

Name: _____

Critical Evaluation of a Website: Middle School Level

Directions: Circle or write your response as appropriate.

1. What type of connection do you have to the Internet?

    _____ Dial-in access: modem speed   2400   9600   14.4K   28.8K   33.6K   56K

    _____ Direct connection: 56K   T1   T3   other: _____

2. What Web browser are you using? _____

3. What is the URL of the Web page you are evaluating?

    http:// _____

4. What is the name of the site? _____

Part One: Looking At and Using the Page

1. Does the page take a long time to load?   YES   NO

2. Are the pictures on the page helpful?   YES   NO   NOT APPLICABLE

3. Is each section of the page labeled with a heading?   YES   NO

4. Does the author sign his/her real name?   YES   NO

5. Does the author give you his/her e-mail address?   YES   NO

6. Is there a date on the page that tells you when it was last updated?   YES   NO

7. Is there an image map (big picture with links) on the page?   YES   NO

8. Is there a table (columns of text) on the page? (Check the source code.)   YES   NO

9. If so, is the table readable with your browser?   YES   NO

10. If you go to another page on the site, can you get back to the main page?   YES   NO

11. Are there photographs on the page?   YES   NO

12. If so, can you be sure that the author has not changed photographs?   YES   NO

13. If you're not sure, should you accept the photos as true?   YES   NO

Critical Evaluation of a Website: Middle School Level *(cont.)*

Summary of Part One

Using the data you have collected for the previous page, write a paragraph explaining why you would or would not recommend this site to a friend for use with a project.

_____

_____

_____

_____

_____

_____

_____

_____

Part Two: What's on the Page and Who Put It There?

1. Does the title of the page tell you what it is about?   YES NO

2. Is there a paragraph on the page explaining what it is about?   YES NO

3. Is the information on the page useful for your project?   YES NO

   If not, what can you do next? _____

4. Would you have gotten more information from an encyclopedia?   YES NO

5. Is the information on the page current?   YES NO

6. Does up-to-date information make a difference for your project?   YES NO

7. Does the page lead you to some other good information (links)?   YES NO

8. Does the author of the page present some information you disagree with?   YES NO

9. Does the author of the page present some information that you think is wrong?   YES NO

10. Does some information contradict information you found elsewhere?   YES NO

11. Does the author use some absolute words like "always" or "never"?   YES NO

12. Does the author use superlative words like the "best" or "worst"?   YES NO

Critical Evaluation of a Website: Middle School Level *(cont.)*

13. Does the author tell you about him/herself?   YES   NO

14. Do you feel that the author is knowledgeable about the topic?   YES   NO

15. Are you positive the information is true?   YES   NO

16. What can you do to prove the information is true?

_____

_____

_____

Summary of Part Two

Looking at the data you have collected in part two, compose a note to the author of the website explaining how you are going to use the website in your project and what your opinion is of the page's content.

_____

_____

_____

_____

_____

_____

_____

_____

_____

_____

_____

My School, Your School

Technology Required

Internet access, e-mail, scanner (optional), chat (optional), video conference (optional)

Grade Levels: 4–8

Subjects: history/social science, language arts

Duration: 4 to 6 weeks

Description

During this activity, students will interact with peers in other schools to explore differences in the educational systems of other regions.

Objectives

In this activity students will:

- compare school cultures with respect to a defined list of areas.
- explore differences in educational systems.

Materials

- maps
- list of potential partners (from local contacts or a website)
- software programs for creating/using e-mail, chat, and/or Instant Messaging, video conferencing (optional), scanner, spreadsheet, and word processor documents

Procedure

1. Before beginning this exchange, ask students to gather the information below as it relates to their own school. The activity page (page 131) will be helpful in getting this information organized.

2. Here are some possible areas for discussion:

   - Typical schedule for your students' grade level
   - Graduation requirements (if applicable)
   - Mode of dress: dress codes, uniforms, etc.
   - Extracurricular activities: sports, community-service requirements, academic recognition, etc.
   - Perceived challenges
   - Role of school in the community
   - School security

My School, Your School *(cont.)*

3. Exchange information with selected partners. Try to get a "snapshot" that reflects the views of an entire class rather than a selected student. This will help you get more balanced information. Using chat, Instant Messaging, or video conferencing would enhance exchanging this type of information.

4. Be sure to allow time for your students to synthesize, analyze, and summarize what they have learned. Does this information impact the students' thinking about their school and the educational system in general?

5. A final report might take the form of a Web page, a *PowerPoint* presentation, or a graphical analysis of information gathered.

Assessment

Using a rubric that assesses the process and knowledge gained will help students look at the information both as students and as researchers. As students, they may simply compare the perceived good and bad about each partner's school. As researchers, they will be able to see the connections among community, culture, and school.

Internet Resources

Web66 has a comprehensive international list of schools that are online. The listing will take you to each school's website.

http://web66.coled.umn.edu

Yahooligans has a list of school sites organized by geographic regions.

http://www.yahooligans.com/School_Bell/School_Sites/

Name _____

My School, Your School

Directions: Gather the information below as it relates to your own school. Then to explore differences in the educational systems of other regions, gather this information about other schools.

Topic	Notes on Your School	Notes on Other Schools
Typical schedule		
Graduation requirements		
Mode of dress: dress codes, uniforms, etc.		
Extracurricular activities		
Perceived challenges		
Role of school in the community		
School security		

On the back of this page, explain how this information impacts your thinking about your school and the educational system in general.

Search Engines

What Is a Search Engine?

A search engine, such as *Yahoo* (**http://www.yahoo.com**) or *AltaVista* (**http://www.altavista.com**), contains a detailed listing of information found on the Internet. When you use one of these search engines, it will electronically search its collection of catalogued information that it has already located for its users on the Internet.

There is currently no charge for utilizing most search engines. The owners of these sites generate revenue by selling advertising space on their pages to companies. Thus, when you access their site to perform a search, you see those advertisements. Some users object to being faced with all that advertising. However, think of viewing the advertisements as the lesser of two evils; if they weren't there, you would have to pay to use the search engine!

Once you have arrived at a search engine, you can either search or browse the information stored in that location. Searching would involve a specific topic or item being entered into the search dialogue box, while browsing would involve investigating the site via the directories presented on the first page of the site.

What Are You Really Searching?

Each search engine site that you use has its own database (or list) of information it has gathered from the Internet. The listing has been created using information either "harvested" from the Internet or submitted by users. When you use a search engine on the Internet, you are not searching the entire Internet. The Internet consists of millions of computers containing trillions of items of information. You can imagine the scope of an exhaustive search of the complete collection. Instead, you are searching the database maintained by that particular search engine.

Why Might You Get Two Different Sets of Results for the Same Search Terms?

The collection of information from the Internet gathered by many of the more popular search engines could have as much as 70% of the same information. However, that leaves 30% of the information to differ between two search engines. So, while the majority of the information will be the same, you will also find a percentage of unique information at each. Thus, a search at *Yahoo* will provide many of the same results as a search at *AltaVista*, but there will also be many differences.

Search Engines *(cont.)*

AltaVista is a search engine. It uses crawlers to locate its websites, which means it has computer programs that go out at night and find websites. Using *AltaVista* results in an extensive search, which is why you always get so many hits with it. It is not selective or picky, in any way, shape, or form. It wants to catalog everything out there. Good, bad, or ugly. It is best used when you want to locate something that might be tough to locate about a particular topic. An AltaVista search will most often turn up far more hits than you can ever possibly review, which can be overwhelming to some people.

Yahoo, on the other hand, is considered a search directory. It employs people to locate websites to catalog; then they select what they determine to be "good" sites. Using *Yahoo* will give you more quality searches, especially on broad topics like "dogs." You won't get as many hits as you would with *AltaVista*, but a lot of the poorer quality sites will not come up. They have weeded those out. Some people don't like this approach. Others find it much more manageable and helpful to have had someone already select the better sites. It just depends on the particular search you are doing, in terms of which type of search tool is best to use.

Web authors also have the option of submitting their websites to any and all search engines to request that they be listed in the databases. This is another way that websites are added to search engines.

Search Strategies

Many people become easily frustrated when performing searches on the Internet for the first time. The following will focus on some structured searches using various techniques and search engines. There are four parts to this section:

1. General searching
2. Refining your general search
3. Metasearching
4. Real language searching

General Searching

Performing searches is the most common starting point for Internet users. It involves simply going to a search engine and typing your topic into the appropriate box or field. Unless you are very specific with your topic, this method most often yields large numbers of matches or what we call "hits."

Search Engines *(cont.)*

Let's try some general searches using a few of the more popular search engines. Go to *Yahoo* (**http://www.yahoo.com**) and do a search for *penguins*. How many matches or hits did you get?

While still using *Yahoo*, type in the search box the words *"emperor penguins"* using quotation marks as shown. What effect does this have on your results?

Now, go to *AltaVista* (**http://www.altavista.com**) and do the same search for *"emperor penguins."* How did the number of matches or hits "harvested" at this site compare to *Yahoo*?

Refining Your General Search

Our previous source yielded many, many results, most likely, too many to rifle through. This is a critical moment for teachers and students. How do you proceed when you have thousands of matches? The easiest way to proceed is to refine your search, thus eliminating many of the results that do not pertain to your research.

Most of the popular search engines have some method of refining your search. Currently, one of the easiest to use is at *Lycos*, so we will use this for our example.

Go to the *Lycos* website (**http://www.lycos.com**) and perform a general search for the term *penguins*. When I performed this search, I got over 200 thousand hits!

Scroll back to the top of the page where the results from your Lycos search will still be on your screen. Here you will find a blue box that allows you to refine your search. First, click in the little box next to **Search within these results**. That way, the next search will only be based on the hits you got on the first search.

Delete the word *penguins* and type the word *emperor* in the box. Click **Go**. This will refine your search to those that also contain the term *emperor*. When I typed *emperor*, it filtered me down to about 80,000 hits. This is a considerable reduction from the 200 thousand located earlier. Only those that had both *penguins* and *emperor* remained.

Although this should have narrowed your search significantly, we're not there yet. Once again, using the same refining technique, search within your results for *Antarctic*, and then within those results for *pictures*. With each refinement, you should end up with fewer and fewer hits. What was your final number of hits? Whatever it was, it was sure to be greatly reduced from 200 thousand. This is one way to pare down the number of hits you get as well as giving you a more focused result.

Search Engines *(cont.)*

Metasearching

As mentioned earlier, searching for information on a specific topic at different sites usually results in a significant number of different results. Knowing this fact, if you are like most users, you will want to search more than one search engine to ensure that you have all the results possible. However, visiting *Yahoo*, *Lycos*, and *AltaVista*, among others, can be a time consuming task.

Metasearch engines will conduct a search on a topic for you by using a number of various search engines. Then, it reports the results back to you—most often presented in a very organized, logical manner. In essence, it is a "search engine of search engines."

Let's try using two metasearch engines. First, go to *Metacrawler* (**http://www.metacrawler.com**) and do a search for *"Betsy Ross"* (in quotation marks). Note that your results come from a variety of search engines, so it lists the ones that were actually used. *Metacrawler* has searched all their respective databases and reported those hits back to you, in one easy step. Think of all the time and effort you just saved!

Now go to *Dogpile* (**http://www.dogpile.com**). Perform the same metasearch for *"Betsy Ross"* at Dogpile and compare your results to those obtained at *Metacrawler*. Since *Dogpile* lists the matches by search engine, you'll need to scroll all the way down the page to make your comparisons.

Real Language Searching

One of the best innovations in the area of searching on the Internet is the use of "real language." This breakthrough has greatly simplified the whole process of searching, which can provide a huge benefit for students and teachers.

One of the leading sites that uses real language searching is called Ask Jeeves. It combines the ease of real language searching with a metasearch engine, making it a wonderful site to use. Go to *Ask Jeeves* (**http://www.askjeeves.com**) and notice that the usual box/field for entering your search topic looks very similar to those found at the other sites. However, if you look above the box, you will find the instruction, "What can I help you find?" Much more personal than the other search engines. Simply type your question in the box and click the **Ask** button.

Search Engines *(cont.)*

How Does a Search Engine Work?

Name: _____ Date: _____

Search Engines *(cont.)*

Boolean Search Strategies

How do I narrow a search using "and"?

- Using *and* will only provide links to sites which have BOTH of these words present

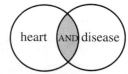

How do I narrow a search using "and"?

- Using *and* twice will limit the search even more

- You will only get pages that include all THREE of the terms

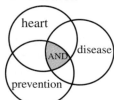

How do I broaden a search?

- Use of the word *or* will broaden a search

- Use *or* if two words may be used interchangeably

- Can use *or* more than once to get very broad

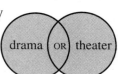

How do I narrow a search using "not"?

- Using *not* twice narrows the search by telling search engine to exclude certain words

- Alta Vista uses the form *and not*

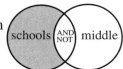

Name: _____ Date: _____

Search Engines *(cont.)*

Search Engines and Mr. Boole

When using the search engines, it is best to start with the page that allows you to use some Boolean search strategies to limit or broaden your search.

Go to *AltaVista* (**http://www.altavista.com**), type the term(s) on line A, and record the number of results that are returned for each entry. Then choose the *Advanced Search* menu item and type the term(s) on line B in the large search box, as written, and record the number of results obtained with this type of search for each entry.

Terms to Search	Number of Results
Line A: endangered species	
Line B: endangered and owls	
Line A: middle school	
Line B: middle school and students	
Line A: cars	
Line B: cars and Toyota	
Line A: toys	
Line B: toys or games	

1. What can you predict about the number of results that will be returned for the advanced searches?

   _____

2. Why is this true?

   _____

   _____

   _____

Teaching Little Fingers to Keyboard

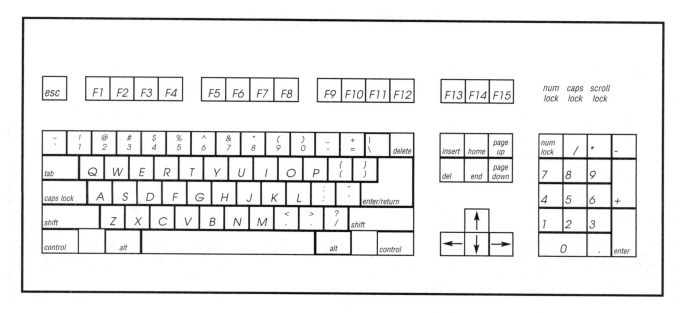

Corey is a seventh-grade student living in southwest Florida. This fall he entered a technology applications class. During the first week of school, Corey and his classmates took a timed keyboarding skills assessment. Corey scored 45 words per minute. His teacher was shocked because Corey couldn't even demonstrate the proper finger placement for the home row keys (a, s, d, f and j, k, l, ;). Corey's teacher insisted that he take the timed keyboarding skills assessment again. Corey did, scoring 47 words per minute.

Playing on the computer since the age of three, Corey managed to formulate his own keyboarding skills. Although this may sound like a wonderful achievement for Corey, it is not. His teacher's greatest concern is that Corey's potential keyboarding speed may be limited unless he learns the proper finger placement and the traditional keystrokes associated with each finger. Because of not receiving proper keyboarding instruction at an earlier age, Corey has a huge two-fold task at hand—breaking his old keyboarding habits and "getting up to speed" with his new keyboarding habits.

What is the lesson to be learned here? Don't let this happen to your students! The minute that your students' fingers touch the computer keyboard, they should begin to learn keyboarding skills appropriate for their age and grade level, so they don't form bad habits. Just as you immediately teach your students to read and write from left to right, they need to learn basic finger placement on the home row keys, how to use the space bar, how to use the Shift key to access upper case letters and special symbols, and more.

"Oh, no!" you sigh. "Am I responsible for teaching keyboarding skills, too?"

Not to worry! There are numerous keyboarding software applications in the educational software marketplace that can foster your students' emerging keyboarding skills and subsequent habits. Many of the software applications teach the mouse skills your students need as well.

On the next page is a table of several keyboarding software applications for students that are currently on the market, including their publishers and the grade levels for which they were designed.

Teaching Little Fingers to Keyboard *(cont.)*

Keyboarding Software Applications for Students

Keyboarding Software Application	Publisher	Grade Levels
Disney's Adventures in Typing with Timon and Pumbaa	Disney Interactive	1 through 2
JumpStart Typing	Knowledge Adventure	2 through 5
Kid Keys 2	Knowledge Adventure	Pre-K through 2
Mavis Beacon Teaches Typing 12 Deluxe	Mindscape and The Learning Company	3 through 12
Mavis Beacon Teaches Typing 12 Standard	Mindscape and The Learning Company	3 through 12
Mavis Beacon Teaches Type 9 for Macintosh	Mindscape and The Learning Company	3 through 12
Mavis Beacon Teaches Typing for Kids	Mindscape and The Learning Company	K through 3
Phonics Alive 6 for Typing	Quickmind	Pre-K through 12
Read, Write and Type!	Talking Fingers	1 through 4
Roller Typing	Edventure	2 through 12
Stickybear's Typing	Optimum Resource	1 through 12
Type to Learn Jr.	Sunburst Communications	K through 2
Typing Instructor 11 Deluxe	Individual Software Incorporated	3 though12
Typing Tutor 10	Simon and Schuster Interactive	Pre-K to 12
Typing Workshop	Optimum Resource	3 through 12

Okay, so now what do you do? Well, remember that you don't have to teach keyboarding per se. Rather, plan to facilitate your students' learning of keyboarding skills by integrating a grade-level appropriate keyboarding software application into your technology time—even if it is only for five minutes or so each week.

Check to see what keyboarding software applications are already available in your school or school district. Ask your fellow teachers, media specialist, computer lab attendant, or technology coordinator to help you obtain and install legal copies of an appropriate keyboarding software application onto the computer systems in your classroom.

Alternatively, if you are in a school where your students go to the computer lab for technology-related instruction, speak with the computer lab attendant about providing your students with a few minutes of keyboarding skill-building activities each visit. You may find that your students are already receiving keyboarding instruction. If so, that's great! If not, the computer lab attendant will be thrilled that you are taking an interest in the activities he or she provides for your students.

Teaching Little Fingers to Keyboard *(cont.)*

Then explore and play with the selected keyboarding software application yourself. (Most children's keyboarding software applications are really fun! They are full of graphics, music, sound effects, and words that reinforce your good actions.) See what skills the application teaches. As you are doing so, create a simple tracking sheet that will allow you and your students to watch their keyboarding skills progress.

As I opened *Kid Keys 2.0*, a pre-K through grade 2 keyboarding software application, I discovered that I could print a manual of how to use the program by clicking the **Manual** button on the opening (Launcher) screen. After signing in, I found myself in a main room with five doors-each with a different type of keyboarding learning activity, including the following:

- Keystone Keyboard
- Dragon Tunes
- Magic Mirrors
- Castle Keys
- Mouse Chase

Each learning activity had four different levels of difficulty. After completing a few of the activities (and receiving an attractive Certificate of Achievement for each), it became clear how to create a tracking sheet for this keyboarding software application. You will see the *Student Keyboarding Tracking Sheet for Kid Keys* on the following page. The keyboarding tracking sheet is also available on the CD-ROM [filename: *keyboard.doc*].

So, have fun teaching little fingers to keyboard. Add your name to the keyboarding tracking sheet you design and complete the activities right along with your students. Watch your own keyboarding skills improve, too!

Teaching Little Fingers to Keyboard *(cont.)*

Student Keyboarding Tracking Sheet for Kid Keys

Name	Keystone Keyboard				Dragon Tunes				Magic Mirrors				Castle Keys				Mouse Chase			
	L1	L2	L3	L4	L1	L2	L3	L4	L1	L2	L3	L4	L1	L2	L3	L4	L1	L2	L3	L4

Installing Software onto Your Computer System

Wow! You just bought a new educational software application and can't wait to try it out. Looking for someone to help you install the program, you check the computer lab and find that the attendant isn't there. You cross the hall to another computer-using teacher and quickly retreat when you see there's a parent-teacher conference going on. You duck into the media center and spy the media specialist at one of the computer systems, surrounded by a group of students.

"Oh, no," you sigh. "I don't know if I can install this myself."

Well, sure you can. Every year it seems that the publishers of educational software applications make it easier and easier to install their products. In fact, most educational software applications automatically begin to install themselves once you place the CD into the CD-ROM drive of your computer system. You simply have to respond to dialog boxes that prompt you to make decisions about where you would like the program installed, whether or not you would like a short cut to the program displayed as an icon on the desktop, and more.

Don't let all those decisions cause you stress. When you don't understand what the publisher is asking and, therefore, don't want to make a decision, then don't! It's that simple. Publishers typically display the options and then pre-select (as a default) the option they recommend (and most people use). So, go with the publisher's recommendation whenever you are not sure what to do. You just click the **Next** button on the screen to move on.

"But what do I do if I put the CD into the CD-ROM drive of my computer system and nothing happens?" you ask.

If, after placing the CD into the CD-ROM drive of your computer system, the educational software application does not automatically begin the installation process, you may have to start the installation yourself.

Installing Software onto Your Computer System *(cont.)*

It really isn't too difficult. Here's how:

PC Machine Installation:

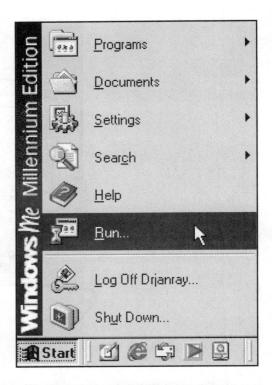

- First, exit any software applications that you may be running on your computer system.

- Place the educational software CD into the CD-ROM drive of your computer system.

- Wait a minute or so for the installation process to begin automatically—even though it may seem like hours.

- If the installation process does not automatically begin after a few minutes, click **Start** on the task bar, and select **Run**.

- At the **Run** dialog box, click **Browse**.

- At the **Browse** window, click the **Look in** list arrow and select **My Computer**.

- Once **My Computer** is displayed in the **Look in** text box, you will see all the drives on your computer system, such as A: (your floppy disk drive), C: (your hard drive), D: (normally your CD-ROM drive), E:, F:, and maybe even more listed. Click on your CD-ROM drive to select it. (You should see the name [or an abbreviated name] of the educational software application you are installing listed next to the drive letter.)

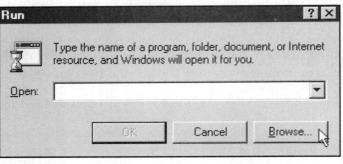

- Then click **Open**.

- You will return to the **Browse** window. This time, the name (or the abbreviated name) of the educational software application and the files and folders found on the CD are displayed. Look for a file named **SETUP** or another term related to installation. Click on that file to select it.

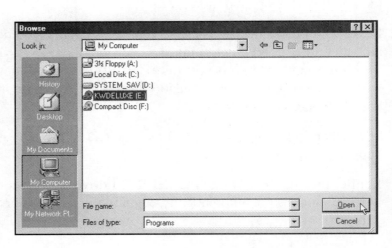

Installing Software onto Your Computer System *(cont.)*

• Then click **Open**.

• You will return to the **Run** dialog box. This time, the name of the setup or installation file you selected is displayed. Click **OK** to begin the setup or installation of the educational software application.

Macintosh Installation:

• If you have a Macintosh, you need to put the CD in your CD-ROM drive and give it a moment to open on its own.

• If it doesn't open, double-click on the CD icon.

• Find the file labeled **Install**, **Setup**, or **ReadMe** and double-click on it to begin the process.

General Installation:

• At the **Welcome** screen, read the messages carefully.

• Then click **Next**.

• At the **Choose Destination Directory** window (or a window with a similar name), you are asked where you would like the educational software application installed. Notice that the publisher has already determined where to place the program (C:\KWDELUXE). If that is fine with you, click **Next**. If that is not fine with you, because you have another place in mind, click **Browse**. Then navigate to and select the location you prefer.

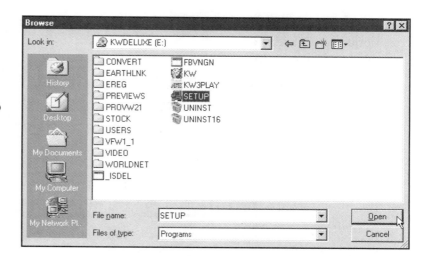

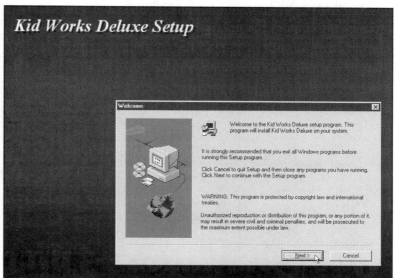

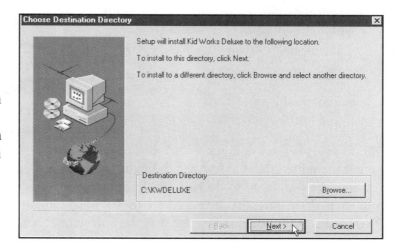

Installing Software onto Your Computer System *(cont.)*

- You may be provided with the option to register your educational software application online. If you haven't already sent in your registration card, feel free to do so. Click **Yes** and follow the instructions on the screen or screens that follow. (Please note that if you want to register electronically, your computer system must have an Internet connection.) If you already registered your educational software application, simply click **No**.

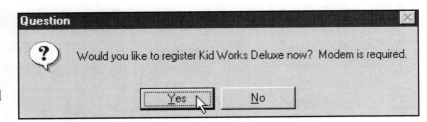

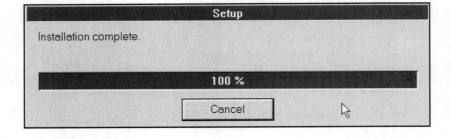

- Soon the **Setup** window will indicate that the installation of your educational software application is complete.

Of course, it is always a good idea to launch the educational software application immediately after installation, to make sure it runs okay. You may be prompted to do so after the setup or installation is complete. If not, launch the program on your own. You may also be asked to restart your computer after loading the software. This is always a good idea so that you can be sure that the software is working correctly.

Installing Software onto Your Computer System *(cont.)*

To launch the program follow these steps.

Windows Machines:

- Click **Start** on the task bar.

- Click **Programs**.

- Click the folder for the educational software application you just installed.

- Click the executable file for the educational software application to launch it.

Macintosh:

- Click on your hard drive folder.

- Click the folder for the educational software application you just installed.

- Double-click on the icon labeled with the name of the software program.

General:

- Once the program launches, click on the opening (Launch) screen to bypass it.

- Log into the educational software application and play with it for a while.

- Once you are satisfied that the program is running okay, exit or close it.

Congratulations! See, installing an educational software application is not that difficult after all.

Special Note: If you did experience any problems during or after installing your educational software application, don't let it upset you. Walk away from the computer system and contact someone from your circle of support who can help you as soon as possible.

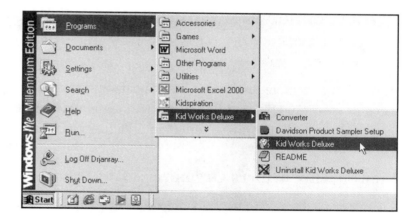

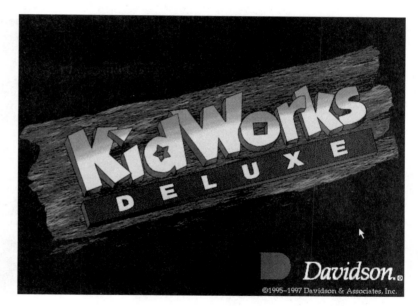

Managing Your Classroom Software Library

"Good order is the foundation of all good things."

Edmund Burke

As you acquire more and more educational software programs for your students to use, managing every piece of it—from CDs and floppy disks to registration cards and teacher's manuals—can become daunting. Make a determined effort to organize your software library now.

Viewing How Others Organize Software

Visit your media specialist, the computer lab attendant, and other computer-using teachers to see how their software is organized. How and where do they store their CDs? How accessible are the user's guides and teacher's manuals? How do they keep track of the registration number, login name(s), password(s), and technical support number(s) associated with each piece of software?

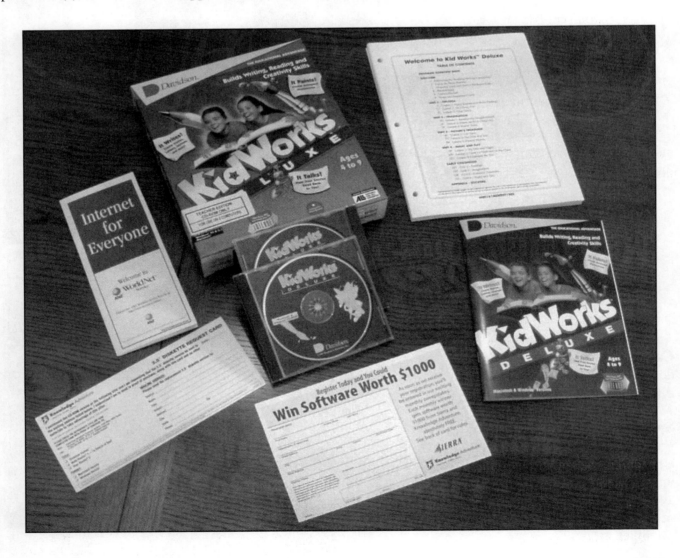

Managing Your Classroom Software Library *(cont.)*

Take notes as you view each person's system of managing software. What techniques did they use that appeal to you the most? Then apply these techniques to organizing your own software library.

Here are some techniques that work for me, as I continually strive to keep my software library well organized. Maybe they will work for you as well.

Using Notebooks to Organize Software

When I received *Kid Works Deluxe (Teacher Edition)* from Knowledge Adventure, the package included the following:

- the box
- a teacher's guide
- a user's guide
- a registration card
- a disk request card (just in case I needed the program on floppy disk, rather than on CD)
- some Internet advertising (for AT&T WorldNet Service)
- two *Kid Works Deluxe* CDs—one for my students to use and one for me to use

Here's how I organized each piece. (Grab an educational software box that you have in the classroom and follow along, making adjustments for its unique contents.)

- From experience, I know that software boxes have a very short shelf life. After one or two students tear into it to retrieve the user's guide, the software box is usually destroyed. So I typically cut up and store the software box in the following manner.

  - Remove the contents of the software box.

  - Open all box flaps.

  - Press the box with your hands until it is flat.

  - Make three cuts: cut up both sides of the box front cover and cut up one side of the box back cover.

  - Fold under the flaps.

Managing Your Classroom
Software Library *(cont.)*

- Although you may be tempted, do not cut off any of the informational flaps. It is best to keep as much of the software box intact as possible. Feel free to cut off non-informational flaps, if you wish.

  - Place the box front cover in the front clear plastic pocket of a three-ring binder.

  - Place the box back cover in the back clear plastic pocket of the three-ring binder.

  - Place the box side panel in the spine clear plastic pocket of the three-ring binder.

- Inserting the box side panel into the spine clear plastic pocket can be tricky, because the fit is tight if the three-ring binder is in its normal closed position. Hold the three-ring binder in such a way that the clear plastic front and back covers touch each other in order to maximize the opening of the pocket. Slip the box side panel into the spine pocket. If it doesn't fit because it is too wide, trim the box side panel a little more (without cutting away any information) or change to a three-ring binder with a wider spine clear plastic pocket.

  Although cut up into pieces, the software box will be forever intact and protected in the clear plastic pockets of the three-ring binder.

Managing Your Classroom
Software Library *(cont.)*

- Remove the shrink-wrap from the teacher's guide. Place the teacher's guide in the three-ring binder.

- User's guides come in a variety of sizes. Place the user's guide in the three-ring binder, if it is large enough. For a smaller user's guide, place it in a pocket folder and then in the three-ring binder.

- Fill out your registration card immediately. Before mailing the registration card, make a copy of it. Date the copy, place it in a clear plastic sheet protector, and then in the three-ring binder.

- For any other literature that came with the software, decide whether or not you really need to keep it. If you do, place the literature in the clear plastic sheet protector as well.

- Slip the software CD into the pocket found in the inside front cover of the three-ring binder for quick and easy retrieval.

- If the software is used frequently or if you are provided with a duplicate copy, consider storing the CD near the computer system(s) in a small storage rack.

Managing Your Classroom Software Library *(cont.)*

Using Magazine Boxes to Organize Software

When I received *HyperStudio 4 (Teacher Edition)* from Knowledge Adventure, the package included the following:

- a teacher's guide

- a user's guide

- a Knowledge Adventure Educational Software catalog

- a *HyperStudio* registration card

- two *HyperStudio* CDs—one for my students to use and one for me to use

I could immediately see that the three-ring binder method of organizing my educational software was not going to work with this version of *HyperStudio*.

- The two guides—the teacher's guide and the user's guide—were too short to three-hole punch and place in a three-ring binder.

- The two guides were also too thick and heavy for placing in a pocket folder.

- The software box front and back covers were too large for the clear plastic covers of a three-ring binder.

So, I needed a different organizational strategy. I decided to use a magazine box.

The *HyperStudio* box was emptied, opened, flattened, and cut-just like the *Kid Works Deluxe* box. The side panel of the *HyperStudio* box was glued to the tall end of the magazine box. All the contents of the *HyperStudio* box were placed inside the magazine box. The remaining portions of the software box itself were trimmed, folded, and placed in the magazine box as well.

Managing Your Classroom Software Library *(cont.)*

Using Media Pouches to Organize Software

When I received *Kid Pix Activity Kit—Sea Animal Activities (Ages 5–9)* and *Kid Pix Activity Kit—Insect Activities (Ages 8–12)* from Teacher Created Materials, each package included the following:

- an activities CD
- a user's guide

I could immediately see that the three-ring binder and magazine box methods of organizing my educational software were not going to work with the *Kid Pix Activity Kits*.

- There were no software boxes to cut up to make the front cover, back cover, and spine for each three-ring binder.

- There were too few materials to justify using either a three-ring binder or a magazine box, especially if I decided to keep the CDs in the small storage rack near the computer system.

Once again, I needed a different organizational strategy. I decided to use media pouches. Media pouches have clear plastic fronts (except for the top two inches); colorful, sturdy nylon fabric backs; zippers; and grommets for easy hanging (with "S" hooks). They are perfect for just a few items. They are also durable enough for your students to take home, if your educational software license agreement includes student take-home rights.

Managing Your Classroom Software Library *(cont.)*

The media pouches can be placed on a shelf with the other educational software in your classroom or hang from a rack. **Special Note:** Your media specialist can help you order media pouches and racks from his or her media center supply catalogs.

Keeping a Software Inventory

Before putting any of your educational software away, record all the information about your software in the *My Software Library Inventory* sheet that is shown on page 156. (The *My Software Library Inventory* sheet is also available on the CD-ROM [filename: swlbry.xls in *Microsoft Excel* and swlbry.doc in *Microsoft Word*].) The information you need includes the following:

- the title of your software application

- the version number of your software application

- the publisher of your software application

- the date you acquired your software application

- the registration number of your software application

- the date you submitted the registration for your software application

Managing Your Classroom
Software Library *(cont.)*

- the telephone number for sales and/or customer service for your software application

- the telephone number of technical support for your software application

- the type of media for your software application, such as CD, floppy disk, and more

- the terms of the licensing agreement for your software application

- any login information necessary to run your software application

- any password(s) necessary to access your software application

If you can't find all of the information about your software application to "fill in the blanks" on the *My Software Library Inventory* sheet, that's okay. Fill in what you can. Keep the *My Software Library Inventory* in a safe place, such as in your top desk drawer, since it has registration, login, and password data. Then, if you need to call a technical support number because an application isn't working properly, you have the information you need at hand.

So, how are you going to organize YOUR classroom software library?

My Software Library Inventory

Software Number	Software Title	Version	Publisher	Date Acquired	Registration Number	Registration Submitted	Sales and/ or Customer Service	Technical Support	Media	Licensed For	Login(s)	Password(s)
Sample	Kid Works Deluxe	NA	Knowledge Adventure	10/1/2001	NA	10/6/2001	1-800-545-7677	1-800-556-6141	2 CDs	2 Computers	NA	NA
Sample	HyperStudio	4	Knowledge Adventure	10/1/2001	HST629ZHS4	10/6/2001	1-800-542-4240	1-800-497-3778	2 CDs	2 Computers	NA	NA

Managing Your Computer Placement

One computer, 30 or more students, absolutely no shelf space, nowhere to put all those portfolios, and a filing cabinet ready to explode! Furthermore, as fate would have it, the one and only plug in the entire room is next to the coat rack. And they want you to be a computer-using educator under these conditions?

Take heart. Sometimes half the battle of getting comfortable with using technology is figuring out where to put the stuff in the first place. If whatever form of technology you want to use is not in a convenient, sensible location, chances are you will never use it.

The following section illustrates several different ways to physically manage the technology in your classroom. You may be in a situation where the only technology you will use all year will be the one computer in your room. You may be fortunate enough to have use of a laserdisc player and a TV monitor from time to time. Maybe you are really lucky and have a "pod" of computers in your classroom and just need some strategies about setting up this area. Or, perhaps the only access you will have to computer-related technology is your weekly trip to the computer lab.

One thing you will want to keep in mind is accessibility to a phone or cable line (if you have one) for a MODEM setup. Often a surge protecter with a taped down extension cord is all that is needed. Whatever the case may be and however the situation changes over time, these suggestions are designed to help you conquer some of the less glamorous, but necessary, details in dealing with technology—where to put it.

One-Computer—Thirty Students?

It is quite possible to run a "high-tech" classroom with only one computer. This computer will wear a variety of hats as it is used as a teacher's personal assistant, presentation tool (for both teacher and students), and as an individual work station. Because this lone computer will serve many different roles, its physical placement in your class is very important. You will probably want to place the computer on a mobile cart for easy transportation around your class. This creates a situation that affects the rest of the class items, such as desks, chairs, tables, shelves, etc. These items will need to be placed in a way to create one or two paths for easy computer-cart movement.

Before setting up your classroom for this technological addition, it is important to ask yourself this question—*What will I primarily use the computer for?* The answer to that question will greatly determine the "home base," where your computer will be located most of the time. If you will mostly be using the classroom computer as a presentation and cooperative learning tool for your lessons, then you will want to set up your classroom similar to diagram #1 below. This type of setup will also be beneficial for student presentations. If the fundamental use for the classroom computer is more of a work station for independent work, research, or long-term group projects, then you will want to set up your classroom similar to diagram #2 on page 159. Let an extra table remain near the computer station so cooperative learning groups will have a place to meet. Or, if your computer-using plans mostly entail record keeping, correspondence, electronic portfolio management, and overall personal assistance to help manage your day, look to diagram #3 on page 159.

While each of the diagrams are set up with the primary function in mind, you can see the paths for easy flow into the other computer uses as well. Most educators in one-computer classrooms find the computer is used for a variety of purposes and ends up being moved around quite a bit. How fortunate we are to teach at a time when we can control where our technology tool will be kept, unlike our nineteenth century predecessors who did not have a choice about where the blackboard went.

Diagram #1 (The Presenter)

One Computer—Thirty Students? *(cont.)*

Diagram #2 (Work Station)

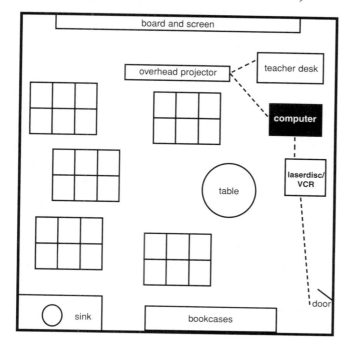

Diagram #3 (Teacher Assistant)

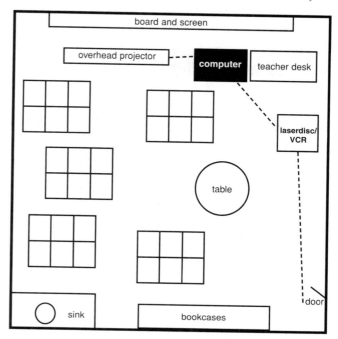

Unless your school holds the world's record for "Most Lucrative Bake Sale," chances are there may be only one computer in your classroom. Maybe you have several computers, or maybe you share one with the rest of your grade level. Whatever the case may be, it is unlikely that every student in your class has a monitor and keyboard at his/her own desk. At first glance, this seems a tragedy. "How can I truly teach using technology when everyone does not have access?" or "What do I do with the other 29 students when Aimee is using the computer?" are common questions. A second glance at the situation may lead us to another assessment, however. Perhaps having access to only one computer is really an advantage in disguise. Perhaps there are actually more meaningful and authentic activities that students can do cooperatively by means of just one computer.

This section will address the vitally important issue of teaching in a classroom with a single computer. A variety of suggestions will be provided, some of which may apply to your current situation and some of which may not. Every teacher, classroom, technology base, and group of students is different. Experiment with a few different strategies until you are comfortable with the one that matches your style and equipment resources. As technology continues to change, schools update equipment, and your technical expertise expands, you will create your own strategies which work best for you. Let these ideas serve as a springboard for you and your resourcefulness. Remember, technology is nothing more then a teaching tool, not an end to itself.

One Computer—Thirty Students? *(cont.)*

The Key to One-Computer Teaching is Large Group Projection!

Just like those teachers who began many years ago to realize the value of using the chalkboard during their lessons, you can use a computer and a large group projection device to add a whole new dimension to your lessons. Imagine finding a terrific piece of software offering a simulation for social studies. Instead of sending small groups of kids to the computer at timed intervals throughout the day (creating disruptions, juggling your entire lesson schedule to accommodate the computer, and struggling to maintain the rest of the class's attention), you will now be able to manage the entire class at one time while still using the appropriate software program.

LCD Panel

Liquid crystal display (LCD) panels work using the same technology as the digital watches many of us own. The difference is that the liquid crystals float between two sheets of glass embedded with electrodes. This panel is then placed on an overhead projector, connected to a computer or video source, and projected onto a large screen. These devices are still pretty pricey for use in a single classroom. In addition, most of these panels will require a special, extra-bright overhead projector which is an additional cost. The most cost effective use of an LCD panel is to share it among a number of classes. The price of these devices has dropped dramatically in the past few years, and industry experts believe they will continue to decrease. Many suppliers will loan panels on a trial basis to schools who are in the market to buy. One disadvantage of LCD panels is that they don't support the number of colors found in most of today's CD-ROMs.

Projecting on the Television

A more affordable option for large-screen projection is the television. You can purchase digital analog converters to convert your computer images to your television screen. If you have a newer television, you can sometimes even skip the convert box and simply attach the computer directly to the television. This allows the computer to be seen on both its monitor and on the television. You can also videotape anything that is seen on the television. If you do not have a VCR or a television that has video input of S video input, you will need to purchase an RF converter from an electronic store.

One Computer—Thirty Students? *(cont.)*

Cooperative Learning with the Computer

The advantages of using cooperative learning techniques are well documented and known among educators. This practical, authentic, and useful tool can be easily transferred when utilizing technology in the classroom. The strategies highlighted are so successful and meaningful for teachers and students that often using one computer in a cooperative learning fashion is preferred over using several computers at once.

The lesson suggestions provided are organized with the premise that one computer and a large-screen projection device are available. While it is certainly possible to conduct a cooperative learning lesson without a large-screen projection device, it is much more manageable for a teacher and easier for student focus if one is used.

Primary grade level teachers typically use small groups and center rotation for classroom lessons. In this case, a projection device is not necessary as the computer could be set up at one of the centers. This is a popular use for CD-ROM players at the primary level. The teacher is set up at the CD-ROM center while small student groups rotate. Perhaps your students are learning about butterflies. At the CD-ROM center, you show a clip of the metamorphosis of a cocoon to your students. Then have them complete an activity (such as a drawing or creating a butterfly, completing a study page, or writing some vocabulary words). With the handy access of a CD-ROM, you can show the clip as many times as necessary without having the trouble of rewinding a film projector or a tape on a VCR.

As students move into the upper grades (3–6), the need for a large-screen projection device increases. Students begin to work more independently, and the teacher then becomes more of a facilitator.

The following pages provide a step-by-step cooperative learning lesson using the Macintosh, LCD Panel (any projection device will do), and a social studies software program. In this particular example, a large-group projection device is not mandatory, but it would definitely be handy. The techniques can be used for virtually any cooperative learning lesson and computer/projection device/software combination.

One Computer—Thirty Students? *(cont.)*

Cooperative Learning with the Computer *(cont.)*

Topic: Social Studies

Grade: 4–6

Software Program
Decisions, Decisions—The Environment (Tom Snyder Productions, 800-342-0236)

Software Background

Decisions, Decisions is the name of a series of role-playing software packages designed for classrooms using only one computer. The software is set up for whole-group discussion with the teacher leading the entire class while managing small groups (just as in nontechnology situations). There are several titles in the *Decisions, Decisions* series highlighting many relevant issues for students. The primary level counterpart to this series is called *Choices, Choices*. *Decisions, Decisions* is the recipient of several educational and technology-related awards. This software package is available for both Macintosh and Windows machines with a few variations in format for each.

In addition to the software, each package comes with a class set of student reference books, teacher's guide, lesson plans, reproducibles, and a critical-thinking supplement. The majority of the simulation revolves around small-group discussions, reading of the printed material, role-playing, and student writing. This simulation does not focus on watching the computer. The computer in this case acts as a resource by providing additional background, setting up scenarios, showing consequences for group decisions, and keeping track of points (if you choose this option). The teacher acts as facilitator for the simulation, directs discussion, paces the activity, and manipulates the computer.

Class Size: 30 students

Small Groups: Six groups of five students each. (There are four roles available for students to role-play, so groups of four would be the simplest configuration. If your class size does not allow for this, see the suggestions under Student Preparation.)

Teacher Preparation

As with any new material or format, it is always a good idea for the teacher to become familiar and comfortable with the activity by previewing it before introducing it to students. Run through the program one time either by yourself or with a colleague; then run through it again, opting for some different choices. This will not take a great deal of time and is well worth the investment.

Student Preparation

Note to the teacher: There is no predetermined formula for preparing a group to use this or any other software. The intellectual, emotional, and social factors for each class are different. You know your class better than anyone else and will make the most appropriate decisions and adjustments as needed.

One Computer—Thirty Students? *(cont.)*

Cooperative Learning with the Computer *(cont.)*

1. **Content Background**: Perhaps you are using "The Environment" program as a culmination of a unit on the environment. If this is the case, your students will be familiar with environmental issues, such as recycling, landfill, urbanization, and the like. If you are using the program as an introduction to an environmental unit, then you will probably want to familiarize your students with some relevant terms and issues. Whatever the case may be, this particular simulation brings up some other important issues not often thought of when learning about the environment. These issues include economics, politics, and commerce, which are all addressed during the simulation. Be sure to familiarize your students with some of the related terminology before beginning the simulation.

2. **Review Cooperative-Learning Rules and Decision-Making Strategies:** True cooperative learning is not placing a few kids in a group and telling them to work together. There are distinct strategies, problem-solving techniques, and specific tactics used to create a productive environment where the students work in an interdependent fashion. Before starting the simulation, review with your students cooperative-learning rules. If you have not had much experience with cooperative learning, this is a great time to begin. The following is a suggested list of group rules to be used as a guide. Ideally, it is best to hold a whole-class discussion with your students beforehand and incorporate their input into the rules list as well.

Cooperative Learning Group Rules

1. Every person has the right to an opinion.
2. Every person has the right to be heard and not interrupted.
3. Every person is expected to be an active listener.
4. Every person is expected to participate fully and finish his/her assigned job(s).
5. Every person will respect the other group members and use constructive language.

Note to the teacher: Be sure to provide your students with some suggestions on how to come to a group decision. These tools will especially be needed in simulation situations where each person assumes a distinct role with a very specific perspective. When all else fails, employ the foundation of democracy and take a vote.

One Computer—Thirty Students? *(cont.)*

Cooperative Learning with the Computer *(cont.)*

3. **Start the Program:** When the program has been started, it will ask the teacher to select the mode of use—whole group or multigroup. For this lesson design, choose multigroup. Next you and your students will be led through a short, graphic introduction to the situation, showing the dilemma and setting up the simulation. This introduction gets the attention of the students but does not reveal all the necessary information. Students will then need to refer to their *Student Reference Books* for the bulk of the material needed to make an informed decision.

4. **Assigning Roles**: The entire simulation is based on helping the mayor of the town of Alpine make a decision about a recent problem involving dead fish in the town's most popular recreational area. Many of the citizens are pointing fingers at the town's largest employer, Malaco Mining Company, as the culprit. In order to help the mayor make a decision, a team of advisors is brought in to research information and present different perspectives. These advisors are the campaign manager, economic advisor, independent scientist, and representative from the environmental council. Each of the *Student Reference Books* contains information relating to each advisor's area of expertise.

   Your students then must choose what role they wish to play. If you have a class of 30 with five students per group, one group member will act as the recorder/facilitator. This individual keeps track of decisions, directs the conversations/debates, monitors discussion and group rules, and reports to the whole class any decisions made. If you have groups of four, then the recorder/facilitator role will need to be shared among group members.

   Depending on your preference as teacher, you may wish to pre-assign roles, assign roles in a random format, or let your students choose. The more opportunities that students have to make their own decisions, the stronger their problem-solving and critical-thinking skills become.

5. **Setting Priorities and Making Decisions:** The next screen on the computer will then instruct the user to listen to all points of view from the mayor's advisors. Each student will then independently read his/her information about the situation and then report back to the small group.

Reading Suggestions

- **Peer Tutor:** If you have a non-English reading student or lower level reader, the recorder/facilitator could pair up with this individual to act as a peer tutor.

- **Jigsaw Format:** Further divide the class up into four groups, one for each role. By placing all the campaign managers together, for example, slower reading students have the opportunity to participate in group reading. All of the campaign managers also have the chance to hear the opinions of others in their roles, creating a brainstorming session and laying the foundation for greater comprehension.

One Computer—Thirty Students? *(cont.)*

Cooperative Learning with the Computer *(cont.)*

Once the information has been shared, the next screen on the computer (and next page in the *Student Reference Book*) asks the groups to make an overall goal.

Choose your #1 priority:

Protect the environment.

Preserve Alpine's economy.

Get reelected.

Keep town expenses low.

Once each team decides upon its goal, the computer will ask for each team's response. Depending on the choice made, a distinct path of options and consequences will appear, asking the team to further research and make new decisions. The cartoon picture of each advisor will appear with a context word. This refers the advisors back to their *Reference* books to continue further reading.

One Computer—Thirty Students? *(cont.)*

Cooperative Learning with the Computer *(cont.)*

While the team being highlighted is deciding and going through the process, the remaining teams continue their reading, research, and discussions about what to do next. A benefit of this method is that other teams get the chance to observe some possible consequences of decisions before they actually make their decisions. (**Hint:** By selecting the Random Picker, the computer will automatically pick groups in a random order, thus eliminating the commonly student-perceived disadvantage of "having to go first.")

During this entire process, the teacher is acting as "ringleader" by facilitating and managing the group process.

6. **Conclusions**: At the end of the decision-making loop that all groups experience, the computer will tabulate a score. This score represents how well the groups achieved the goals they set for themselves at the beginning of the simulation. There is no "right or wrong" goal to the simulation, so each set of scores will be different and apply only to that particular group.

As with all cooperative learning strategies and authentic learning situations, it is very important to provide students with an opportunity to self-evaluate and reflect on the process both as individuals and groups. The computer offers a self-evaluation mode whereby each group's goals appear on the screen one at a time with a maximum point value attached to it. Students are asked to indicate whether they "Succeeded," "Sort of Succeeded," or "Did Not Succeed" at meeting these goals. The value of keeping score in this kind of situation is very subjective.

Some students are highly motivated by scoring, while others feel too much pressure to make "right" decisions. The real value in this particular scoring setup, however, lies in goal setting— asking students to set goals, keep their goals in mind all throughout the process and then at the end determine if the goal met was valuable. Goal setting is a skill that should be taught to students of all ages. It is up to you to decide the benefits of using the point scoring system with your unique class.

Whether you decide to use the point scoring setup or not, some form of reflection should be allowed in order for students to truly construct their own learning. The final phase of the traditional model for cooperative learning allows for the group participants to talk about what was successful, as well as what needed some improvement for next time. Praising the other group members for their efforts is also a positive and empowering tool for students.

Equally important in a simulation whole-group activity such as *Decisions, Decisions* is the process of debriefing. With controversial subjects and diversity of opinions, your classroom is likely to "heat up" a bit. This is perfectly normal and fine. Not only is it reflective of real life, but this kind of atmosphere also lends itself to many opportunities for growth of all students. Be sure in your debriefing session to discuss any departures from reality that took place and put the simulation in proper perspective.

One Computer—Thirty Students? *(cont.)*

Cooperative Learning with the Computer *(cont.)*

7.   **Time Management:** Once you spend a little time previewing the simulation, it becomes quite apparent that the process could go on for some time. The amount of time allotted to "The Environment" is entirely up to you as the teacher. By using the whole class discussion mode and really sticking to the clock, it would be possible to complete the program between one and two hours. By doing this, however, the benefit of cooperative learning and value of discussions becomes very limited. Some teachers will use *Decisions, Decisions* and other such simulations over the course of a month-long unit. (Any portion of the program can be saved.) Again, there is no predetermined time allotment for the simulation, but rather it is the unique needs of each teacher and class which dictate this.

Teaching with Technology

After reading this lesson, you may ask yourself, *How is this so different from what I already do?* This is a good question in that it reveals the answer to the prevailing question of *How do I use technology in my classroom?* As you can see, this lesson is virtually no different from any other lesson you may teach using a simulation, game, or whole-group activity. The only obvious difference is that there is now a computer sitting at the front of the room and you the teacher are pressing a few buttons every now and then. In this case (as is true with proper classroom technology use) the computer is used merely as a tool. The technology takes a back seat to the real action. The real action is the students interacting with one other amid tremendous learning opportunities.

The next logical question would be, *If this lesson is really no different from what I already do, why bother using it?* The answer is efficiency and student motivation. It would be entirely possible to conduct this simulation using printed material only. By doing this, however, storage space becomes a pivotal concern. With a file of student reference books and a small disk, all the information required to play is easily stored in a small area. Another advantage of using software is the neatness factor. Instead of having to flip back and forth through a binder, or spreading all the papers and options all over a desk, front table, or chalkboard, the teacher selects a button on the computer and information is immediately brought up. This is a much less frustrating and much more organized manner of plowing through a program. The computer keeps track of each group's scores—one less management item to contend with. And of course, student motivation is a large factor. Students enjoy using the computer in virtually any capacity imaginable. Even though the bulk of this simulation relies on student work instead of computer entertainment, most students believe that if they are using the computer even for a short period of time, work becomes fun.

It is easy to see in this example how the computer acts as a helpmate to the teacher instead of taking center stage and running the show. Remember the motto, *Curriculum is the engine, technology is but one of the tools.*

Classroom Computer Pod

A computer pod consists of three or more computers, usually five, in one area. A pod could be as many as ten computers, but much more than that constitutes a lab. An obvious advantage to having a computer pod in your classroom is that several students can work on computer projects at one time, thus creating more time for scheduling other activities. An efficient way for students to use computer time with the pod is to set up a "centers" schedule. One center could be for a technology project at the computer pod and other centers for different curricular areas.

In a computer pod setup in the traditional classroom with limited electrical outlets, the computers are generally close together and connected via several cords and power strips. With this configuration, it can be difficult to remove one computer for other uses unless a little foresight is used. Since a computer serves many uses for both the teacher and student, you will want one computer accessible for your own needs. This means that in setting up the pod, you will want to leave one computer available for quick and easy mobility. Set this computer up on its own power strip or outlet or identify the cord with a colored sticker so you will always know which one to use.

Another consideration for the computer pod (as with all kinds of setups) is proximity to the phone or cable line for MODEM use. Of course, an extension cord can be used, but you may want to avoid the "spider web" of excess cords and wires by having your pod near the telephone line source.

You can choose to put your computer pod in the front of the room. This strategy is beneficial in that it allows for easy flow of a mobile computer to be connected with an overhead projector, to be used for class presentations, to be used as a teacher's assistant, or to hook up to the laserdisc player. With the computer pod located in the front of the room, however, there is the potential challenge of keeping noncomputer-using students focused on the task or lesson at hand. If this is a concern, try setting your classroom up with the computer pod away from the front of the room.

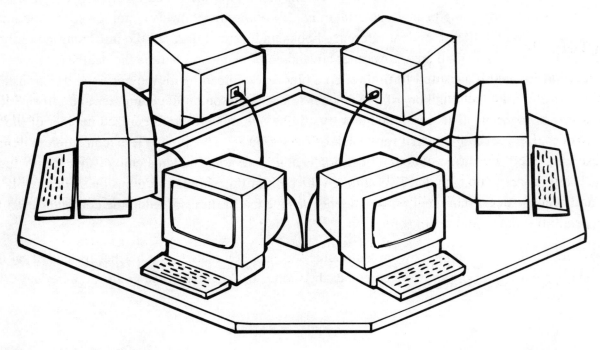

168

Team Teaching with Technology

Team teaching is nothing new in education. For a number of years, teachers have known of and reaped the benefits of sharing ideas, curriculum, work load, and schedules in order to make hectic professional lives a bit easier. Using educational technology is no different. More often than not, most teachers end up sharing technology with the entire school and staff purely from a cost-effective standpoint. The "tech team teaching" strategy is an alternative to the otherwise universal sign-up schedule for equipment.

Have you ever had the experience of wanting to use the VCR/TV on a Friday afternoon only to find all the boxes checked off on the signup weeks in advance? Or perhaps you are allotted only three days with the mobile computer and your students need an additional day? As cooperative and positive as all the teachers on campus can be, these kinds of situations create frustration and sometimes lead to a condition of "no use" at all.

The tech team teaching strategy is helpful for a number of reasons. First, the same teacher-partners (or group of teachers) are always working together. This allows for easier flow of communication and opportunities for flexibility in scheduling, since fewer people are affected. Second, team teachers generally teach in the same area, so transportation of equipment is less time consuming and easier to manage than when sharing with the entire school. Third, by creating lessons with a team, the research and preview time that teachers spend before actually using a program with students is shortened with the division of labor.

The keys to effective tech team teaching are communication and ease of equipment mobility. A weekly schedule for just a few teachers is much easier to manage and remember than one for an entire staff. If you feel your students are responsible enough, choose a "tech toter" each day to move the equipment on to the next room. If your students are too young to handle the task, use an aide or parent helper. Remember, be flexible, be mobile, and keep your sense of humor.

Tech Team Teaching Classroom Setup

Easy accessibility and freedom of movement are vital for a smooth running tech team teaching situation. If all of the teaming teachers create technology spaces in their classroom, which have plenty of "in and out" room, as a well as clear paths to get there, this will help make equipment transitions much easier. If the technology area for each room is somewhat close to the main door, this will greatly increase efficiency. For those reasons, it is suggested that each classroom be set up in the "work station" format shown on page 159. This format allows for easy access because the equipment path is short and near the door. This will keep classroom disruption to a minimum, since the equipment will be dropped off quickly and at the back of the room. Also, the "work station" format lends itself to easy evolution into presentation and teacher assistant formats too. Whatever setup each teacher creates, be sure that it is established with the rest of the team where the technology area is and/or where the equipment should be delivered.

Team Teaching with Technology *(cont.)*

Tech Team Teaching Schedule

Week of: _____

Day	Teacher	Hardware	Software	Time
Monday				
Tuesday				
Wednesday				
Thursday				
Friday				

Team Teaching with Technology *(cont.)*

Mobile Technology

Mobile technology means any form of technology that is readily transported from one place to another. A computer on a cart is mobile technology. The VCR/TV on a cart is mobile technology. A cordless phone is mobile technology. (Chances are, there are not too many of those floating around your campus.) Mobile technology is mobile for the sole purpose of sharing equipment. For virtually every elementary campus across the continent—even schools with a computer in every classroom—there is some form of mobile technology on site.

Many of the tips for managing this type of situation are mentioned earlier in the section about "tech team teaching." However, this particular situation is a bit different—in most cases an entire school is involved, not just a small group of teachers. With that many people, a variety of schedules and a spread-out area, there are definite challenges to creating a system which is effective for everyone. Here are some tips for devising a positive, workable, and successful system.

Mobile Technology Tips

Grade Level Division: If possible, divide all available technology among grade levels. For example: if there are seven VCR/TV carts at the school, assign one per grade level. Each grade level is responsible for creating its own schedules. The carts could be stored in an area central to that grade level to eliminate extra transportation time. If there is not enough technology for each grade level to have its own (perhaps there are four laserdisc players for seven grade levels), set priorities. Generally speaking, the upper grade levels use the laserdisc player more than the lower levels.

In this case, the fifth and sixth grades can share one laserdisc player, third and fourth grades can share one, and the primary grades can share the last. Of course, these arrangements are not set in stone, and flexibility in sharing is a key factor for success. However, grouping technology in this fashion allows for easier communication, fairness in sharing, and more universal use of the equipment.

Tech-Toters: Remember when you were in elementary school and there was a special group of students in charge of the AV equipment? This elite group of students seemed so unique, mature, and knowledgeable in their handling of such complex equipment. They were the envy of the entire student population because—best of all—they got excused from class. A "tech toter" is basically the modern-day version of the "AV runner."

Valuable time is often gobbled up with the continued transportation of shared technology equipment. It is difficult (and in some cases illegal) for teachers to leave their classrooms unattended. This makes passing along the laserdisc player to a teacher down the hall a bit troublesome. If just one teacher gets even ten minutes behind schedule, every other teacher planning to use the same equipment that day must readjust. A solution to keep the transportation of mobile technology flowing is to enlist the help of student tech-toters.

Mobile Technology *(cont.)*

Tech-Toters *(cont.)*: A tech toter should be a responsible student, able to work independently, able to easily catch up with any work or instructions missed, and be able to move equipment that is heavy. Always send two tech toters at a time to help each other with any potentially awkward transportation problems. Since being a tech toter is a privilege, create a special club called the Tech Toter Team or some other creative name. This group of students receives special training about the equipment—how to set it up and proper mobility guidelines. Make this a special club for just fifth and sixth grade students to give them something enjoyable and distinctive to look forward to. The tech toters could rotate their schedules so they would be available for all of the other grades to move equipment.

NOTE: Technology equipment is indeed expensive, and there are some educators who would rather that students not be responsible for moving such high-priced items. This is understandable. However, those old film projectors we used in our school days were quite the costly items too. Using tech toters is a decision that will require some serious thought and entire staff agreement.

Tech-Checkers: With any piece of electronic equipment or fine machinery, routine maintenance is vital. Computers, VCRs, laserdisc players, MODEMs, LCD panels, and any other piece of technology needs to be dusted frequently. It takes but a few dust particles to wedge themselves in a strategic position to wreak havoc on a piece of electrical equipment. Also, with so many people sharing one piece of technology, cables and wires may become disconnected and/or hooked into wrong ports. This can be a source of frustration for the next person to use the equipment.

An easy and educational way to eliminate these and other mobile technology problems is to assign a team of "tech checkers" to maintain and monitor the equipment on a regular basis. Preferably, tech checkers should be students. Using students for this task not only provides them with positive self-esteem but is also a great way for them to learn more about technology. (Many students already know much more than teachers when it comes to this area.) The adult supervisor for this group (the technology mentor teacher, parent volunteer, or aid) should be familiar with the technology at your site, especially the maintenance for each item. Set up a schedule for the tech checkers to routinely follow up on these and other items:

- dusting of equipment
- securing of cables
- correct cables to correct ports
- plug in, boot up, and check for proper start up

- software boxes in order
- laserdiscs in proper covers
- cases securely closed and latched
- cords wrapped neatly

Tech Checker Jobs

Dust the equipment daily

Check the cables to see that they are secure

Turn the computer on each morning

Turn the computer off each afternoon

Organize software boxes

Make sure that CDs are in their proper cases

Straighten the keyboard and mouse

The Computer Lab

Ideas for Involving Parents in Using the Computer Lab

Parents can be a powerful resource to both you and your students. In addition, they will be able to keep in touch with classroom projects and technology. (Please refer to pages 251–254 on more extensive ways to involve parents in technology.)

If you must divide your class in half so that every student has a computer in the lab, bring a parent in to supervise lab activities. This allows you to stay with the remainder of the class, continuing other lessons. Or use a parent to supervise the entire class in the lab, freeing you for some preparation and research time for other technology projects.

If possible, keep the lab open during recess and lunch periods to allow for more access. A parent helper could volunteer during this time to supervise.

Clean Work Areas

Keep the lab tidy. Since several students will be coming in and out of the lab, each time your class goes, be sure to assign a tech checker for the session. This person will put away disks, cover up hardware with plastic covers, be sure chairs are pushed in, and switch off any equipment.

Create Two Labs from One

Space permitting, and if there are enough computers, your school might want to consider creating a primary-level lab and an upper-grade lab. There are several advantages to this kind of arrangement.

1. With two labs, more students have more access.

2. Computer tables can be set to proper heights to avoid improper posture and poor typing habits.

3. Locations may be more convenient.

4. Software can be grouped more efficiently for age appropriateness.

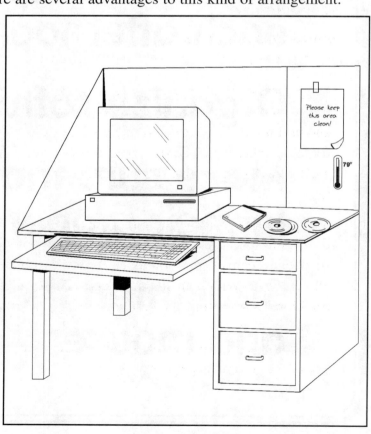

Community Lab

Foster a community-school effort and open your lab to parents and other community members to come in and view software. This not only helps to train more adults but also gets community members more interested in technology. This becomes very helpful during times of local elections and school funding initiatives.

The Computer Lab *(cont.)*

Often when computers first make their presence known in schools, the computer lab is the place where these creatures are kept. There is usually one computer lab teacher, and the entire student population rotates through a schedule, allowing equal computer time for each teacher. The ideal situation for students and teachers of course, is to have all forms of necessary technology right in the classroom so that lessons can be fully integrated. When the student's only exposure to technology is one week out of the month for a short time each day, it is difficult to fully prepare students for the twenty-first century. Nonetheless, some computer time is better than no computer time. Fortunately, more schools are purchasing technology, and additional computers are making their way into classrooms. This is allowing for a greater number of students to have access to technology.

With these additional computers brought to campus, the computer lab's role will begin to evolve. Instead of being the one and only place for technology, the lab now shifts to a resource area for students and staff. Even if you have a computer in your room and feel that all your technology needs are met, do not underestimate the power of that computer lab. Some labs are full of the older Apple IIe and IIgs models, so teachers feel there is not much value in students using these machines. There are plenty of uses for those old Apple computers. The majority of students are just so happy sitting down at a computer that they will not complain about the model. Additionally, the more systems that students (and teachers) know how to use, the more versatile and prepared they are for further education and the future job market.

Physical Setup

Established Computer Lab: Most schools already have a lab set up and running. This section will include a few tips for the established lab arrangement.

a.   Keep cords concealed. If at all possible, keep the cords organized, grouped, and out of foot traffic. Not only is it dangerous for students to play with electrical cords, but they may also trip and hurt themselves. Also, if one cord gets disconnected, it is frustrating and time consuming to try to decipher which cord belongs to what computer. Inexpensive cord tubes (snakes) are available. These hollow, flexible tubes can hold several cords, thus creating one cord instead of ten.

b.   Computer arrangement will largely depend on the size of room, number of computers, and desk/table space. For proper posture and keyboarding, the computer tables should be low enough so students can sit comfortably at eye level with the monitor, their hands resting on the keyboard, elbows bent. With both sixth graders and first graders using the lab, this can be a tough task. In traditional classrooms, the best use of space for a computer lab would be the rows format. However, sometimes a circular table is a better use of space. The circular tables (or two instruction centers placed back to back) can hold up to six computers and provide a bin at the center for cord management.

Checklist Technology vs. Integrated Technology

What do we mean when we speak of integrating technology into the curriculum? Perhaps the best place to start in developing an answer to this question is to get an idea of what each of the key components—***technology, integration, curriculum***—is.

Webster's defines ***technology*** as...

- the practical application of knowledge, especially in a particular area,
- a capability given by the practical application of knowledge,
- a manner of accomplishing a task, especially using technical processes, methods, or knowledge, and
- the specialized aspects of a particular field of endeavor.

In sum, **technology is the means to task completion.**

As it applies to education, Webster's defines ***integrate*** as...

- to form, coordinate, or blend into a functioning or unified whole,
- to unite with something else, and
- to incorporate into a larger unit.

In sum, **integration is the combining of tasks to complete a productive system.**

Curriculum is defined as...

- the course offered by an educational institution, and
- a set of courses constituting an area of specialization.

In sum, **curriculum is a productive system of combined tasks.**

Integrating technology into the curriculum means combining tasks (objectives) to achieve learning outcomes (goals). These goals compose the curriculum. Technology is the means by which objectives are completed, and integration is a purposeful co-utilization of various technologies toward attaining the curriculum.

The curriculum represents what we feel is most worthwhile for our students to learn. We as educators are in a constant process of writing, revising, evaluating, and rewriting the curriculum. Because technology continually advances, the process never quite reaches equilibrium.

A natural consequence of technology is that the more we use it, the more we become accustomed to it. We get set in our ways, nostalgic about what has come before, and wary of something new. This is especially true in education. How often have we encountered the instructional mentality that the "old" ways of teaching were good enough, so why change things?

Checklist Technology vs. Integrated Technology *(cont.)*

There has always been resistance to new technologies in education. The following quotes from history clearly bear this out. (These quotes from the work of David Thornburg were shared at the 3rd Annual *HyperStudio* Festival in San Diego, California.) How many of us would be willing to go back to the days of writing on tree bark, as was the established educational technology in 1703?

"Students today can't prepare bark to calculate their problems. They depend on their slates which are more expensive. What will they do when the slate is dropped and it breaks? They will be unable to write!"

(Teacher's Conference, 1703)

"Students today depend on paper too much. They don't know how to write on a slate without getting chalk dust all over themselves. They can't clean a slate properly. What will they do when they run out of paper?"

(Principal's Association, 1815)

"Students today depend too much upon ink. They don't know how to use a pen knife to sharpen a pencil. Pen and ink will never replace the pencil."

(National Association of Teachers, 1907)

"Students today depend upon store bought ink. They don't know how to make their own. When they run out of ink they will be unable to write words or ciphers until their next trip to the settlement. This is a sad commentary on modern education."

(The Rural American Teacher, 1928)

"Students today depend on these expensive fountain pens. They can no longer write with a straight pen and nib. We parents must not allow them to wallow in such luxury to the detriment of learning how to cope in the real business world which is not so extravagant."

(PTA Gazette, 1941)

"Ballpoint pens will be the ruin of education in our country. Students use these devices and then throw them away. The American values of thrift and frugality are being discarded. Business and banks will never allow such expensive luxuries."

(Federal Teachers, 1950)

Checklist Technology vs. Integrated Technology *(cont.)*

New technologies, while eagerly welcomed by a few pioneering souls, are resisted by many. But our most basic educational goals and objectives (learning to access and communicate ideas and information effectively) have always stood the test of time and are nourished by technological innovation. As each technology comes of age, it is gradually welcomed by all. The technologies mentioned above were each originally condemned by a segment of the educational community. But none of these brought the demise of education that was initially predicted. Each, in fact, helped to enhance the quality of education. Computers are the latest in a continuing technological evolution that is helping to improve the means by which teachers teach and students learn.

As the computer comes of age, it is transforming the way information and ideas can be transmitted and received. It is merging and synthesizing multiple types of media in ways never before possible. This mediamorphosis is making the computer a tool far greater than just the sum of its parts.

But as great a technological wonder as the computer is, it is a tool. The computer is a means to an end. School districts across the nation are expending vast amounts of time and energy developing computer curricula. But in so doing, they are placing the computer into a position of a learning outcome, removing it from its rightful position as a means of achieving learning outcomes. As a result, many teachers see the computer as just another add-on, as just one more thing they've got to teach in an already packed school day.

If the mastery of computer skills becomes the focus of the curriculum, then true integration is hindered. The result will often be a checklist approach to the teaching of computers, where the skills may have little or no relevance to the rest of what students are learning. True integration of technology only occurs when the subject matter composes the curriculum, and technology is woven in as a means of achieving it. This was just as true of tree bark in 1703 as it is for computers in the 21st century.

Problem solving, information gathering, data analysis, comparison and contrast, artistic expression— these are just some of the important learning outcomes that compose the curriculum from subject to subject. For example, what good is learning to do a spreadsheet if it is just being done to fulfill a "computer" goal or objective? However, if learning to do a spreadsheet is incorporated as part of a math goal for organizing information, then doing a spreadsheet is an invaluable skill. Or it might be used as part of a Social Studies goal for presenting and analyzing survey results. When computer skills are separate curricular goals of their own, then they are often done as disjointed, meaningless tasks. As integrated components within existing curricula, they can provide greater overall learning.

Word processing, database, spreadsheet, graphics, animation, digital imaging, Internet, and yes—even multimedia authoring with *HyperStudio*—are of little value in and of themselves. Separated from the acquisition and conveyance of ideas and information, they are skills without application. The computer is poised to take its place as another tool available to teachers and students to help them attain these outcomes. Its effectiveness in doing so has everything to do with where it is placed in the grand scheme of things.

Technology Standards

"Who dares to teach must never cease to learn."

John Cotton Dana

As a teacher, you know the importance of life-long learning—especially in the dynamic field of educational technologies. Just picking up this book indicates that you are willing to learn and grow in your abilities to manage and use the technologies that are available to you in your classroom.

There is a non-profit professional organization, the International Society for Technology in Education (ISTE), which strongly supports your endeavors. ISTE is dedicated to promoting the appropriate use of information technology to improve teaching in K–12 education. ISTE develops standards in educational technology for students, teachers, administrators, and more.

"Oh, no! More standards," you moan. "With all the content standards I have to meet, all I need is another set of standards."

Actually, the ISTE standards are a foundation upon which you can stand to get the technology, support, and training you need to meet them. The ISTE standards have been adopted by state boards of education across the country. With that in mind, as a conscientious educator, you can lobby, so to speak, for everything you need to help you meet those standards—for yourself and for your students.

ISTE Standards for Teachers

Take a look at the *ISTE National Educational Technology Standards and Performance Indicators for Teachers* that are located on the ISTE website (http://cnets.iste.org/teachstandintro.html).

On page 181 is a chart that you can utilize to evaluate how well you meet the ISTE standards. There are four columns in the chart: Standard Category, Standard, Performance Indicators, and Self-Assessment. (The CD version of the chart is entitled chart.pdf.)

Copy the chart from page 181 and use it to evaluate yourself. As you read through the *ISTE National Educational Technology Standards and Performance Indicators for Teachers*, complete the chart by writing the various standards and performance indicators. Then, rate yourself in the Self-Assessment column for each Performance Indicator using the following scale.

- 4—I can demonstrate mastery of this Performance Indicator.
- 3—I am close to being able to demonstrate mastery of this Performance Indicator.
- 2—I am far from being able to demonstrate mastery of this Performance Indicator yet, but I am working on it.
- 1—I have not even started to work toward mastery of this Performance Indicator, but now I am aware of it.
- 0—I don't even understand what the Performance Indicator means.

Technology Standards *(cont.)*

Now add up your score. Then see where you stand with the *ISTE National Educational Technology Standards and Performance Indicators for Teachers*.

Out of a possible 92 points, if you scored

- 83 points to 92 points—Great going! Are you viewed as a technology leader in your school? Thought so!

- 74 points to 82 points—Good going! Looks like you are well on your way to meeting all the standards.

- 65 points to 73 points—You're doing okay. Focus on achieving one standard at a time and soon you'll be "up to speed."

- 64 points and below—Looks like you have a ways to go, but don't beat yourself up over your score. Take a technology class that will help you address your weakest standards. Be sure to sign up for any technology-related teacher inservice your district offers as well.

Now that you know there are *ISTE National Educational Technology Standards and Performance Indicators for Teachers*, know how many of the standards you have mastered, and know how many of the standards you have yet to master, take your knowledge one step further. If you have a less than perfect score, identify one, two, or three technology goals and a simple action plan for how you plan to meet each goal.

You will find a *My Technology Goals and Action Plan Sample* on page 182. You will find the *My Technology Goals and Action Plan* form for you to fill out on page 183. The *My Technology Goals and Action Plan* form is also available on the CD-ROM [filename: *techgoal.pdf*].

To complete the *My Technology Goals and Action Plan* form, list one, two, or three standards that you would like to master under the column heading *Standard That Needs Improvement*. Then list the following under their appropriate column headings.

- What you plan to do to achieve each goal.

- How you plan to do it.

- The resources you will need to achieve each goal.

- A reasonable target date for each goal that will keep you motivated.

The last column in the *My Technology Goals and Action Plan* form provides you with space to note how you are doing. Imagine how good you will feel when you can write, "Done!"

Once you have accomplished one, two, or three goals, gradually add more until you have accomplished them all.

Technology Standards *(cont.)*

Directions: Use the standards and performance indicators listed on the ISTE website (http://cnets.iste.org/teachstandintro.html) to complete the following chart using the ratings on page 179.

Standard Category	Standard	Performance Indicators	Self Assessment
I. TECHNOLOGY OPERATIONS AND CONCEPTS			
II. PLANNING AND DESIGNING LEARNING ENVIRONMENTS AND EXPERIENCES			
III. TECHNOLOGY, LEARNING, AND THE CURRICULUM			
IV. ASSESSMENT AND EVALUATION			
V. PRODUCTIVITY AND PROFESSIONAL PRACTICE			
VI. SOCIAL, ETHICAL, LEGAL, AND HUMAN ISSUES			

My Technology Goals and Action Plan Sample

Standard That Needs Improvement	What I Plan to Do	How I Plan to Do It	Resources I Will Need	When I Plan to Achieve This Goal	How I Did
1 A. use technology resources to engage in ongoing professional development and lifelong learning.	I will take a technology class for professional development. The class will teach me how to build my own classroom Web page.	I will sign up for an online course that gives me college credit and allows me to work at my own pace.	I will need my computer system, access to the Internet, software for building a Web page, time, and money.	I hope to have the class completed by spring.	
2 D. use technology to communicate and collaborate with peers, parents, and the larger community in order to nurture student learning.	I will start a classroom Web page so that other teachers and classes, my students and their parents, and the community can see what we are learning.	I will take a class at the university that will teach me how to build my own classroom Web page.	I need everything listed above. Plus, I need to find out the school district guidelines for building classroom web pages.	I will build my classroom Web page as I am taking the class. After that, it is just a matter of keeping it going.	
3 E. facilitate equitable access to technology resources for all students.	I will make sure that all of my students have equal time at the computer.	I will stop using the computer as a reward only. I will set up a schedule that allows every student use of the computer on a rotating basis.	I need to design a rotating schedule of computer use that will work for my students and me.	I will do this right away. I will try to have it implemented by the end of the month.	

My Technology Goals and Action Plan

Standard That Needs Improvement	What I Plan to Do	How I Plan to Do It	Resources I Will Need	When I Plan to Achieve This Goal	How I Did
1					
2					
3					

ISTE Technology Foundation Standards for Students

ISTE Standards for Students

Take a look at the *ISTE National Educational Technology Foundation Standards for Students* that are located on the ISTE Website (http://cnets.iste.org/sfors.htm).

These standards are linked to the more detailed *Profiles for Technology Literate Students* for the following grade ranges: PreK–2; 3–5; 6–8; and 9–12.

The *Profiles for Technology Literate Students* describe specific competencies that students should be taught and subsequently exhibit. If you are interested in seeing the detailed *Profiles for Technology Literate Students*, visit the ISTE Internet site (**http://www.iste.org**). From ISTE, you may also obtain the booklet *National Educational Technology Standards for Students*, which includes the *Foundation Standards for Students* as well as the *Profiles for Technology Literate Students* at all grade ranges.

Standard Categories

BASIC OPERATIONS AND CONCEPTS

SOCIAL, ETHICAL, AND HUMAN ISSUES

TECHNOLOGY PRODUCTIVITY TOOLS

TECHNOLOGY COMMUNICATION TOOLS

TECHNOLOGY RESEARCH TOOLS

TECHNOLOGY PROBLEM-SOLVING AND DECISION-MAKING TOOLS

Simple Student Projects

Wherever you may find yourself on the Techno-Continuum, there are always plenty of ideas for student projects using some form of technology. These activity suggestions are easy enough to use for the Techno-Phobic while being very relevant for the Total-Techno. While the activities are targeted for specific grade levels, they can easily fit the needs of all elementary grades by adding your own creativity and age-appropriate ideas. Have some fun, explore new ground, and enjoy watching the creativity of your students take on new directions.

In the pages that follow you will find student projects already mapped out for you to use in your classroom. There are also two additional pages at the end of the student projects section to jot down your own ideas to use for student project sheets. You may want to make copies of these pages and keep them in your "Techno Binder" for quick and easy reference.

Summary of Student Projects

Techno T-shirts: Adaptable for grades K–6, students will turn their computers and printers into T-shirt decal-making machines.

Interactive Banners: Adaptable for grades K–3, students will create posters or banners on a particular theme and then supplement their work with pictures and/or videos from the Internet.

Walk the Hall of Time: Adaptable for grades K–6, students will create hall banners combining art work and technology for Back-to-School and Open House Nights.

Internet-Related Class Books: Adaptable for grades K–6, students will create books on particular themes and then use information found on the Internet to supplement their work.

Oral Presentations: Adaptable for grades K–6, students will develop speeches and presentations on topics of their choosing and include a multimedia program to enhance their presentations.

Keep in mind that many of these projects can be made exclusively on the computer by designing them in a paint, draw, and graphics program or a multimedia presentation rather than presenting them on paper or poster board.

Student Projects *(cont.)*

Techno T-Shirts (Grades K–6)

Turn your computer and printer into a T-shirt decal-making machine.

Materials

- printer
- heat transfer sheet
- computer
- graphics program (such as *Print Shop*® or *Kid Pix*)
- cotton T-shirt for each student
- computer paper
- iron

Directions

1. Create a design on a computer, using a graphics program.

2. Replace the paper in your printer with the heat transfer sheet.

3. Set up the print options to print the image in reverse. Most graphic programs will allow you to print in reverse.

4. Print the image.

5. Allow the printed image to dry to avoid smearing.

6. Using a hot iron, place the printed image face down on a T-shirt. Secure the printed image with pieces of masking tape in the corners to avoid smearing when ironing.

7. When ironing on the image, use a pressing motion, not a rubbing, circular motion.

8. Allow the T-shirt to cool and wear it with pride.

Tips

1. For the first washing of the T-shirt, soak it in vinegar to help the image set. Wash the T-shirt inside out to preserve color.

2. Heat transfer sheets can be purchased at your local computer product supplier.

Student Projects *(cont.)*

Interactive Banners (Grades K–3)

Students create a poster or banner on a particular theme and supplement their work with pictures and/or videos from the Internet.

Materials

- poster board or butcher paper to make a banner
- paint, crayons, and colored markers
- computer connected to the Internet

Directions

1. Make sure that the Internet browser software is already loaded onto the computer and you are comfortable with how to use the program.

2. Choose a theme around which students will center their banner/poster. A possible use of the Interactive Banner activity is using it as a culminating activity and student presentation. Suggestions for themes include weather, animals, plants, Earth, and the solar system.

3. Using the animal theme, for example, students create a banner on animals they have studied. Working in partners or groups, students create their banners with pens, crayons, or paint. When their pictures are finished, students write the names of their animals near their pictures.

4. With the help of an adult or upper-grade techno buddy, students view websites for still photos or videos of the animals on their banner/poster.

5. With the continued help of a techno buddy, when the stills and/or video have been selected, the respective website addresses (URLs) need to be recorded.

6. Students cut out the individual URLs and paste them next to their animal illustrations on their banner/poster.

7. During the class presentation, students will post their banners/posters on the front board for the entire class to view. Be sure that the computer and Internet are loaded and ready to go.

8. When your students orally give their presentations and refer to their illustrations, they can enter the bar code to show their pictures or video selections for added creativity and information in their speeches.

9. Leave the banners up for a few days so other students can interact with the banners, too.

Student Projects *(cont.)*

Interactive Banners (Grades K–3) *(cont.)*

Tips

1. Laminating the banners with the pasted URLs will help them last longer.

Extension

Interactive Story Boards (Grades K–3)

Interactive Story Boards use the same idea as Interactive Banners, except the story board will tell a story instead of showing isolated pieces of information. This technique is a good strategy for K–1 grades after the teacher has read a story to their class. For the retelling of the story, divide a piece of paper into eight blocks and have students draw sequential pictures of their interpretation of the story. Later, students can help to choose website images (both still and video) to insert into their story boards for a multimedia experience.

Student Projects *(cont.)*

Walk the Halls of Time (Grades K–6)

This activity enables your entire class to create a presentation for the school or community. Hall Banners are a terrific technology show-off for Back-to-School and Open House Nights. Students of all ages can participate, but with the younger students more adult supervision will obviously be needed.

Materials

- large pieces of mural paper (Depending on size, you may need to tape two long strips horizontally.)
- paint, colored markers, and/or crayons
- computer connected to the Internet

Directions

1. Choose a theme for the hall banner.

2. Determine which students will be responsible for illustrating and/or writing specific parts of the banner.

3. With a pencil, lightly frame areas for students to work in.

4. Choose websites which contain information related to your theme.

5. Preview with your students the frames, links, and images which you think will work with your topic. Begin keeping track of website addresses.

6. Students will work in small groups on their respective sections on the banner. As they work, remind them that they should keep in mind any Internet images which they feel would relate to their work.

7. When the student banner is complete, choose the corresponding images from the Internet to add to the text on the banner.

8. Some students may not find an appropriate frame from the Internet, which is perfectly fine. (Curriculum comes first, not technology.)

9. Print and cut out individual images. Have the students attach the images to their sections of the banner.

10. Determine where the Hall Banner will be located (in the hall, cafeteria, gym, library, etc.) and hang up the banner.

Tips

Make a Holiday Hall Banner. This is an enjoyable way to create even more enthusiasm around a holiday. Post the Hall banner in the cafeteria, assign students to monitor, and as the school rotates through for lunch, all can enjoy a show.

Student Projects *(cont.)*

Internet-Related Class Books (Grades K–6)

This activity can be as simple or as complex as you desire. Students of all ages can participate in this activity. For a first grade class studying plants, each student can illustrate one facet of plant life. On the bottom of the page (possibly with the help of an adult) have each student write a sentence telling about his/her illustration. The student will later look at a website on plant life and choose a movie or still frame which helps to explain or supplement his/her picture. Take the URL from that segment and paste it to the picture. A sixth grade class studying ancient civilizations can create an interactive class book in the same fashion. Perhaps the upper-grade students may want to include the built-in quizzes on some websites for the reader to take at the end of the book.

Materials

- white construction paper 8.5" x 11" (22 cm x 28 cm) for each student

- colored construction paper for the cover

- colored markers, crayons, and/or paint

- computer connected to the Internet

Directions

1. Choose a theme or topic for your class book.

2. Have the students view websites to get ideas and gather information.

3. Have the students draw their own pictures for the class book and each write a sentence or short paragraph sharing information about these illustrations.

4. Then, have them choose which pictures or movies they want to coincide with their book pages.

5. Select the corresponding URLs for respective pictures or videos.

6. Copy, cut, and paste the URLs on the student pages.

7. Bind the book together, hook up the computer, and enjoy the teamwork as students share their books and visit the websites.

Tips

1. Laminate each page to make the book more durable.

2. Display your book in the library, school board room, or front office to share with other people.

Student Projects *(cont.)*

Oral Presentations

Student speeches and oral presentations have a new dimension when using a multimedia program. Timely use of video or still images can greatly enhance an oral presentation. Tell your students that most presentations in the work place today are done with some form of technology to provide visuals for more audience interest.

Materials

- index cards for speech
- multimedia software program
- computer with large-screen presentation device

Directions

1. Assign a topic to your students for oral presentations. Give them guidelines as to how long the presentations should be and how many visual images they are expected to use.

2. Students prepare their speeches, using index cards for outline notes.

3. Give students time to visit websites in order to select the images they wish to use to enhance their presentations.

4. Students need to design their visual presentations in a mutlimedia program using pictures, videos, sounds, and clip art.

5. Students write down when to advance their multimedia slides on their speech cards.

6. Give your students plenty of time to practice doing their speeches using the computer. It takes some time to create smooth transitions and successfully interject visual images into an oral presentation.

7. Plan to give the presentations over the span of one week, doing six a day. Otherwise, students begin to lose interest.

Tips

1. When students are giving their presentations, be sure they use the multimedia presentation as an addition to their presentations, not the focus of the presentation.

2. Set up the computer player before school, during recess and lunch, and after school so students can practice in private.

3. Video tape your students giving their presentations so they may view them later. This is a helpful tool for self-evaluation.

Student Projects *(cont.)*

TECHNO PROJECT

Project Name _____   Project Purpose _____

Beginning Date _____   Due Date _____

HARDWARE NEEDED

_____

_____

_____

SOFTWARE NEEDED

_____

_____

_____

ADDITIONAL MATERIALS

_____

_____

_____

_____

DIRECTIONS

_____   _____

_____   _____

ADDITIONAL INFORMATION, TIPS, ETC.

_____   _____

_____   _____

_____   _____

Student Projects *(cont.)*

Project Name _____

Project Purpose _____

Subject Area _____

Approximate Time Needed _____

Materials Needed

_____   _____

_____   _____

_____   _____

_____   _____

Directions and Procedure

_____   _____

_____   _____

_____   _____

_____   _____

Culminating Activity

_____   _____

_____   _____

_____   _____

_____   _____

Possible Extensions

_____   _____

_____   _____

_____   _____

_____   _____

Name:_____

Computer Basics

Computer

A *computer* is a machine that can do many things. A computer is a very helpful tool to people. You can write a story on a computer. You can learn many new things on a computer. You can even play games on a computer. All computers have two parts, a monitor and a keyboard. A *monitor* is the screen of the computer. It is like watching TV. The *keyboard* is a rectangle with many letters, numbers, and symbols on it. The keyboard is a way for you to talk with the computer. Computers are fun!

Write these words.

computer _____

monitor _____

keyboard _____

Write this sentence.

Every computer has a monitor and a keyboard. _____

_____

_____

Name:_____

Computer Basics 2

Computers have a mouse and a mouse pad. A *mouse* is a friendly tool to help you talk with the computer. You can move the mouse with your hand. The mouse must always stay on its special place. This place is called a *mouse pad.* Be sure to keep your mouse on its pad.

Write these words.

computer

mouse

mouse pad

Write this sentence.

A computer has a mouse and a mouse pad.

Name:_____

Disk Drive Basics

A *disk drive* is a special place to put your floppy disk. A *floppy disk* is a square-shaped component that helps the computer think. Be very careful when you touch the floppy disk.

Write these words.

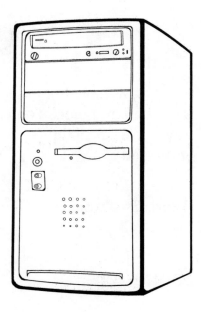

floppy disk

disk

drive

Write this sentence.

A disk drive holds a floppy disk.

Name:_____

CD-ROM Basics

A *CD-ROM* is an enjoyable part to a computer. A CD-ROM lets the computer show movies, play sounds, and hold lots of information. A CD is a *compact disk*. The *CD* is kept in a hard container to protect it. The CD goes into the CD-ROM drive. Be sure to only touch the edge of the CD.

Write these words.

CD-ROM _____

_____

compact disk _____

_____

CD _____

_____

Write this sentence.

A CD-ROM drive lets the computer play a CD, or compact disk.

_____

_____

_____

Name:_____

Modem Basics

A *modem* is a very useful type of technology. By using a modem, two people at different computers can "talk" with each other. You can even communicate with someone in a different country. It is like talking on the telephone, except you are using a computer. Modems can be inside the computer or they can be a small box on the outside. A modem is connected to a telephone line, and the messages travel over telephone wires. Once you have connected your modem and are using it to talk with another computer user, you become *online*. When talking with other computer users with your modem, you will be using an online *network*.

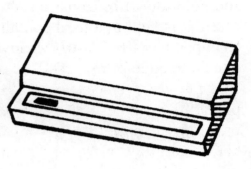

Write these words.

modem

_____
- -
_____

online

_____
- -
_____

network

_____
- -
_____

Write this sentence.

Using a modem helps me to go online and talk on a network.

_____
- -
_____
- -
_____

Name: _____

Laserdisc Player Basics

A *laserdisc player* looks almost like a VCR. Like a VCR, the laserdisc player is used with a television set. Instead of putting in a video tape, though, a *laserdisc* is placed in the laserdisc player. The laserdisc is a large, round, flat shiny disc. You can watch movies from a laserdisc or look at pictures. You can use a *remote control* to direct the laserdisc player. You can also use a bar code reader. A bar code reader looks like an ink pen. By running the bar code reader over a small bar code, you can program the laserdisc player.

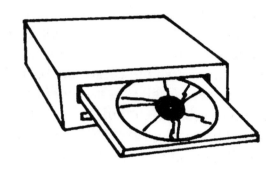

Write these words.

laserdisc player

---

laserdisc

---

remote control

Write these sentences.

A laserdisc player shows movies from a laserdisc. I direct the laserdisc player with a remote control.

Name:_____

Scanner Basics

A *scanner* is a machine that helps you copy a picture and then put the picture into the computer. Scanners come in two styles. One type is a *flat bed* where you place the picture you want copied onto the flat bed scanner. The flat bed is in the shape of a rectangle. The other type of scanner is called a *handheld* scanner. This scanner is much smaller than the flat bed and looks like the mouse from a computer. Use the handheld scanner by rolling it over the picture you want to copy. There are many things which can be scanned for a computer. You can scan photographs, drawings, artwork, and pictures from books.

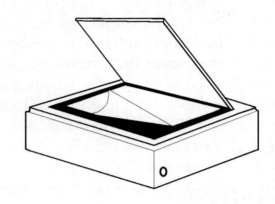

Write these words.

scanner

_____

_____

flat bed

_____

_____

handheld

_____

_____

Write these sentences.

I can copy a picture or drawing with a scanner. I can use a flat bed or a handheld style.

_____

_____

_____

_____

Name: _____

Parts of a Computer

Matching

Draw a line from each of the words to the picture that means the same thing.

keyboard

monitor

CD-ROM

floppy disk

disk drive

mouse

mouse pad

CD

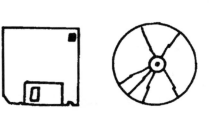

Write each of the words here. Use spaces or commas between words.

_____

- -

_____

- -

_____

- -

_____

Name: _____

Peripheral Devices

Matching

Draw a line from each of the words to the picture that matches.

laserdisc player

laserdisc

remote control

bar code reader

MODEM

flat bed scanner

handheld scanner

Write each word here. Use spaces or commas between words.

_____

- -

_____

- -

_____

- -

_____

Name:_____

Find the Terms

Technology Word Search

Find all of the technology words in the word search. The words can be found written across and down. For extra credit when you are finished, write the words in alphabetical order on the back of the paper.

```
D E O N W Z C O M P U T E R R F C O U P X V D E X R F
U P O L K N G B F H T V H Y U T V F H I Y H N U J M I
D M A C I N T O S H R F L A S E R D I S C P L A Y E R
Y G I L H T U D J K I D E O N J S C W R C L L O P T K
M O N I T O R D E O N G F E R N O E D F Q Q A Z W S X
M O U R N I N G E T H E L A W E S H A Q W R Y M P H N
A D I S K D R I V E R G O J I T D E O N T K V O X Z G
F W E B B E R W D G H Y P J O W T Y U I P I O U T H J
M I L L E R A W R R U I P H H O K E M P E A F S X D T
D E O N L A U C V B U R Y B A R D R T Y R A E I O U
U P D E O N F Y R Z Q A D H J K E R U O D F E L H J K
B F G J T A W E T B N J I D E O N F U L B E W I N G J
D E O N R U N P G Q A W S D F K E Y B O A R D S A S L
E E D F T R O E A D S Q K H P U Y R G J D R E P O C A
O F O H V F E Y U O P A K J K R T I F R C S Z X H A J
N Y J N O E D D H R Q S L X C D R O M T H F R B J N G
R E M O T E C O N T R O L T P I H F R B F I A R Y N J
D E O N F R O H Q Z T G H U J I K G R G E R T Y U E A
U K F R A W S X E D C B A R C O D E R E A D E R X R X
```

Cross off the words as you find them:

LASERDISC PLAYER
COMPUTER
MACINTOSH
MONITOR
DISK DRIVE
BAR CODE READER
KEYBOARD

CD-ROM
REMOTE CONTROL
FLOPPY DISK
NETWORK
MOUSE
SCANNER

Simple Student Activity Sheets

Computer Contract

Computer Contract

I, _____, promise to treat computers with respect. I will follow all of the computer rules. I promise to

1. have clean hands before using the computer.
2. touch the computer in a gentle way.
3. keep food and drinks away from the computer.
4. use my inside voice when I use the computer.

I promise to be a respectful computer student.

_____
Student

_____
Teacher

_____
Date

Name:_____

Parts of a Computer

Computers are made up of many parts, just as we have arms, feet, hands, a head, and more. When all of the different parts of a computer are connected together, it is called a **computer system**. On the picture below you can see all the different parts of the computer system. Each separate part is called a peripheral. Also, each part that you can touch is called hardware.

Activity: Match the parts of a computer system by putting the correct number from the picture of the computer system next to the correct part.

_____   **Keyboard**—used to type information.

_____   **Monitor**—displays visual graphics and information.

_____   **Printer**—makes a paper copy of what is displayed on the monitor.

_____   **CPU**—contains all the parts necessary for the computer to operate.

_____   **Mouse**—moves the cursor around on the screen. You can also draw with it.

_____   **Disk Drives**—hold floppy disks and CD-ROMs.

Extension: Look at an actual computer system in your classroom and identify its parts.

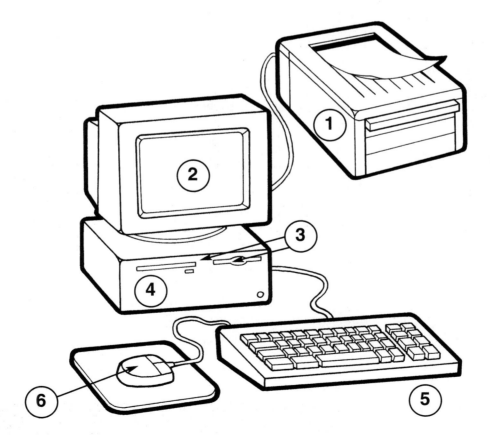

Name:_____

Input Devices

A **peripheral device** is a piece of hardware that you can attach to your computer. One kind of peripheral device is used for input so you can put data into your computer.

Activity: Match the number from each input device with its picture by writing the correct number on the line provided.

___ **Keyboard**—By typing on the keys, you can input letters, numbers, and symbols. You can also use the keyboard to input commands into your computer.

___ **Mouse**—A hand-sized device with one or more control buttons, it is connected to your computer and is used to move the cursor and other objects around on the screen.

___ **Scanner**—It takes pictures from a printed page and changes them into graphics on the screen. It can be a hand-held tool or as big as a small copy machine.

___ **Tablet**—A device upon which you can draw, it looks like a drawing pad. As you draw on the tablet, your picture appears on the computer's screen.

___ **Disks and Disk Drives**—Information from a disk is read into the computer through the disk drive.

___ **Voice Recognition System**—It converts your voice into electronic signals through a microphone. It allows a computer to respond to a set of instructions spoken by your voice.

___ **Modem**—It converts signals from the telephone into digital pulses a computer can understand. It allows you to talk from one computer to another over telephone or cable lines.

___ **Joystick**—It is an input device used for playing computer games.

___ **Touch Screen**—You press the screen with your finger to activate your choices.

___ **Digital Camera**—A digital camera gives you the opportunity to add personal pictures to your documents or presentations. You transfer images to your computer directly from the camera.

Extension: Try to use as many of these input devices as possible.

1.

2.

3.

4.

5.

6.

7.

Amount Requested	
$20	$100
$40	$200
$80	$300

8.

9.

10.

Name:_____

Output Devices

Another type of peripheral device is an **output** device. It is a piece of computer hardware that displays output to you after the computer has processed the data you input.

Try to remember it this way:

input ——> in put ——> put in

output ——> out put ——> put out

Activity: Match the number from each output device with its picture by writing the correct number on the line provided.

1.

___ **Monitor**—This is the screen on which words, numbers, and graphics are displayed for you to see. The cathode ray tube (CRT) is found inside the monitor. The monitor is the most common output device.

2.

___ **Printer**—This output device prints whatever is on the monitor onto paper. Printers will print words, numbers, and graphics. There are a variety of printers from which you can choose.

3.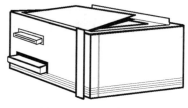

___ **Modem**—This acts not only as an input device but also as an output device when it sends messages from your computer to other computers.

___ **Disks and Disk Drives**—When you save your data onto a disk for future use, disks and disk drives act as output devices.

4.

___ **Speakers**—Sound is output from your computer through speakers. They are either built inside your computer or are external, like those in a stereo system. Some computers have the ability to imitate human speech and can actually be programmed to talk with speech and voice synthesizers.

5.

Extension: Try to use as many of these output devices as possible.

Name:_____

Computer Parts and Peripherals

Using the words from the Word Bank, fill in the names of the items pictured in the spaces provided.

Word Bank			
monitor	mouse	keyboard	floppy disk
laser printer	CPU box	mousepad	cable
connector	flatbed scanner	CD-ROM or DVD	

_____   _____

_____   _____

_____

_____   _____

_____   _____

_____   _____

Name:_____

Memory Brain Teasers

1. I am the amount of memory that is equal to 1,024 megabytes. What am I?

   _____

2. I am shiny and round but you can only use me once to save information in my spiral grooves. What am I?

   _____

3. I am square and stiff on the outside but round and flimsy on the inside. What am I?

   _____

4. I am the amount of memory that is equal to 1,024 bytes. What am I?

   _____

5. I am the amount of memory that is equal to 8 bits. What am I?

   _____

6. I am shiny and round and you can use me over and over again to save information in my spiral grooves. What am I?

   _____

7. I shimmer and shine, am reflective and bright. On my mountainsides and in my valleys you can record what you like. What am I?

   _____

8. I am the amount of memory that is equal to 1,024 kilobytes. What am I?

   _____

BONUS:

How many pages full of words could each form of memory hold?

   a. one megabyte

   b. one gigabyte

Assume a page is 80 characters by 66 rows, and 1 character is 1 byte, then there are 80 x 66 = 5,280 characters, or bytes, on a page.

Remember that

   1,024 bytes = 1 kilobyte

   1,024 kilobytes = 1 megabyte

   1,024 megabytes = 1 gigabyte

Use the space below to calculate your answer.

Show your work for the BONUS question here.

Crossword Puzzle

ACROSS

1. 1,024 ___ = 1 megabyte
2. 1,024 ___ = 1 gigabyte
4. looks like a television
6. a standard binary code
8. a LAN is a network that is _____
10. network that passes between buildings
11. has a tail
14. where the mouse sleeps
15. short for "bytes per second"
16. looks like a typewriter
18. floppy _____
19. what you ask if you can't figure something out
20. short for "read only memory"
21. places to visit on the Internet
23. short for "central processing unit"
24. a unique number assigned to a computer on the Internet

DOWN

2. short for "megabyte"
3. 1,024 ___ = 1 kilobyte
5. short for "electronic mail"
7. a _____ strike could damage a computer
9. a Web file named after a dessert
10. short for "World Wide Web"
11. converts binary (digital) signals to analog (sound) signals
12. largest memory measurement
17. the protocol that makes sure data is transferred smoothly between two modems
20. _____ only memory
22. short for "Internet service provider"

Name: _____

Word Search

Words go in all directions! (backwards, too)

COOKIE
INTERNET
COMPUTER
LINK
LAN
WAN
MONITOR
CPU
MOUSE
CABLE
MODEM
SCANNER
WEBSITES
KEYBOARD
PC
ASCII
RAM
ROM
CD
DVD
MEMORY
BITS
BYTE
KILOBYTE
MEGABYTE
GIGABYTE
SOFTWARE
HARDWARE
CHIP
FLOPPY

```
A E L G I G A B Y T E I
Q C A I R B G X F Z S N
W A N B N M A S C Y U T
B D Q P W K L E P A B E
Q C B H C O M P U T E R
A D V Q C B O E I X A N
R X Y A Q B N S A W O E
C O O K I E I R I P Z T
E H Q S I M T U D G E C
D B I Q V E O P S Z B X
W A L P P B R D W D Q D
K I L O B Y T E E S L E
Q X K A Q B P T B M A J
U C P O T B S A S Z W D
A B E C A B L E I C A R
L Q B R M S D B T W C A
C Y M E S B C T E Y D O
Q P A N D B X I S T I B
M P B N Z B C Q I D V Y
H O Q A A E Y E S F E E
A L U C B R Q T H Q T K
R F B S Q A R A E Z Y B
D A D Q E W Y T R A B O
W R B F Q T R A J K A F
A O C K N F O D V D G C
R M Q A B O M Q D P E E
E F S Q K S E A Q F M J
Q A D Q R A M R B A E B
```

Name: _____

Hardware and Peripherals Test—PC

Objective

Identify specific computer hardware.

Standard

• Using pencil and ruler, correctly label components of the computer by drawing lines and writing the corresponding letter as shown in the example done for "monitor."

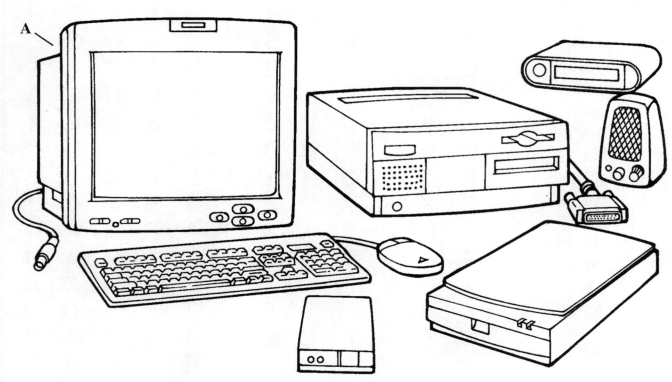

Components to Identify

A. Monitor	E. Mouse Button	I. Numeric Keypad	M. External Modem
B. Function Key(s)	F. Floppy Disk Drive	J. External Hard Drive	
C. Scanner	G. Scanner Cable	K. Speaker	
D. CD-ROM Door/Drive	H. Brightness Adjust Knobs	L. CD-ROM Drive	

What key or keys would be used to restart the computer? _____, _____, _____

How would you "quit" using an application? _____, _____, _____

If a computer's CPU is rated at 333, what does the 333 represent? _____

Name: _____

Hardware and Peripherals Test— Macintosh

Objective

Learn components of the Macintosh computer.

Assignment

Correctly identify specific items on the Macintosh computer.

Standards

- Using pencil and ruler, correctly label components of the computer by drawing lines and writing the corresponding letters as shown in the example done for "monitor."

Components to Identify

A. Monitor

B. Function Keys

C. Input/Output ports

D. CD-ROM Door/Drive

E. Floppy Disk Drive

F. Volume Buttons

G. Brightness Buttons

H. Command Key

I. Microphone

J. CD-ROM Drive Button

K. Keyboard Input/Output Cable

L. Keyboard Elevators

M. Reset Key

What three keys are used to restart the computer? _____, _____, _____

What three keys are used to "force-quit" an application? _____, _____, _____

Name(s) _____

Internet Fun Scavenger Hunt

Objective

Find a variety of information on the Internet.

Assignment

Find the following. 1 point for each find—20 points maximum. Have your teacher (or someone designated by the teacher) initial each of your finds on the line provided.

Teacher Initials

_____ 1. a picture of Abraham Lincoln

_____ 2. a picture of Rosa Parks

_____ 3. a picture taken by the Hubble Space Telescope

_____ 4. a map of California

_____ 5. today's weather forecast for Levittown, Pa

_____ 6. how do you catch a bubble? (*Hint:* Science Museum of Minnesota)

_____ 7. picture of a giant sea tortoise

_____ 8. text of Lincoln's Gettysburg Address

_____ 9. the first chapter of *The Red Badge of Courage*

_____ 10. picture of the space shuttle in orbit

_____ 11. picture of Michael Jordan as a rookie

_____ 12. a picture of Phoebe, one of Saturn's moons

_____ 13. a recipe for slime

_____ 14. a copy of the poem "The Road Not Taken" by Robert Frost

_____ 15. the number of soldiers killed in the Civil War

_____ 16. a map showing the route of the Underground Railroad

_____ 17. a picture of one of the Seven Wonders of the World

_____ 18. text explaining how immune cells get involved when we get a splinter (*Hint:* Cells Alive)

_____ 19. the year William Shakespeare wrote *Romeo and Juliet*

_____ 20. a picture of the Great Wall of China

Name(s) _____

Internet Business Website Search

Objective

Find Internet sites that show stores or merchandise that are related to a business you would like to own.

Assignment

Find the following sites. Write the URLs on the lines provided. Have your teacher initial (or someone designated by your teacher) each of your finds on the line provided.

1. one Web site of a business that sells the same category of merchandise that you do

   URL _____

   Teacher Initials _____

2. a second Web site that sells the same category of merchandise that you do

   URL _____

   Teacher Initials _____

3. a graphic item on a Web site showing an item similar to one sold in your business

   URL _____

   Teacher Initials _____

4. a map of the state in which your store is located

   URL _____

   Teacher Initials _____

5. a map of the city in which your store is located

   URL _____

   Teacher Initials _____

6. today's weather forecast of the city in which your store is located

   URL _____

   Teacher Initials_____

7. the population of the city in which your store is located

   URL _____

   Teacher Initials _____

Name: _____

Internet Search—People in History

Use your choice of Web browsers and search engines to locate the answers.

1. President Lincoln gave his first inaugural address on what date (month, day, year)?
   Answer _____

2. Jackie Robinson, the first African-American professional baseball player, played his first year for what major league team and in what year?
   Team _____   Year _____

3. In what year did Susan B. Anthony demand that women be given the same civil and political rights (the right to vote) as all men?
   Answer _____

4. How many Jewish people were thought to have died in the Holocaust?
   Answer _____

5. Who was the prime minister of Israel from 1977–83?
   Answer _____

6. Claude Monet, the great French Impressionist painter, lived from
   _____ to _____.

7. What was Dr. Seuss's first book for children? In what year did he write it?
   Name of book _____ Year _____

8. In what year did Thomas Edison invent the electric light ?
   Year _____

_____ **out of 8 correct.**

Name _____

Internet Science Scavenger Hunt

Science Scavenger Hunt

Have fun trying to find the solutions to these science questions. Go to the suggested Web site and search for the answer. You may also use search engines such as *Lycos, Infoseek,* or *Yahoo.* Answers must be in the form of a URL for the site. All locations must be verified by the teacher (or someone designated by the teacher) and initialed. Add a bookmark when you find the correct page.

Teacher Initials

1. What is the recipe for slime?
   Hint: U.S. Department of Education   _____
   Answer :

2. Where can I find a video clip on the hatching of a baby worm?
   Hint: Yuckiest Site on the Internet   _____
   Answer :

3. Why do feet smell?
   Hint: Beakman and Jax   _____
   Answer :

4. How do you catch a bubble?   _____
   Hint: Science Learning Network: Thinking Fountain or Science Museum of Minnesota
   Answer :

5. What material do you need to make a fossil of your own?   _____
   Hint: Bill Nye the Science Guy Episode
   Answer :

6. Why do some fruit flies have white eyes?   _____
   Hint: Exploratorium
   Answer :

7. How do immune cells get involved when we get a splinter or a scratch?   _____
   Hint: Cells Alive
   Answer :

8. How does Albert Einstein look when seen through the eye of a bee?   _____
   Hint: B-Eye
   Answer :

9. What liquid was used in the solubility test with Twinkies?   _____
   Hint: T.W.I.N.K.I.E.S. Project
   Answer :

PowerPoint Storyboard

Directions: Plan your slide show by sketching where you want text and pictures to appear. Number the slides in the squares on the bottom right of the slide. Ask for additional pages if needed.

Name_____

HyperStudio Card Design Sheet

My Card Design

1. Complete a detailed card design in the space above. Show any **artwork**, **text**, and **buttons** that will be seen on your card. Draw your design in **color**.

2. Write a paragraph explaining the **purpose** of your card. Include reasons why you feel the card's design relates well to the project. Write neatly, and use proper spelling and correct grammar.   Use the back of this sheet if you need additional space.

_____

_____

_____

_____

_____

_____

_____

_____

Spreadsheet Planning Sheet

Directions: Plan your spreadsheet worksheet by entering data and formulas in the correct cells.

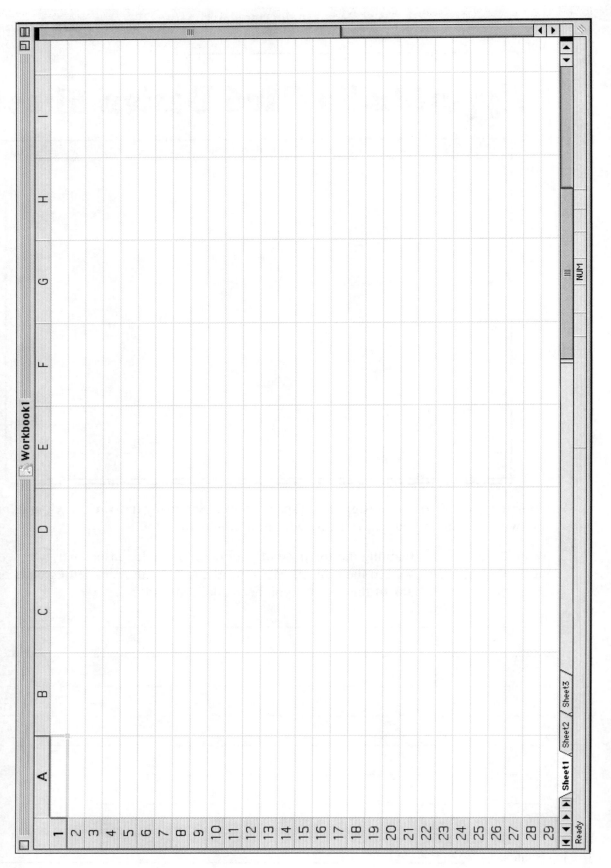

Group Project Planning Sheet

1. Names of group members _____

    _____   _____
                Project Manager   Graphics Pro

    _____   _____
                Internet Pro   Scanning Pro

2. Assignment or group goal: _____

    _____

    _____

3. List the things that need to be done to complete this goal.

    1. _____

       _____

    2. _____

       _____

    3. _____

       _____

    4. _____

       _____

    5. _____

       _____

    6. _____

       _____

    7. _____

       _____

    8. _____

       _____

Due dates: _____

Group Project Evaluation Form

1. Write the names of your group members _____

_____

_____

_____

_____

_____

2. What do you think you learned? _____

_____

_____

_____

_____

_____

_____

3. What do you think your group learned? _____

_____

_____

_____

_____

_____

_____

4. Did everyone in your group get a chance to use the computer?   O Yes   O No

5. Were the members of your group cooperative?   O Yes   O No

6. Did your group have any problems working together? If so, what caused the problems?

_____

_____

_____

_____

_____

Name_____

Book Reference Sheet

Author's last name _____ First name _____

Name of book_____

Where published_____

Publisher_____ Copyright date_____

This source was used for... O Text   O Graphics   O Sound   O Video   O Animation

_____

Author's last name _____ First name _____

Name of book_____

Where published_____

Publisher_____ Copyright date_____

This source was used for... O Text   O Graphics   O Sound   O Video   O Animation

_____

Author's last name _____ First name _____

Name of book_____

Where published_____

Publisher_____ Copyright date_____

This source was used for... O Text   O Graphics   O Sound   O Video   O Animation

_____

Use this format when listing books on your reference card...

Author's last name, first name. *Name of book.* Where published: Publisher, Copyright date.

Here are some examples...

Dickens, Charles. *Great Expectations.* New York: Washington Square Press, Inc., 1963.

Hopper, Grace Murray and Mandell, Steven L. *Understanding Computers.* St. Paul: West Publishing Co., 1984.

HyperStudio Planning Sheets

Name_____

CD-ROM Reference Sheet

Name of CD-ROM_____

Where published_____

Publisher_____ Copyright date_____

This source was used for… O Text   O Graphics   O Sound   O Video   O Animation

_____

Name of CD-ROM_____

Where published_____

Publisher_____ Copyright date_____

This source was used for… O Text   O Graphics   O Sound   O Video   O Animation

_____

Name of CD-ROM_____

Where published_____

Publisher_____ Copyright date_____

This source was used for… O Text   O Graphics   O Sound   O Video   O Animation

_____

Use this format when listing CD-ROMs on your reference card…

Name of CD-ROM. CD-ROM. Where published: Publisher, Copyright date.

Here are some examples…

The Animals! A True Multimedia Experience. CD-ROM. Novato, CA: The Software Toolworks, Inc., 1993.

Corel Gallery for Macintosh 10,000 Clipart Images. CD-ROM. Ontario: Corel Corporation, 1994.

Name_____

Dictionary & Encyclopedia Reference Sheet

Name of article_____

Name of source _____

Edition copyright date _____

This source was used for…   O Text   O Graphics   O Sound   O Video   O Animation

_____

Name of article_____

Name of source _____

Edition copyright date _____

This source was used for…   O Text   O Graphics   O Sound   O Video   O Animation

_____

Name of article_____

Name of source _____

Edition copyright date _____

This source was used for…   O Text   O Graphics   O Sound   O Video   O Animation

_____

Use this format when listing dictionaries or encyclopedias on your reference card…

"Name of article." *Name of source.* Edition copyright date.

Here are some examples…

"Software." *The American Heritage Dictionary of the English Language.* 1982 edition.

"Computer." *The New Grolier Multimedia Encyclopedia CD-ROM.* 1993 edition.

Name_____

Internet Reference Sheet

Name of site _____

Date posted at site _____

Site address_____

Date you visited the site_____

This source was used for…   O Text   O Graphics   O Sound   O Video   O Animation
_____

Name of site _____

Date posted at site _____

Site address_____

Date you visited the site_____

This source was used for…   O Text   O Graphics   O Sound   O Video   O Animation
_____

Name of site _____

Date posted at site _____

Site address_____

Date you visited the site_____

This source was used for…   O Text   O Graphics   O Sound   O Video   O Animation
_____

Use this format when listing Internet sites on your reference card…

"Name of Internet site." Date posted. <Internet site address> (Date you visited the site).

Here is an example…

"Home Page for *HyperStudio* by Roger Wagner Publishing, Inc." 7 January 1998.
<http://www.*hyperstudio*.com> (24 January 1998).

≣ **HyperStudio Planning Sheets** ≣

Name _____

Magazine Reference Sheet

Author's last name _____ First name _____

Name of article_____

Name of magazine _____

Date _____ Pages _____

This source was used for…   O Text   O Graphics   O Sound   O Video   O Animation

_____

Author's last name _____ First name _____

Name of article_____

Name of magazine _____

Date _____ Pages _____

This source was used for…   O Text   O Graphics   O Sound   O Video   O Animation

_____

Author's last name _____ First name _____

Name of article_____

Name of magazine _____

Date _____ Pages _____

This source was used for…   O Text   O Graphics   O Sound   O Video   O Animation

_____

Use this format when listing magazines on your reference card…

Author's last name, first name. "Name of article." *Name of magazine.* Date: Pages.

Here is an example…

Battersby, Jeff. "Believe the Hype—Multimedia Programming Made Easy." *MacHome.*
    February 1998: 48.

Name _____

News Article Reference Sheet

Name of article_____

Name of newspaper _____

Date (day/month/year) _____

Section of newspaper where article appears _____

This source was used for…   O Text   O Graphics   O Sound   O Video   O Animation

_____

Name of article_____

Name of newspaper _____

Date (day/month/year) _____

Section of newspaper where article appears _____

This source was used for…   O Text   O Graphics   O Sound   O Video   O Animation

_____

Name of article_____

Name of newspaper _____

Date (day/month/year) _____

Section of newspaper where article appears _____

This source was used for…   O Text   O Graphics   O Sound   O Video   O Animation

_____

Use this format when listing newspaper articles on your reference card…

"Name of article." *Name of newspaper* and Date: Section.

Here is an example…

"Fifth-grade class has 'Flecknology' focus." *Beavercreek News-Current* 31 May 1997: 1A, 3A.

E-Mail Directory

Name: _____

E-mail Address:_____

Information: _____

_____

_____

_____

_____

Name: _____

E-mail Address:_____

Information: _____

_____

_____

_____

_____

Name: _____

E-mail Address:_____

Information: _____

_____

_____

_____

_____

Acceptable Use Policy

Dear Parents,

We are pleased to offer computer technology to our students. To ensure that every student benefits from the time spent with the computers, and to prevent technical problems, please review the following technology contract with your child. It is important that these rules are clearly understood and followed.

Student use of the school's technology is a privilege which, at the discretion of the school administration, may be revoked by the school at any time. The school reserves the right to seek financial restitution for any damage(s) caused by a student or other users.

(1) I **will** use only the computer that is assigned to me and will not attempt access to any unauthorized computer.

(2) I **will not** attempt to use any software or hardware without the approval of the instructor.

(3) I **will not** vandalize any software or hardware.

(4) I **will not** modify any system settings on any computer.

(5) I **will not** disrupt the privileges of other computer users or misrepresent other computer users.

(6) I **will not** copy, change, read, or use anyone else's software or files without prior permission from the instructor.

(7) I **will** use the Internet exclusively for activities which are specified by the instructor.

(8) When on the Internet, I **will not** reveal any personal information about myself or anyone else.

(9) When on the Internet, I **will not** send messages that contain inappropriate content. This includes profanity and any other non-academic activity.

(10) When on the Internet, I **will not** purchase any goods or services.

(11) When on the Internet, I **will not** download, upload, or otherwise gain access to any unauthorized material(s).

- -

Please retain the above for your records and return the bottom portion to your child's teacher.

I understand and will abide by this Acceptable Use Policy.
I understand that violating any part of this agreement will result in disciplinary action.

STUDENT: _____ DATE: _____

I have explained and discussed this agreement with my child and he/she understands and agrees to abide by the aforementioned conditions for use of school computers and computer equipment.

PARENT/GUARDIAN SIGNATURE: _____ DATE: _____

Grading Rubrics for Technology Projects

As the avenues which students use to complete their class work change, so do the methods of evaluating their work. Teachers wonder "How do I grade a multimedia project?" "How do I evaluate a group presentation?" "How can I assess neatness when the work is done on the computer?" "Each *HyperStudio* project is so unique, what guidelines do I use?" and "What strategies do I use to combine technology projects with student portfolios?" These are all practical questions.

Keeping in mind that technology does not drive the curriculum but is rather a tool to assist teachers in reaching their curricular goals, the area of student assessment is no different. Rather than asking yourself, "How am I going to grade a multimedia presentation?" ask instead, "What are the goals that I want my students to reach by completing this project?" In the same way teachers assess all other student work, evaluating a student project involving technology begins by asking this question. Once those learning objectives have been established, a set of criteria is created that serves as guidelines in evaluating student projects.

One meaningful method of utilizing this set of criteria is by creating a rubric. The word *rubric* literally means "rule." When the word is used in connection with assessment, it means a set of criteria that can be used to judge a sample of student work. By assigning points to various elements of a project, students earn a cumulative point total which then serves as their overall "grade" for the work done. This type of evaluation is very helpful to students because they are able to see the various parts of their project and the importance of each area in relation to their overall score.

The following pages contain some generic sample rubrics for various technology projects. These are also available on the CD-ROM in the *Teacher Sheets* folder (filename: rubrics.pdf). You can use these as guidelines or as a "skeletal" foundation when designing your own rubrics. As your students become more familiar with projects involving technology (or any other curricular area for that matter), give them the opportunity to assist in designing the rubrics. When a rubric is used as a teaching tool, assessment becomes part of the instruction, and students are provided with clear directions and focus.

Grading Rubrics *(cont.)*

Paint, Draw, and Graphics Rubric

Competent

The student can independently apply special effects to a graphic, such as rotate, stretch, and perspective, in a paint program.

The student can independently use the line tool, shape tools, and text tool in a draw program.

The student can independently change the size or shape of an object using the edge handles in a draw program.

The student can independently change an object's pattern or color in a draw program.

The student can independently move and duplicate an object in a draw program.

The student can independently group and change the stacking order of objects in a draw program.

The student can independently apply special effects, such as rotate and flip horizontal/vertical, in a draw program.

The student can independently copy a graphic to the clipboard and paste or insert it into another document.

Emergent

The student can usually apply special effects to a graphic, such as rotate, stretch, and perspective, in a paint program.

The student can usually use the line tool, shape tools, and text tool in a draw program.

The student can usually change the size or shape of an object using the edge handles in a draw program.

The student can usually change an object's pattern or color in a draw program.

The student can usually move and duplicate an object in a draw program.

The student can usually group and change the stacking order of objects in a draw program.

The student can usually apply special effects, such as rotate and flip horizontal/vertical, in a draw program.

The student can usually copy a graphic to the clipboard and paste or insert it into another document.

Beginner

The student requires assistance to apply special effects to a graphic, such as rotate, stretch, and perspective, in a paint program.

The student requires assistance to use the line tool, shape tools, and text tool in a draw program.

The student requires assistance to change the size or shape of an object using the edge handles in a draw program.

The student requires assistance to change an object's pattern or color in a draw program.

The student requires assistance to move and duplicate an object in a draw program.

The student requires assistance to group and change the stacking order of objects in a draw program.

The student requires assistance to apply special effects, such as rotate and flip horizontal/vertical, in a draw program.

The student requires assistance to copy a graphic to the clipboard and paste or insert it into another document.

Grading Rubrics *(cont.)*

Word Processing Rubric

Competent

The student can independently save and retrieve word processing files.

The student can independently format the text of the document by changing text size, font, and style.

The student has a clear understanding of the concept of text/word wrap.

The student can independently cut, copy, and paste text.

The student can independently use the spell checker.

The student can independently manipulate the layout of a document, using margins, justification, and line spacing.

The student can independently move or copy text between two or more word processing documents.

Emergent

The student can usually save and retrieve word processing files.

The student can usually format the text of the document by changing text size, font, and style.

The student has a basic understanding of the concept of text/word wrap.

The student can usually cut, copy, and paste text.

The student can usually use the spell checker.

The student can usually manipulate the layout of a document, using margins, justification, and line spacing.

The student can usually move or copy text between two or more word processing documents.

Beginner

The student requires assistance to save and retrieve word processing files.

The student requires assistance to format the text of the document by changing text size, font, and style.

The student has little understanding of the concept of text/word wrap.

The student requires assistance to cut, copy, and paste text.

The student requires assistance to use the spell checker.

The student requires assistance to manipulate the layout of a document, using margins, justification, and line spacing.

The student requires assistance to move or copy text between two or more word processing documents.

Grading Rubrics *(cont.)*

Spreadsheets Rubric

Competent

The student can independently recognize the parts of a spreadsheet.

The student has a clear understanding of the purpose of a spreadsheet.

The student can independently open a spreadsheet program.

The student can independently recognize new menus within the spreadsheet environment.

The student can independently move to a specific cell on a spreadsheet.

The student can independently enter text or numbers into a spreadsheet.

The student can independently save and retrieve spreadsheet files.

The student can independently select a cell or block of cells.

The student can independently change the order of information within a column by sorting.

Emergent

The student can usually recognize the parts of a spreadsheet.

The student has a basic understanding of the purpose of a spreadsheet.

The student can usually open a spreadsheet program.

The student can usually recognize new menus within the spreadsheet environment.

The student can usually move to a specific cell on a spreadsheet.

The student can usually enter text or numbers into a spreadsheet.

The student can usually save and retrieve spreadsheet files.

The student can usually select a cell or block of cells.

The student can usually change the order of information within a column by sorting.

Beginner

The student requires assistance to recognize the parts of a spreadsheet.

The student has little understanding of the purpose of a spreadsheet.

The student requires assistance to open a spreadsheet program.

The student requires assistance to recognize new menus within the spreadsheet environment.

The student requires assistance to move to a specific cell on a spreadsheet.

The student requires assistance to enter text or numbers into a spreadsheet.

The student requires assistance to save and retrieve spreadsheet files.

The student requires assistance to select a cell or block of cells.

The student requires assistance to change the order of information within a column by sorting.

Grading Rubrics *(cont.)*

Multimedia Presentations Rubric

Competent

The student can independently place text into a simple, static screen/card.

The student can independently paste a graphic copied from clip art into a simple, static screen/card.

The student can independently create a graphic using basic graphics tools and place it into a simple, static screen/card.

The student can independently add photos from a CD-ROM, Photo CD, or a floppy disk, into a simple, static screen/card.

The student can independently add scanned images to a simple, static screen/card.

The student can independently add images from a digital camera to a simple, static screen/card.

Emergent

The student can usually place text into a simple, static screen/card.

The student can usually paste a graphic copied from clip art into a simple, static screen/card.

The student can usually create a graphic using basic graphics tools and place it into a simple, static screen/card.

The student can usually add photos from a CD-ROM, Photo CD, or a floppy disk, into a simple, static screen/card.

The student can usually add scanned images to a simple, static screen/card.

The student can usually add images from a digital camera to a simple, static screen/card.

Beginner

The student requires assistance to place text into a simple, static screen/card.

The student requires assistance to paste a graphic copied from clip art into a simple, static screen/card.

The student requires assistance to create a graphic using basic graphics tools and place it into a simple, static screen/card.

The student requires assistance to add photos from a CD-ROM, Photo CD, or a floppy disk, into a simple, static screen/card.

The student requires assistance to add scanned images to a simple, static screen/card.

The student requires assistance to add images from a digital camera to a simple, static screen/card.

Grading Rubrics *(cont.)*

Databases Rubric

Competent

The student can independently determine what items to use in a physical database and an electronic database.

The student can independently retrieve a record from a physical database and an electronic database—single field, exact match.

The student can independently use a public database.

The student can independently add new records to a file.

The student can independently enter new information to one or more fields of an existing record.

The student can independently save updated records on disk.

The student can independently organize a file by sorting alphabetically, numerically, or chronologically in a chosen field.

The student can independently print sorted records and use the information.

Emergent

The student can usually determine what items to use in a physical database and an electronic database.

The student can usually retrieve a record from a physical database and an electronic database—single field, exact match.

The student can usually use a public database.

The student can usually add new records to a file.

The student can usually enter new information to one or more fields of an existing record.

The student can usually save updated records on disk.

The student can usually organize a file by sorting alphabetically, numerically, or chronologically in a chosen field.

The student can usually print sorted records and use the information.

Beginner

The student requires assistance to determine what items to use in a physical database and an electronic database.

The student requires assistance to retrieve a record from a physical database and an electronic database—single field, exact match.

The student requires assistance to use a public database.

The student requires assistance to add new records to a file.

The student requires assistance to enter new information to one or more fields of an existing record.

The student requires assistance to save updated records on disk.

The student requires assistance to organize a file by sorting alphabetically, numerically, or chronologically in a chosen field.

The student requires assistance to print sorted records and use the information.

Grading Rubrics *(cont.)*

Internet/Telecommunications Rubric

Competent

The student can independently attach a document to an e-mail message.

The student can independently create and use a signature file.

The student can independently participate in Acceptable Use Policy design.

The student can independently use the directory buttons and tool bar in a Web browser.

The student can independently use a variety of ways to get to another Web site.

The student can independently save sites using a bookmark, hotlist, or favorite.

The student can independently use required software and complete required tasks for projects.

The student can independently develop and implement a project using online resources.

Emergent

The student can usually attach a document to an e-mail message.

The student can usually create and use a signature file.

The student can usually participate in Acceptable Use Policy design.

The student can usually use the directory buttons and tool bar in a Web browser.

The student can usually use a variety of ways to get to another Web site.

The student can usually save sites using a bookmark, hotlist, or favorite.

The student can usually use required software and complete required tasks for projects.

The student can usually develop and implement a project using online resources.

Beginner

The student requires assistance to attach a document to an e-mail message.

The student requires assistance to create and use a signature file.

The student requires assistance to participate in Acceptable Use Policy design.

The student requires assistance to use the directory buttons and tool bar in a Web browser.

The student requires assistance to use a variety of ways to get to another Web site.

The student requires assistance to save sites using a bookmark, hotlist, or favorite.

The student requires assistance to use required software and complete required tasks for projects.

The student requires assistance to develop and implement a project using online resources.

Computer Setting Adjustments You Can Make

The students love the computer-learning center in your classroom. They take turns playing with interactive CD-ROM storybooks, drawing pictures in the paint program, and exploring the Internet sites you have bookmarked for their use.

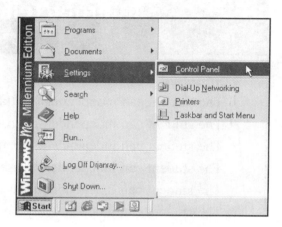

You recently noticed that two of your students, Anisa and Reggie are having trouble controlling the mouse and using the keyboard. After watching them closely, you determine their difficulties are developmental. They will soon outgrow them; however, in the meantime, there are some things that you can do with the computer system to help them.

Adjusting the Double-click Speed of the Mouse

Anisa has a difficult time double-clicking the mouse. As hard as she tries, Anisa's little fingers don't move fast enough to get the two quick, consecutive clicks necessary to launch a program or to activate the characters on her storybook screen. Anisa is frustrated! You can help Anisa by slowing down the double-click speed of the mouse.

If your computer system is a PC you can:

- Click **Start** on the task bar.

- Click **Settings**.

- Click **Control Panel**.

- At the **Control Panel** window, double-click **Mouse**.

- At the **Mouse Properties** window, click the **Buttons** tab to bring it to the forefront.

- Click and drag the indicator bar for the Double-click speed to the left, toward Slow.

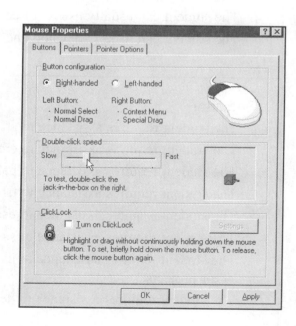

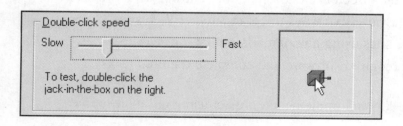

Computer Setting Adjustments You Can Make *(cont.)*

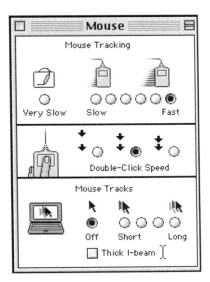

- Have the student (for whom you are adjusting the double-click speed of the mouse) double-click on the jack-in-the-box.

- If the speed is adjusted to meet the needs of the student, Jack will pop up!

- If Jack didn't pop up, keep adjusting the double-click speed slower and slower until he does.

- Click the **Apply** button.

- Then click **OK**.

If your computer is a Mac, you can:

- Click on the **Apple Menu** icon in the upper-left corner of your screen.

- Pull down to and click on **Control Panels**.

- Click on **Mouse**.

- When the window opens, you can change the double-clicking speed of the mouse.

Adjusting the Keystroke Rate

Reggie has different problems. Reggie's keystrokes are so deliberate and so intense that his little fingers seem to stick to the keys. When Reggie tries to type his name, it typically comes out RRReggggiiie. You can adjust the keyboard settings for Reggie so that he gets a little more time to lift his fingers from the keys before they repeat.

If your computer is a PC, you can:

- Click **Start** on the task bar.

- Click **Settings**.

- Click **Control Panel**.

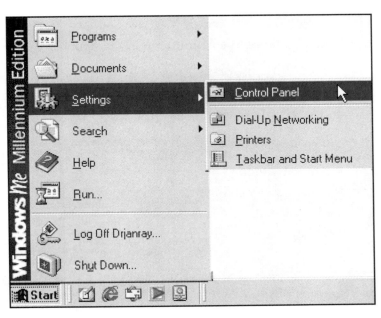

Computer Setting Adjustments You Can Make *(cont.)*

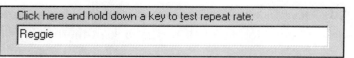

- At the **Control Panel** window, double-click on **Keyboard**.

- At the **Keyboard Properties** window, click the **Speed** tab to bring it to the forefront.

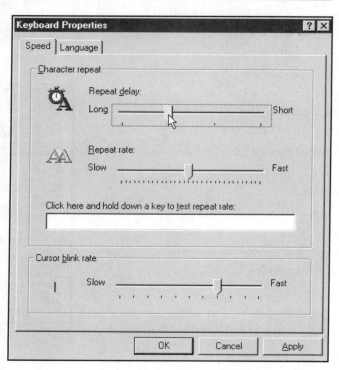

- Click on the **Repeat Delay** indicator bar and move it from the Short position on the right to a longer position toward the left.

- Have the student (for whom you are adjusting the keyboard speed) type his or her name in the **Character Repeat** text box.

- If the student's name does not display any repeated letters, the **Repeat Delay** is set correctly.

- If the student's name still displays repeated letters, make the **Repeat Delay** longer and try again.

- When you are finished adjusting the **Repeat Delay**, click the **Apply** button.

- Then click **OK**.

If you computer is a Mac, you can:

- Click on the **Apple Menu** icon in the upper-left corner of your screen.

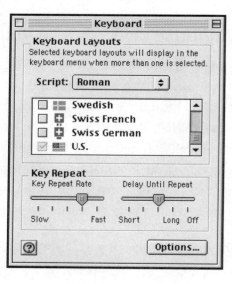

- Pull down to and click on **Control Panels**.

- Click on **Keyboard**.

- When the window opens, you can change the keystroke rate of your keyboard.

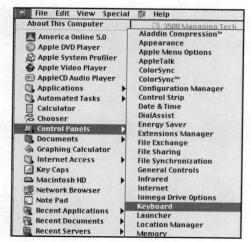

Computer Setting Adjustments You Can Make *(cont.)*

Adjusting the Mouse for Left-Handed Students

One morning you sit down at the computer and realize that the mouse is on the left side of the keyboard. "Wow," you sigh to yourself. "I forgot that two of my little ones are left-handed. I bet it was Maggie who did this."

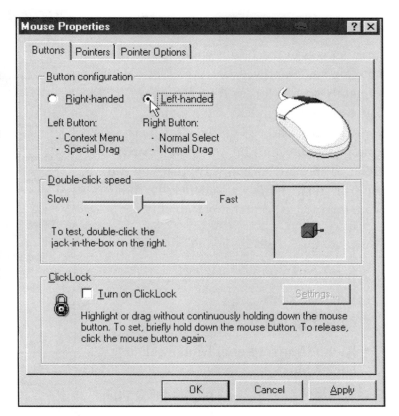

Students who are left-handed will naturally move the mouse from the right side to the left side of the computer keyboard. However, on a PC, they will still be clicking with their middle fingers, rather than with their index fingers unless you change the button settings on the mouse. It is pretty easy to do. Keep in mind that this is not necessary for Macintosh computers because there is only one mouse button.

If your computer system is a PC, you can:

- Click **Start** on the task bar.
- Click **Settings**.
- Click **Control Panel**.
- At the **Control Panel** window, double-click **Mouse**.
- At the **Mouse Properties** window, click the **Button** tab to bring it to the forefront.
- Under **Button configuration**, click **Left-handed**.
- Click **Apply**.
- Click **OK**.

Special Note: Adjusting the button configuration for the mouse works well if you have a mouse designed for use by either hand. If you have a mouse that is shaped in such a way that you know it was designed for right-handers only, you should purchase a mouse that was designed for left-handers only as well. Alternatively, you can purchase a symmetrical mouse, so that either your right-handed students or your left-handed students can use it.

Computer Setting Adjustments You Can Make *(cont.)*

Adjusting the Mouse Pointer

Christian is a sweet, bright young boy with an engaging smile and very thick glasses. He frequently spends lots of time rolling the mouse around in circles on the mouse pad. When asked what he is doing, Christian explains that he can't find the pointer on the screen. There are several ways that you can help Christian, and other students like him, locate the mouse pointer more quickly.

If your computer system is a PC, you can:

- Click **Start** on the task bar.

- Click **Settings**.

- Click **Control Panel**.

- At the **Control Panel** window, double-click **Mouse**.

- At the **Mouse Properties** window, click the **Pointers** tab to bring it to the forefront.

- Click the **Scheme list** arrow and select a different style of pointer for your students, such as **Windows Standard** (extra large).

- Click **Apply**.

- Next, click the **Pointer Options** tab to bring it to the forefront.

- Under **Visibility**, click **Show** pointer trails.

- Under **Visibility**, click **Show** location of pointer when you press the **CTRL** key.

- Click **Apply**.

- Click **OK**.

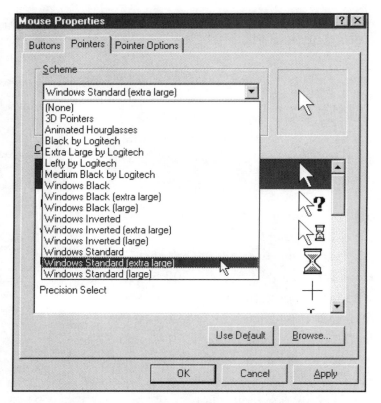

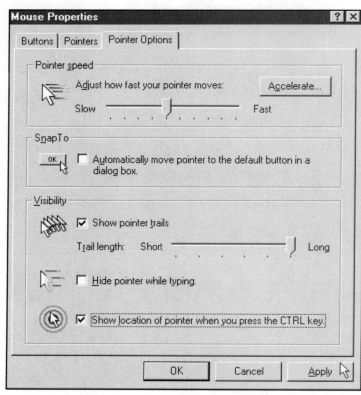

Computer Setting Adjustments You Can Make *(cont.)*

Be sure to show your students that they can always find the location of the pointer by pressing the **Control** key on the keyboard. When the **Control** key is pressed, a large ring appears on the screen and becomes increasingly smaller as it isolates the mouse pointer or insertion beam.

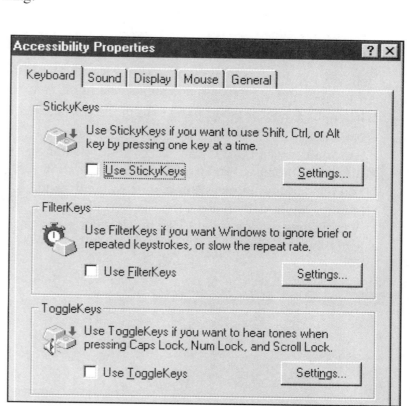

Other Adjustments You Can Make

There is also a full range of adjustments you can make under **Accessibility Options** within the **Control Panel**. To view these options, complete the following:

- Click **Start** on the task bar.

- Click **Settings**.

- Click **Control Panel**.

- At the **Control Panel** window, click **Accessibility Options**.

- At the **Accessibility Options** window, click the **Keyboard** tab to bring it to the forefront.

- Notice that there are three options—StickyKeys, FilterKeys, and ToggleKeys. Explore these options by clicking on their **Settings** buttons. When you do, you will notice that you already worked with FilterKeys when you adjusted the Repeat Rate earlier.

Computer Setting Adjustments You Can Make *(cont.)*

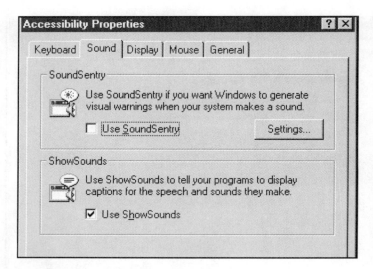

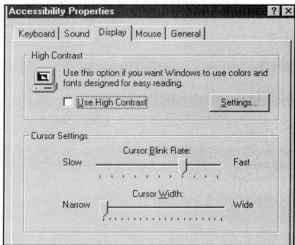

- Click the **Sound** tab to bring it to the forefront.
- Notice that there are two options—SoundSentry and ShowSounds. The **SoundSentry** displays a visual warning when the computer system makes a sound. The **ShowSounds** displays a caption for speech and sounds.
- Click the **Display** tab to bring it to the forefront.
- Notice that there are two options—High Contrast and Cursor Settings. The **High Contrast** allows you to select a Black on White, White on Black, or custom screen display. The **Cursor Settings** allows you to change the Cursor Blink Rate and the Cursor Width.
- Click the **Mouse** tab to bring it to the forefront.
- Notice that there is one option—MouseKeys. The **MouseKeys** option allows you to control the pointer settings, such as speed and acceleration, with the arrow keys on your keyboard.
- Click the **General** tab to bring it to the forefront.
- Notice that there are three options—Automatic reset, Notification, and SerialKey devices. The **Automatic** reset turns off any accessibility features you selected after a designated number of minutes of nonuse. The **Notification** option allows you to see warning messages and hear sounds when features are turned on and off. The **SerialKey** devices option allows you to set up alternate keyboards and mice.

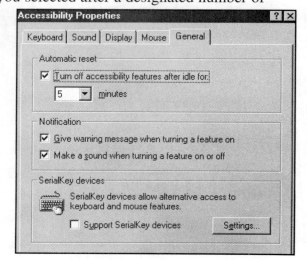

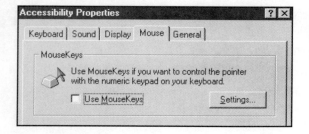

Computer Setting Adjustments You Can Make *(cont.)*

There is another change that you can make to the screen display to meet the special needs of your students-enlarging the icons on the desktop. This change is made through the **Display** settings within the **Control Panel**.

If you are working on a PC computer, you can:

- Click **Start** on the task bar.

- Click **Settings**.

- Click **Control Panel**.

- At the **Control Panel** window, click **Display**.

- At the **Display** window, click the **Effects** tab to bring it to the forefront.

- Click **Use large icons**.

- Click **Apply**.

- Click **OK**.

- Now the icons on your desktop will appear larger.

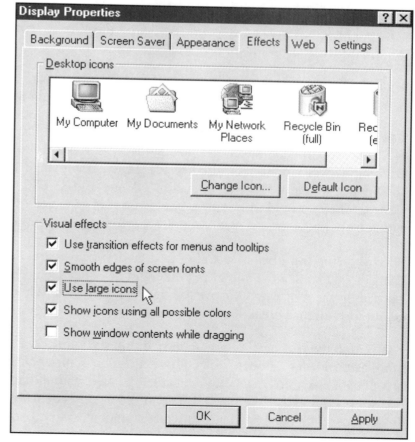

Managing Technology for Special Needs Students

When I first began my teaching career, I worked as a speech and language pathologist. The bulk of my caseload included hearing-impaired students, and I loved working with them so much that I became a teacher of the hearing impaired.

My first hearing-impaired classroom was quite a challenge! Students ranged in age from seven years to 13 years and in academic performance from pre-K through 8th grade.

One day, when I was working with Tammy, a seven-year-old profoundly deaf student, I wondered how she compared to other seven-year-old students in regular classrooms. I found that I didn't have enough teaching background to measure her academic performance against other students her age. I wanted to know what a "normal" seven-year-old student could do. So, I resolved to teach all the elementary grades. Then I would truly understand what was expected of students at each grade level. Then I would truly know how students actually performed at every age. (Ah, those youthful, teaching years!)

The following fall I began teaching first grade. During the first six to eight weeks, we reviewed all the skills the students were taught in kindergarten. That seemed to go pretty well. After all, the students worked on most of the skills over an entire school year. Granted, there were some lapses in memory due to the summer break, but every student seemed to perform well.

Then came the regular first grade curriculum. Wham! I was hit with the reality that there is no such thing as a "normal" student. The physical, social, emotional, and academic differences among a group of students that were relatively the same age were astounding. It seemed like every student in the class had some type of "special need." The most socially adept student, Leslie, had severe academic difficulties. The most academically adept student, Larry, had severe social difficulties.

Managing Technology for Special Needs Students *(cont.)*

The point is that when I speak of special needs students, it doesn't mean just those students who have been identified as visually impaired, hearing impaired, A.D.H.D., and more who you are teaching. It doesn't mean just those students for whom you have attended an I.E.P. It doesn't mean just those students who have special reading classes, special mathematics classes, or access to the Resource Room.

In this section, you will learn about assistive devices for your special needs or young students, as well as resources for assistive devices and related educational software.

Assistive Devices for Your Special Needs Students

Assistive devices are products designed to help your special needs students access and use the computer systems in your classroom. The assistive devices that can help you manage technology use in your classroom include the following.

- special keyboards
- keyboard labels
- keyboard overlays
- special mice
- special screen devices
- special furniture

Special Keyboards

The keyboard you are using in your classroom probably has the traditional QWERTY layout. If you have a student who seems overwhelmed by this layout, you can order a special keyboard that displays the letters in ABC order.

The keyboard you are using in your classroom probably is tan or gray with black lettering. If you have a student who needs additional visual clues to find specific keys, you can order a special keyboard with brightly colored keys.

Managing Technology for Special Needs Students *(cont.)*

The keyboard you are using in your classroom probably has keys that are .5 inches wide and just over .5 inches tall. If you have a student who lacks fine-motor control, you can order special keyboards with much larger keys.

There are alternate keyboards that look nothing like the traditional QWERTY keyboard. They are designed as learning input devices for special needs students. These keyboards typically are used with a variety of keyboard overlays that allow students to touch their selections.

Keyboard Labels

Did you ever notice that the letters on your keyboard are all capitalized? If this is confusing to your special needs or younger students, you can purchase lowercase keyboard labels. The lowercase keyboard labels also have color-coded vowels and numbers. You can also purchase high-contrast keyboard labels (with white letters on a black background).

Keyboard Overlays

Keyboard overlays change the input configuration of the covered keyboard. Overlays are placed over special, touch-sensitive, flat keyboards. These alternative keyboards act like touch windows, giving direct access to screen content. They are typically made with moisture-proof paper and high-contrast colors. In addition, keyboard overlays may include symbols, pictures, numbers, or simply colors rather than letters.

Special Mice

Do any of your special needs or young students have trouble controlling the cursor? If so, you can purchase a special mouse, designed with a large trackball mounted on top, which helps make positioning the cursor easier. Another option is to purchase a children's mouse that is specially designed for little hands.

For students who have difficulty staying within the confines of a mouse pad, you can use an optical mouse. The optical mouse has an optical sensor rather than a trackball underneath, which allows it to operate on almost any surface.

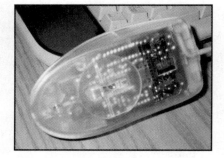

Managing Technology for Special Needs Students *(cont.)*

Special Screen Devices

Did you know that there are special software programs that place the keyboard or a large calculator on the screen? Then students can use a mouse to select the letters or numbers they want.

There are also touch windows that allow your special needs or younger students to use the computer screen as an input device. Using their fingers, rather than a mouse or the keyboard, students can select menu items, draw pictures, and more.

Switches

For a special needs student who is unable to use a mouse, try a pressure-sensitive switch. This input device can be either hand activated or head activated. Hand activated switches come in a variety of shapes (round, oval, rectangular), sizes (for young children, as well as for teens), and colors (red, yellow, blue, and more). If necessary, switches can be attached to adjustable arm-like mounts that are locked onto your student's wheelchair or onto your computer workstation.

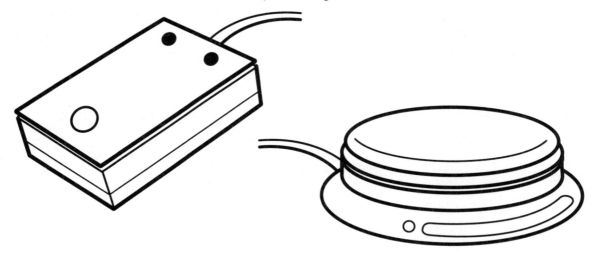

Special Furniture

If you work with very young children, you are already familiar with the special furniture that is scaled for their activities. Make sure your computer workstation or multimedia table is adjusted so that your students maintain correct posture while viewing the monitor and using the mouse and keyboard.

If you have a special needs student who uses a wheelchair, you may find it necessary to purchase a computer workstation or multimedia table that meets ADA (Americans with Disabilities Act) requirements. This special furniture allows you or your students to easily adjust the level of the keyboard tray. The desktop can be raised, lowered, or tilted as well.

Managing Technology for Special Needs Students *(cont.)*

Resources for Assistive Devices

Many educational software applications for special needs students are designed to interface with alternate or special keyboards, touch screen devices, and switches. From interactive CD-ROM storybooks to "intelligent" word prediction programs, you will find a wide variety of educational software programs available for your special needs students.

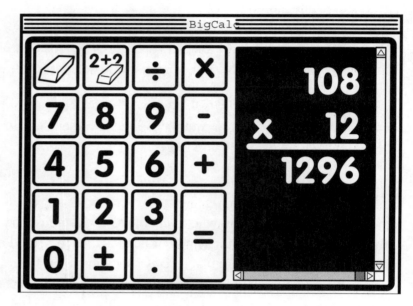

Most major educational software vendors, such as Learning Services and Educational Resources, provide several of the most popular assistive devices for special needs students. The Internet addresses for these vendors are as follows:

- Learning Services **http://www.learnserv.com/**, 1-800-877-9378
- Educational Resources **http://www.edresources.com/er/**, 1-800-860-7004

These companies specialize in providing a full range of assistive devices and educational materials for special needs students.

- IntelliTools, Inc. **http://www.intellitools.com**, 1-800-899-6687
- Don Johnston Incorporated **http://www.donjohnston.com/index.htm**, 1-800-999-4660

Check with your district technology coordinator, as well as your director of special education. Either of these persons (or their designees) should be able to help you select, order, install, and learn how to use the computer-related assistive devices your students need in the classroom.

Now you are familiar with several assistive devices that can help your students access the computer system in your classroom. You also have the information you need to make changes to the keyboard, mouse, display, and accessibility options settings, making computer use more comfortable for your students—because they are all very special!

Getting Parents Involved

Keeping positive and open lines of communication with parents will always be an important facet of good teaching. When it comes to the classroom, parents are concerned that their children have access to the latest in technology. Like teachers, they want their children to be prepared for the twenty-first century and the future job market. The team effort between parents and teachers can be a terrific experience and great benefit to both parties, but the greatest winners are the students. Here are some ideas on ways to involve parents in technology for your classroom program and school.

Technology Nights

Once a month (or more), offer a "Technology Night" to parents. This is an evening set aside where parents come to your class, the computer lab, or a large group presentation to learn about the different technologies in which their youngsters are participating. Share with parents the software programs that you will be using with their children and how they support the curriculum and learning outcomes for your program. Set up a hands-on environment so parents can actually try out the technology. Not only can teachers lead these meetings but they can encourage groups of students to do the same. When parents see their children demonstrating programs and applying their knowledge, their enthusiasm and level of support becomes even greater.

Parent Hands-On Time

Put that computer to overtime use by opening it up for parents after school. Parents can sign up to use a computer (with their child) and learn about various software applications. This situation not only benefits the parents and increases their knowledge but it also creates for you a larger resource for parent technology helpers. Perhaps the lab could be open one or two nights a week for parents who work outside of the home. Custodians are usually on campus until 10:00 PM and could lock the lab before leaving for the evening.

Getting Parents Involved *(cont.)*

Parent Technological Helpers

When parents volunteer to help in the classroom, focus that energy toward technology. Even if parents tell you they do not know a thing about computers, gently encourage them to learn more by offering them free time on your class computer or computers in the school lab. If you can plan some time to spend with a handful of your interested parents, your efforts will be rewarded. Allot one or two afternoons to meet with parents, showing them the computer basics (turning on and off, starting up programs, how to print), and in no time they can supervise the computer pod or computer center in your class. The more help you have, the more time is made available for you to help students one on one, research other projects, and design lessons.

Technology-Picnics

When students have completed a few projects (such as hyperstacks, oral presentations, bar-coded posters and books, and other multimedia presentations), give them the opportunity to show off to mom and dad. Host a "Technology Picnic" in your classroom. Parents and their children can share a blanket and lunch while your budding technological geniuses take turns sharing their projects with the rest of the group. Parents will be impressed with the work not only of their own child but also that of other students. Students will enjoy the chance to share their projects with a large audience. Just be sure to keep the crumbs (and ants) away from the technology.

Parent-Student Projects

After your students have had some experience with creating multimedia and other technology-using projects and presentations, assign a "Parent-Student" technology project. This is probably best done the last quarter of the school year as students will be more familiar with certain programs. Parent and student will work together to plan a project based around a theme or topic of your choosing. Parents would need to set aside at least an hour during class time to come in and work with their child before the project is due. In primary grades for example, parents could bring some old family photographs which could be scanned into a hyperstack about "The Smith Family Tree." The child could be working on the rest of the stack work during class computer time.

Getting Parents Involved *(cont.)*

Parent-Student Projects *(cont.)*

In the upper grades, parent-student teams could preview laserdiscs, select or create bar codes, and write a presentation about a given topic like the solar system. During their final presentation, both parent and child must share the limelight equally. A special program night could be set aside for the families to come and watch the multimedia masterpieces of students and parents.

Technological Library

For parents who have compatible computer systems at home, share with them the opportunity to check out copies of school software. Create centrally located filing cabinets with small drawers (designed specifically for housing software disks) to keep the software. Assign one drawer the "Parent Check-Out" drawer. Run the check-out system like the card system at the library. Parents sign up for a disk for one or two weeks and must return it before checking out any more. Students can take turns being the technological librarians by maintaining the files, making sure software is returned on time, filling out overdue notices, etc. Not only does this increase parent technology awareness, but it also fosters the parent-child relationship with this shared interest.

Answer Key

Page 203

Page 205

Keyboard—5	Monitor—2
Printer—1	CPU—4
Mouse—6	Disk Drives—3

Page 206

Keyboard—4	Mouse—5
Scanner—2	Tablet—10
Disks and Disk Drives—1	Voice Recognition System—9
Modem—3	Joystick—6
Touch Screen—7	Digital Camera—8
Page 207	Monitor—4
Printer—3	Modem—5
Disks and Disk Drives—2	Speakers—1

Page 208

laser printer	monitor
CPU box	CD-ROM or DVD
connector	flatbed scanner
mouse	mousepad
cable	keyboard
floppy disk	

Page 209

1. a gigabyte	5. a byte
2. CD-ROM	6. CD R/RW
3. a floppy disk	7. DVD-RAM
4. a kilobyte	8. a megabyte

Page 210

Across

1. kilobyte	15. bps
2. megabyte	16. keyboard
4. monitor	18. disk
6. ascii	19. question
8. local	20. ROM
10. WAN	21. websites
11. mouse	23. CPU
14. mousepad	24. IP address

Page 210 *(cont.)*

Down

2. meg	11. modem
3. bytes	12. gigabytes
5. email	17. handshake
7. lightning	20. read
9. cookie	22. ISP
10. WWW	

Page 211

Page 216

1. March 4, 1861
2. Brooklyn Dodgers 1947
3. 1872
4. 6 million
5. Menachem Begin
6. 1840-1926
7. *And to Think That I Saw It on Mulberry Street,* 1937
8. 1879

CD-ROM Index

Page Number	Filename	Folder	Associated Software Application
34	system.pdf	Teacher Sheets	*Adobe Acrobat Reader*
36–38	eval.pdf	Teacher Sheets	*Adobe Acrobat Reader*
42	planning.pdf	Paint Draw Lesson	*Adobe Acrobat Reader*
43	tale.pdf	Paint Draw Lesson	*Adobe Acrobat Reader*
44	example.pdf	Paint Draw Lesson	*Adobe Acrobat Reader*
45	cartoon.bmp	Paint Draw Lesson	*Kid Pix Studio Deluxe*
45	cartoon.kpx	Paint Draw Lesson	*Kid Pix Deluxe 3*
50	conflict.doc	Word Processing Lesson	*Microsoft Word*
50	conflict.pdf	Word Processing Lesson	*Adobe Acrobat Reader*
51	sample.doc	Word Processing Lesson	*Microsoft Word*
55	example.xls	Spreadsheet Lesson	*Microsoft Excel*
55	right.xls	Spreadsheet Lesson	*Microsoft Excel*
63	survey.doc	Spreadsheet Lesson	*Microsoft Word*
63	survey.pdf	Spreadsheet Lesson	*Adobe Acrobat Reader*
67	animal.cwk	Database Lesson	*AppleWorks*
70	plan1.pdf	Database Lesson	*Adobe Acrobat Reader*
71	plan2.pdf	Database Lesson	*Adobe Acrobat Reader*
77	pyramid.pdf	PowerPoint Lesson	*Adobe Acrobat Reader*
77	pyramid.ppt	PowerPoint Lesson	*PowerPoint*
78	plan1.pdf	PowerPoint Lesson	*Adobe Acrobat Reader*
79	plan2.pdf	PowerPoint Lesson	*Adobe Acrobat Reader*
80	apples.stk	HyperStudio Lesson	*HyperStudio*
80	fmtree09.stk	HyperStudio Lesson	*HyperStudio*
80	fmtree12.stk	HyperStudio Lesson	*HyperStudio*
80	fmtree14.stk	HyperStudio Lesson	*HyperStudio*
80	Student Samples	HyperStudio Lesson	Folder of *HyperStudio* files
87	describe.pdf	HyperStudio Lesson	*Adobe Acrobat Reader*
88–89	eval.pdf	HyperStudio Lesson	*Adobe Acrobat Reader*
90	planning.pdf	HyperStudio Lesson	*Adobe Acrobat Reader*
91	template.pdf	HyperStudio Lesson	*Adobe Acrobat Reader*
102	alivest.ins	Inspiration Lesson	*Inspiration*
102	alivetem.ins	Inspiration Lesson	*Inspiration*
102	boysele.ins	Inspiration Lesson	*Inspiration*
102	typestem.ins	Inspiration Lesson	*Inspiration*
102	typestor.ins	Inspiration Lesson	*Inspiration*
108	cone.doc	Kidspiration Lesson	*Microsoft Word*
108	cube.doc	Kidspiration Lesson	*Microsoft Word*
108	cylinder.doc	Kidspiration Lesson	*Microsoft Word*
108	shapes1.kid	Kidspiration Lesson	*Kidspiration*
108	shapes2.doc	Kidspiration Lesson	*Microsoft Word*
108	sphere.doc	Kidspiration Lesson	*Microsoft Word*
120	advanced.pdf	Internet Lesson	*Adobe Acrobat Reader*
121–122	5wslides.pdf	Internet Lesson	*Adobe Acrobat Reader*
121–122	5wslides.ppt	Internet Lesson	*PowerPoint*
123	infoshet.pdf	Internet Lesson	*Adobe Acrobat Reader*
124–125	elementr.pdf	Internet Lesson	*Adobe Acrobat Reader*
126–128	middle.pdf	Internet Lesson	*Adobe Acrobat Reader*
131	school.pdf	E-mail Lesson	*Adobe Acrobat Reader*
136	howwork.pdf	Search Engines	*Adobe Acrobat Reader*

CD-ROM Index *(cont.)*

Page Number	Filename	Folder	Associated Software Application
137	boolean.pdf	Search Engines	*Adobe Acrobat Reader*
138	search.pdf	Search Engines	*Adobe Acrobat Reader*
142	finger.pdf	Teacher Sheets	*Adobe Acrobat Reader*
156	inventry.pdf	Teacher Sheets	*Adobe Acrobat Reader*
170	teaming.pdf	Teacher Sheets	*Adobe Acrobat Reader*
173	techjob.pdf	Teacher Sheets	*Adobe Acrobat Reader*
181	chart.pdf	Teacher Sheets	*Adobe Acrobat Reader*
182	techgoal.pdf	Teacher Sheets	*Adobe Acrobat Reader*
183	techplan.pdf	Teacher Sheets	*Adobe Acrobat Reader*
192	techno.pdf	Teacher Sheets	*Adobe Acrobat Reader*
193	plansht.pdf	Teacher Sheets	*Adobe Acrobat Reader*
194	basics.pdf	Student Sheets	*Adobe Acrobat Reader*
195	basics2.pdf	Student Sheets	*Adobe Acrobat Reader*
196	drives.pdf	Student Sheets	*Adobe Acrobat Reader*
197	cdrom.pdf	Student Sheets	*Adobe Acrobat Reader*
198	modem.pdf	Student Sheets	*Adobe Acrobat Reader*
199	lasrdisc.pdf	Student Sheets	*Adobe Acrobat Reader*
200	scanner.pdf	Student Sheets	*Adobe Acrobat Reader*
201	parts1.pdf	Student Sheets	*Adobe Acrobat Reader*
202	devices.pdf	Student Sheets	*Adobe Acrobat Reader*
203	search1.pdf	Student Sheets	*Adobe Acrobat Reader*
204	contract.pdf	Teacher Sheets	*Adobe Acrobat Reader*
205	parts2.pdf	Student Sheets	*Adobe Acrobat Reader*
206	input.pdf	Student Sheets	*Adobe Acrobat Reader*
207	output.pdf	Student Sheets	*Adobe Acrobat Reader*
208	parts3.pdf	Student Sheets	*Adobe Acrobat Reader*
209	memory.pdf	Student Sheets	*Adobe Acrobat Reader*
210	puzzle.pdf	Student Sheets	*Adobe Acrobat Reader*
211	search2.pdf	Student Sheets	*Adobe Acrobat Reader*
212	testpc.pdf	Student Sheets	*Adobe Acrobat Reader*
213	testmac.pdf	Student Sheets	*Adobe Acrobat Reader*
214	internet.pdf	Student Sheets	*Adobe Acrobat Reader*
215	website.pdf	Student Sheets	*Adobe Acrobat Reader*
216	people.pdf	Student Sheets	*Adobe Acrobat Reader*
217	science.pdf	Student Sheets	*Adobe Acrobat Reader*
218	storybrd.pdf	Student Sheets	*Adobe Acrobat Reader*
219	design.pdf	Student Sheets	*Adobe Acrobat Reader*
220	sprdsht.pdf	Student Sheets	*Adobe Acrobat Reader*
221	group1.pdf	Student Sheets	*Adobe Acrobat Reader*
222	group2.pdf	Student Sheets	*Adobe Acrobat Reader*
223	bookref.pdf	Student Sheets	*Adobe Acrobat Reader*
224	cdref.pdf	Student Sheets	*Adobe Acrobat Reader*
225	dictref.pdf	Student Sheets	*Adobe Acrobat Reader*
226	intntref.pdf	Student Sheets	*Adobe Acrobat Reader*
227	magref.pdf	Student Sheets	*Adobe Acrobat Reader*
228	newsref.pdf	Student Sheets	*Adobe Acrobat Reader*
229	email.pdf	Student Sheets	*Adobe Acrobat Reader*
230	aup.pdf	Student Sheets	*Adobe Acrobat Reader*
232–237	rubrics.pdf	Teacher Sheets	*Adobe Acrobat Reader*